HISTORICAL DICTIONARY

The historical dictionaries present essential information on a broad range of subjects, including American and world history, art, business, cities, countries, cultures, customs, film, global conflicts, international relations, literature, music, philosophy, religion, sports, and theater. Written by experts, all contain highly informative introductory essays of the topic and detailed chronologies that, in some cases, cover vast historical time periods but still manage to heavily feature more recent events.

Brief A–Z entries describe the main people, events, politics, social issues, institutions, and policies that make the topic unique, and entries are cross-referenced for ease of browsing. Extensive bibliographies are divided into several general subject areas, providing excellent access points for students, researchers, and anyone wanting to know more. Additionally, maps, photographs, and appendixes of supplemental information aid high school and college students doing term papers or introductory research projects. In short, the historical dictionaries are the perfect starting point for anyone looking to research in these fields.

HISTORICAL DICTIONARIES OF RELIGIONS, PHILOSOPHIES, AND MOVEMENTS

Jon Woronoff, Series Editor

Historical Dictionary
of the Welfare State

Third Edition

Bent Greve

ROWMAN & LITTLEFIELD
Lanham • Boulder • New York • Toronto • Plymouth, UK

Ref JC 479 .G74 2014
Greve, Bent.
Historical dictionary of the
  welfare state

Published by Rowman & Littlefield
4501 Forbes Boulevard, Suite 200, Lanham, Maryland 20706
www.rowman.com

10 Thornbury Road, Plymouth PL6 7PP, United Kingdom

British Library Cataloguing in Publication Information Available

Library of Congress Cataloging-in-Publication Data
Greve, Bent.
  Historical dictionary of the welfare state / Bent Greve. — Third edition.
    pages cm
  Includes bibliographical references.
  ISBN 978-1-4422-3231-0 (cloth : alk. paper) — ISBN 978-1-4422-3232-7 (ebook)
  1. Welfare state—Dictionaries. I. Title.
  JC479.G74 2014
  330.12'6—dc23
                                                                2013040581

Printed in the United States of America

Contents

Editor's Foreword

Not so long ago, a book on the welfare state would have mainly praised such advantages as enhanced security, greater financial support, and a comfortable old age. The depiction would have been generally positive. But the situation has changed, and although the welfare state is still largely admired and widely aspired to, certain problems have emerged, including unwanted state interference, welfare dependency, a weakening of family and social ties, and especially an excessive fiscal burden. Thus, there is now a serious debate about what kind of welfare state is best and how it should be managed, in a more balanced manner. This deliberation pits those in favor of greater coverage and easier access against those insisting on more economic growth and freedom of the individual and, in so doing, adds the voices of the New Left and the New Right. This is actually healthy, and the result will likely be more rational and also more viable systems in the future.

However, for any debate to be constructive and productive, it certainly helps to know what one is considering, which is the primary purpose of *Historical Dictionary of the Welfare State*, now appearing in a third edition. This edition is even more useful than the last one since the chronology has been updated with the latest events; the introduction offers a detailed overall view of the past and current situation; the dictionary contains new entries, while many older ones have been updated; and the bibliography lists additional resources for further reading. Of particular interest, there are now eleven statistical tables providing some of the basic data. While covering the advanced countries in greater detail, more references are made to the Third World so that readers can more clearly see the progress that has been made and what problems have arisen to form their own opinions of what the future solutions might be.

Bent Greve, the author of all three editions, has continued his active career as a specialist on the welfare state, with some emphasis on Europe. This has included working for the Danish Association of County Councils, followed by the Economic Board of the Danish Labour Movement. More recently, he has been serving as professor of welfare state analysis in the Department of Society and Globalization at Roskilde University. Greve was also director of the Jean Monnet European Centre of Excellence, and as well as a deputy member on the board of the European Institute of Social Security. He remains a longtime member of the Danish Central Board of Taxation. He is also chairman for the Copenhagen Business Academy. All the while, Greve has been writing numerous books and articles on the welfare state, and, since 2007, he has been the regional and special issues editor of *Social Policy and Administration*. This background, combining activity in the public and voluntary sectors, practical experience, and academic research, has allowed him to have a well-rounded view of a subject that is probably of greater importance today than at any other time in history.

Jon Woronoff
Series Editor

Reader's Note

To facilitate the rapid and efficient location of information and make this book as useful a reference tool as possible, extensive cross-references have been provided in the dictionary section. Within individual entries, terms that have their own entries are in **boldface type** the first time they appear. Related terms that do not appear in the text are indicated in the *See also. See* refers to other entries that deal with this topic.

Preface

The goal of *Historical Dictionary of the Welfare State* is to identify, describe, and define the core concepts that are fundamental to an analysis of the welfare state or welfare society. This book focuses on the definitions and concepts that are the most relevant, long-lasting, and important, rather than presenting biographies of the many writers in these different fields. The presentation of biographies is limited to historically important thinkers. To those who feel that other figures should have been included, I apologize.

The central criterion for an entry has been the historical importance of a concept, not the individual researcher's contribution to the analysis of the welfare state and social policy; furthermore, the dictionary describes how history has influenced the current development of theories and the analytical ways of dealing with the welfare state. It also describes the history, transition, and future of the welfare state.

I do not pretend to cover the entire field, but I have tried to present the information so that scholars interested in welfare states and welfare state analysis from different viewpoints will find this dictionary of use. I attempt to provide insights from major areas in social science, including sociology, economics, political science, and social work. I try to combine the different disciplines and, by doing so, present a more complex and integrated view of the welfare state.

One goal is to describe and explain the items as clearly and precisely as possible. Some may find that the result is too simplistic, as many arguments for and against various standpoints and assumptions are left out to make a clear and hopefully crisp presentation.

I have tried to include the most important references to the welfare state literature. A core problem in doing this has been that an entire book could be filled simply with names and titles instead of information. The selection process was a result of my own research and using the databases at libraries about books and journals in the field. I know that this can be a limited and inadequate way of selecting the various authors; however, my argument for using this method is that I needed to narrow the field. Otherwise, the book would have consisted mainly of a bibliography, instead of what I hope to be valuable information and ideas, especially for the many students in the field who can use this dictionary as a first step in identifying areas of interest. Users can find important definitions, historical descriptions, and ways of interpreting welfare state development. Aside from numerous new and expanded entries, this third edition includes two new features—an appendix containing an overview of related websites and a bibliography of even more literature.

This book provides historical descriptions of the development of social security systems in selected countries. The countries chosen are core countries in different welfare state clusters, as well as those where important events for the development of the welfare state have taken place. Countries from different parts of the world have been included to broaden the picture and also indicate the variety of approaches to welfare states and their development. This also implicitly answers the question of why mainly European countries are described. It would not have been possible to include all the countries in the world, and, as the pattern of development has often been more or less the same amongst groups of countries, this seems to be a reasonable way of presenting historical trends in the development of the welfare state. My understanding of what constitutes a welfare state also influenced the choice of countries. This book contains up-to date information, although it can sometimes be difficult to determinate whether recent events are lasting events. This is also due to the fact that data are often two or three years behind current events. Thus, junctures and changes may be difficult to understand and foresee; therefore, only in a number of years will it be possible to prove clearly what has actually happened and in what direction the welfare state has been moving. I found it useful to cover the first year of legislation in many countries concerning central contingencies, for example, pension, industrial injuries, unemployment benefits, sickness and maternity benefits, and family allowances.

Only a few illustrations are included. A short, quantitative, comparative description of the development of the various welfare states—especially since World War II—is also given, which includes some recent data on central aspects relating to welfare state developments. It is difficult to limit the examples while trying to cover the area of social security in the various countries and regions included in this book; however, such material is included as an appetizer to central data and information. Readers interested in this topic can turn to statistics from the European Union, International Monetary Fund, and Organization for Economic Cooperation and Development. Many of the websites listed in the appendixes provide collected data on welfare state issues from a comparative perspective.

Acronyms and Abbreviations

ALMP	active labor market policy
APW	average production worker
CSR	corporate social responsibility
DRG	diagnosis-related groups
ECOSOC	Economic and Social Council
ESF	European Social Fund
EU	European Union
GDP	gross domestic product
HDI	Human Development Index
HMO	health maintenance organization
ICSW	International Council on Social Welfare
ILO	International Labour Organization
ISSA	International Social Security Association
LIS	Luxembourg Income Study
LWS	Luxembourg Wealth Study Database
MISSOC	Mutual Information System on Social Security
NAFTA	North Atlantic Free Trade Agreement
NAIRU	nonaccelerating inflation rate of unemployment
NGO	nongovernmental organization
NPM	new public management
OECD	Organization for Economic Cooperation and Development
OMC	open method of coordination
PAYG	pay-as-you-go
QALY	quality adjusted life years
RCT	randomized control trials
SAP	Social Action Program
SEA	Single European Act
UK	United Kingdom
UN	United Nations
UNESCO	United Nations Educational, Scientific, and Cultural Organization
UNICEF	United Nations Children's Fund
USSR	Union of Soviet Socialist Republics
VAT	value-added tax
WHO	World Health Organization

Chronology

The development of the welfare state has differed among countries, thus the heterogeneous paths and strategies of different countries. This chronology presents only the major core dates and events for the development of the welfare state in general, including the first welfare legislation of the countries included in the dictionary.

Sixth century BC   Greece: A narrow type of social assistance to soldiers is developed in Athens, as what seems to have been the first legislative attempt to cope with a social problem.

1388   United Kingdom: The first Poor Law is enacted in England to deal with the labor shortage.

1601   United Kingdom: The Elizabethan Poor Law Act is introduced in England to establish local areas' responsibility for the poor. This law was the first to give specific groups with specified needs public support.

1698   United Kingdom: The world's first life insurance company is started in England.

1730   The Reformation begins in many Northern European countries. As a result of its changes, many poor are no longer supported by the church, which may have had an indirect impact on the different types of welfare states that later emerged.

1776   Adam Smith's book *The Wealth of Nations* is published. This book has since influenced many liberals' way of thinking about the welfare state.

1791   France: The constitution declares that citizens have a right to social assistance. A specific pension for seamen is also established.

1794   Prussia: A general state law also focusing on the poor is issued.

1798   Denmark: Poor relief laws are introduced.

1824   United Kingdom: A law protecting the establishment of trade unions is enacted.

1833   United Kingdom: A Factory Act is introduced.

1834   United Kingdom: The Poor Laws were changed to more general laws, with a more general level of support.

1838   Germany: Employers are made responsible for the railroad workforce.

1842   Germany: A settlement law is enacted.

1848   United Kingdom: A public health act is passed.

1852   France: Mutual funds covering sickness and invalidity for specified groups are introduced.

1853   Prussia: The Institute of Factory Inspectors is founded to help improve working conditions.

1854   Germany: Compulsory insurance for mineworkers is introduced.

1883   Germany: Sickness insurance is introduced as the first in a series of new Bismarckian reforms establishing new principles for the welfare state structure and how to deliver and finance welfare state activities.

1884   Germany: The first law on industrial injury is passed.

1887   Czech Republic/Austria-Hungary: A law on industrial injury is passed, the first area of social security to be covered in Austria and Hungary.

1888   Czech Republic: Coverage in case of sickness or maternity is enacted. **Denmark:** The first social security law, a law on child maintenance, is introduced.

1889   Poland: An injury insurance system is introduced. **Germany:** The first law on pensions to be passed in any country is implemented.

1891   Sweden: The sickness benefit system is introduced. **Hungary:** A social insurance-based system on sickness and maternity is established.

1894   Belgium: Mutual benefit societies are established to cover sickness and maternity benefits.

1895   Finland/Norway: The first laws on social security in the area of industrial injury are introduced.

1897   Austria: A plan for compensation of workers is implemented. **United Kingdom/Ireland:** Even though Ireland is not yet an independent country, a system covering industrial injury is introduced.

1898   Austria: Legislation on sickness and maternity is introduced. **France:** The first social insurance system is introduced in the area of industrial injury. **Italy:** A law on industrial injury is passed. **New Zealand:** A law on old age pensions is passed.

1900   Spain: A law on industrial injury is passed.

1901   England: The first study on poverty, by B. Seebohm Rowntree, based on an analysis of poverty in York, England, in 1899, is published. **The Netherlands:** A law on industrial injury is introduced.

1902   Australia: Social security in relation to industrial injury is initiated. Total coverage was finally passed in 1946.

1905   France: For the first time in any country, an unemployment benefit system is introduced.

1906   Czech Republic: Old age and disability are covered by legislation.

1907   Hungary: Industrial injury is covered.

1908   Australia: Old age, disability, and survivors' coverage is introduced. **Canada:** Social security coverage is introduced in the province of Quebec for industrial injury; other provinces soon followed. **New Zealand:** Compensation for industrial injury is implemented. **United Kingdom:** The Old-Age Pensions Act is introduced.

1909   Norway: Sickness and maternity laws are established.

1911   Ireland: A disability benefit is enacted. **Japan:** The first social security measures, for industrial injury, are introduced. **Switzerland:** Sickness and maternity benefits and coverage of industrial injury is introduced.

1912 **Romania:** Old-age pension becomes the first form of social security, and a work–injury scheme is implemented. **United States:** Workers compensation is introduced.

1913 **The Netherlands:** Old-age pensions and compensation in case of industrial injury is passed. **Portugal:** The first social security law, covering industrial injury, is passed. **Sweden:** First universal law regarding old age pension is enacted.

1914 **Greece/South Africa:** Laws on industrial injury are introduced.

1915 **Argentina:** The first social security law, on industrial injury, is passed. **United States:** The portion of the workforce covered by compensation reaches approximately 30 percent.

1916 **Chile:** A law on industrial injury is introduced.

1917 **Finland:** An unemployment insurance law is established.

1918 **Bulgaria:** The first law regarding sickness and maternity is decided.

1919 The International Labour Organization (ILO) is established as part of the Versailles Treaty after World War I. **Brazil:** The first law covering industrial injury is passed. **Germany:** The Weimar Republic is founded, securing certain rights for citizens. **Spain:** A pension and unemployment provision is enacted.

1922 **Croatia:** The first law on old-age pension is enacted. **Estonia:** Family allowances are introduced. **Greece:** A law on sickness and maternity is introduced. **Japan:** Sickness and maternity benefits begin being covered.

1923 **Brazil:** Pension and sickness benefits are introduced for railroad workers. Beginning in 1936, coverage would be extended to all workers in the industries.

1924 **Bulgaria:** Laws on old age, disability, and work injuries are introduced. **Chile:** Several social contingencies are covered, including old age, disability, sickness, and maternity. **Estonia:** Laws regarding pension, sickness, maternity benefits, and industrial injury are implemented.

1927 **Canada:** Rules related to old age, disability, and survivors are implemented.

1928   France: The International Council on Social Welfare is founded in Paris.

1929   Spain: Sickness and maternity benefits are implemented. **United States:** The Wall Street Crash has a profound impact on social policy worldwide, with many workers becoming unemployed.

1930   A forced labor convention is adopted by the ILO. **Belgium:** The first law concerning family allowances is passed in Belgium. This was the last social security area to be covered, and it was only gradually introduced in most other welfare states, often not until after World War II. **New Zealand:** An unemployment compensation system is implemented. **Romania:** Sickness benefits are introduced.

1931   Mexico: A law on industrial injury is introduced, the first area to be covered in that country. **Vatican:** The *Quadragesimo Anno*, issued by Pope Pius XI, includes the now-famous description of the concept of "subsidiarity," which states that what can be done at a lower level should not be taken over by a higher level.

1933   United States: The New Deal is initiated under President Franklin D. Roosevelt. These reforms sought to create jobs and introduce various social security laws, legislation that would have a lasting impact.

1934   Argentina: Maternity benefits are provided. **Greece:** Old age and disability is covered.

1936   United Kingdom: John Maynard Keynes publishes his now-famous book, *The General Theory of Employment, Interest, and Money*.

1937   Chile: Unemployment benefits and family allowances are adopted. **Finland:** Pension and disability are covered.

1938   New Zealand: Sickness and maternity benefits are established. **Spain:** Family allowances as the last of the classical social security elements are implemented. **Sweden:** Saltsjøbaden agreement is signed on the corporative involvement of partners.

1940   Canada: Old-age compensation is introduced.

1941   Brazil: Family allowances are introduced. **Japan:** Old age and disability are now also covered by the system. **New Zealand:** A family allowance system is established. **United Kingdom:** Archbishop Temple introduces the concept of the welfare state as an answer to the aggression and power of Germany.

1942   United Kingdom: Lord William Beveridge publishes a report entitled *Social Insurance and Allied Services*, from which the Beveridgian model, characterized by universal provision of welfare, is later developed.

1943   Italy: A family allowance system is adopted.

1944   Argentina: The first pension system to ensure coverage in old age goes into effect. **Canada:** Family allowances are implemented. **Ireland:** Family allowances are the last social area to be covered.

1945   Czech Republic: Family allowances are implemented. **Greece:** Unemployment assistance is introduced.

1947   Japan: Unemployment benefits are established.

1948   The Convention on Freedom of Association and Protection of the Right to Organise is adopted by the ILO. Finland: A law on family allowances is implemented. **India:** A state insurance act goes into effect providing medical care and sickness and maternity benefits, as well as benefits in case of disability or death. A law covering pensions is also passed. **Sweden:** A law on family allowances is the last social insurance element implemented.

1950   Romania: Family benefits are introduced.

1951   The Equal Remuneration Convention is adopted by the ILO. China: Laws on social security are introduced, including those regarding old age, disability, sickness, maternity, and industrial injury. **United States:** Kenneth J. Arrow's impossibility theorem is published.

1952   ILO Convention No. 102 on social security is codified. Croatia: The first law on unemployment compensation is passed.

1953   South Korea: A work-injury social insurance system is established.

1954   Croatia: Sickness benefits are introduced. **Germany:** A law on family allowances is introduced.

1956 Denmark: Universal old-age pension is established, marking a shift toward a universal welfare state.

1957 Argentina: A law on family allowances is passed. **European Union:** The European Economic Community (now the European Union, or EU) is founded by Germany, France, Italy, and the Benelux countries. The treaty includes labor mobility and social security for migrant workers.

1958 The ILO enacts the Discrimination Convention.

1961 India: A maternity benefits law goes into effect.

1963 Finland: Laws on sickness and maternity, the last areas to be addressed, are established. **South Korea:** The first sickness and maternity benefits laws are enacted.

1965 Brazil: An unemployment benefit is implemented as the last of the classical social contingencies.

1966 United States: Medicare, which was created in 1965, is implemented.

1971 Japan: Child allowances go into effect.

1973 The ILO enacts the Minimum Age Convention. **South Korea:** The National Welfare Pension Act, focusing on old age, disability, and survivors, goes into effect.

1989 European Union: The Community Charter of Fundamental Social Rights is passed.

1991 Argentina: Unemployment benefits are made general after having been introduced for construction workers in 1967. **European Union:** The Maastricht Treaty includes the "Protocol on Economic and Social Integration and a Social Dimension." The United Kingdom does not adopt this protocol. **Romania:** Unemployment benefits are introduced.

1993 South Korea: Unemployment insurance is enacted.

1995 United Nations: The fourth United Nations Conference on Women, held in Beijing, decides that gender mainstreaming should be included in all policies.

1996   China: Unemployment benefits are introduced to those in state enterprises. **United States:** Welfare reforms with more contracting are passed.

1997   European Union: The Amsterdam Treaty is concluded by the heads of states, with social integration as part of the agreement, which is endorsed by all members. The treaty also emphasizes to a greater degree than before that both labor market policy and social policy are areas of concern for the EU as whole.

2000   European Union: The Lisbon Agreement, which calls for the use of the open method of coordination (OMC) in social policy, labor market policy, and pension policy in Europe, is adopted. This reflects the balance between the centralized and decentralized levels in the EU.

2001   United States: The contribution and limiting of benefits in occupational pension is increased.

2002   Austria: A family care leave system is introduced. **Netherlands:** The health care system is reformed to improve user influence and equality in access.

2003   Denmark: The normal age of retirement is decreased from 67 to 65. **Estonia:** Family benefits are increased. **Finland:** The age of retirement is made more flexible, along with other changes in the pension system. **Germany:** The Harz reforms of the German labor market begin, including a change in the unemployment benefit system and active labor market policy. **United States:** The Medicare Prescription Drug, Improvement, and Modernization Act is signed, implying more choice in health care plans.

2004   European Union: Ten former Eastern European countries join the EU; nearly all European countries are now members. **Lithuania:** A move is made toward pension-based saving instead of pay-as-you-go plans.

2005   Denmark: Free choice options increase with regard to part of pension investments. **Finland:** Pension reform begins, including a later age of retirement. **France:** A change in rules goes into effect for pension while working. **Italy:** A new pension reform raises the age of retirement.

2006   Bulgaria: A new fourth pillar in the pension system is enacted. **Croatia:** A law on work injuries is implemented. **Poland:** The permanent disability pension is abolished. **United States:** Pension reform related to defined contribution and defined benefit plans goes into effect.

2007 **Bulgaria/Romania:** These two countries enter the EU, now covering 27 member states. **Denmark:** Welfare reform, including gradual later retirement from the labor market and an increase in labor market participation, begins. **Germany:** The pension age increases from 65 to 67. **Hungary:** Health care system reform begins. **Norway:** Pension reform with a more flexible approach begins, but also a later expected age of retirement. **Romania:** A decision moving toward a three-pillar pension system is enacted. **South Korea:** A universal tax-financed pension system is enacted, beginning at the age of 65.

2008 **Czech Republic:** The age of retirement and number of years required in the labor market increase. **Greece:** Pension reform is adopted against the will of the trade unions, with cuts in pension. **Spain:** The pension system is reformed, including more years of employment being required to receive a full state pension. **United States:** The fiscal crisis starts with a collapse of financial institutions and decrease in housing prices. The crisis quickly spreads throughout most of the world, having an impact on welfare states, especially in Europe.

2009 **Germany:** Public pension increases. **Hungary:** Changes are made to calculation pension bonuses and the retirement age is increased. **Latvia:** Social security benefits are reduced. **Russia:** Pension benefits are increased as part of a pension reform package.

2010 **European Union:** The European Commission launches the EU 2020 strategy, with the aim of creating more growth and jobs in Europe. **Greece:** Cuts are made in pension benefits in the wake of the fiscal crisis. **Lithuania:** Benefits are reduced as part of austerity measures. **United States:** A new health care reform is enacted, implying that more people are covered by the national health care system.

2011 **Bulgaria:** Contribution rates for pensions increase, and a later retirement age is introduced. **Ireland:** A new tax is levied on occupational pension, and the age of retirement increases. **Italy:** A 54 billion euro austerity plan is approved. **Spain:** Reforms are put in place to increase labor market participation and the retirement age, as well as the number of years required to acquire a full pension. **Ukraine:** The age of retirement increases to 60 for women and 62 for men. **United Kingdom:** Spending cuts go into effect, mainly with welfare, amounting to £83 billion pounds, as part of efforts to reduce the deficit, and incentives are given to work longer.

2012 An ILO recommendation that developing countries also establish social protection floors is adopted.

2013 **Croatia:** The country becomes the 28th member of the EU.

Introduction

The term *welfare state* is reasonably new, developed in the 1930s and 1940s. Some see it as the opposite of the concept of warfare of World War II—opposite due to the fact that warfare requires that money be spent on military and war, but, with welfare, on social policy, health care, and so forth. This book goes further back than the 1930s and 1940s, and aside from a few references to ancient times and the Poor Laws, the starting point for presenting and discussing what we today would label welfare state activities is Chancellor Otto von Bismarck's reforms in Germany, starting in 1883. Similar reforms quickly followed in most European countries.

It is obvious that the concept has a relative meaning and will be interpreted differently throughout time and in different countries based on their economic, political, social, and cultural legacies and historical development. Definitions of the welfare state often focus on how and why a state intervenes in the economy and welfare of the individual citizen. A welfare state does not, however, have to mean state intervention; it may merely reflect the state's restrictions and the demands of the labor market, families, and the rest of civil society.

Some welfare states are fairly universal in their approach, whereas others have chosen a more selectivist attitude. Different types of the welfare state exist as a result of the way different societies have chosen to develop their systems. Many welfare states came about in response to the Industrial Revolution, while others developed in response to changes in the demographic situation and structure, which gave rise to new demands for new protection. The initiatives were related to specific social areas, for instance, support for pensions, education, housing, and spouses. These developments were often in response to market failure and the market's inability to provide the necessary support for the individual's risk. This contrast between market and state has, to a large extent, also been part of the debate between, for example, the New Right and the New Left.

The systems in various countries are still quite different, and after the rapid expansion of the welfare state in the 1960s and 1970s, the legitimacy of the welfare state was increasingly questioned because of rising unemployment, increasing dependency on the state, ideological pressure for more individualism, state deficits, and state debt. The question related to legitimacy is often an issue dependent on the economic development, ideological preferences, and voter expectations for what the role of the state should be to develop a welfare society.

The economic consequences of the welfare state also often come into question, including how the financing would influence individuals' behavior, as well as how different types of social security systems could have an impact on incentives to work and save. The state's role was, and has been, widely debated by the New Right and public choice theorists, among others. The conflict between handling market failure and government intervention has yet to be resolved. Given this criticism, it is difficult to foresee how the welfare state will develop. It can be argued that the welfare state will continue to exist and evolve, but the form, shape, and structure will also continue to vary among countries.

The interactions and borderlines among state, market, and civil society will presumably shift as time progresses, and the roles of various actors in the development can and will change throughout time and among countries. Thus, there are constant conflicting perspectives on what the welfare states should look like, how to finance welfare states, and how to deal with welfare both in times of crisis and prosperity. The following is a short description of the historical development of the welfare state. More can be found in individual country descriptions, as well as those of relevant organizations. The goal here is to provide a broader overview presenting central themes and elements to grasp the welfare state's development and core reasons and arguments behind this growth.

Welfare states are undergoing constant change for several reasons. In most countries, a change in demography implies movement toward spending more on health and elderly care, while at the same time reducing public-sector involvement and payment to pension, including later retirement from the labor market. The financial crisis, with the need to use money to avoid bankruptcy in the financial sector, increasing levels of unemployment and reducing income from taxes and duties, implied a high level of public-sector deficit. This has once again led to restructuring and retrenchment in public-sector spending. Thus, at least in some countries, this means a weaker role for the welfare state. An external crisis like the financial crisis can, therefore, have a profound impact on welfare states. Whether this continues and permanently changes the preferences of voters is not an easy question to answer, as most people and countries with an increasing level of income have a greater demand for services, including more welfare services. As a result, it is safe to say that the welfare state is here to stay, although it can vary in different countries and welfare regimes, and there are certain instances where it is necessary to have a welfare state. Hence, there may be both economic efficiency as well as ideological arguments for the welfare state. The balance between these arguments, including the willingness to pay for welfare, will continue to have an effect on the welfare states in the years to come.

HISTORICAL DEVELOPMENT

It is difficult to briefly describe the historical development of welfare states in different countries, as the national strategies used when social policy and social security were initiated were highly nation specific. Nonetheless, it seems possible to identify some common features and also see the development of welfare states in a framework in which certain time periods have witnessed decisions that have had a stronger impact and influence on the developments of the welfare state than others. References are made here to certain key people in relation to the thinking about and development of welfare state activities, even though for many countries this means oversimplifying and neglecting the influences of national figures and national responses to changes in economic and social conditions.

When looking at different countries and the complexity of their economic and social development, it becomes obvious why it is not easy to say exactly why and how different welfare states developed. National differences in economic, political, social, and cultural conditions have existed (and still do), and these differences have had an effect on the way the systems developed. This is why so many variations of the welfare state exist, and why there are numerous interpretations of the why and how of welfare states.

The structure of the following discussion reflects the situation found in different historical periods of the development of the welfare state. The first period is ancient times and the development of the Poor Laws. Next comes the period of industrialization in the late 17th and early 19th centuries (1870–1913), followed by the period between World War I and World War II and immediately after World War II. The golden age of the welfare state (1950–1973) is described, trailed by a discussion of the welfare state crisis, retrenchment, and new orientation since 1973. Central thinkers of the various periods are included, and the prevailing ideology of each period is also presented.

The first elements of the welfare state derived from many countries' support of specific groups that were seen as deserving. In ancient times, one particular deserving group was soldiers who had served their country. This implies that a core factor in public-sector involvement has been opinions about who deserves support and who does not. This also indirectly acknowledges that, to involve some people in higher-risk activities, some type of coverage is needed, for example, accident insurance for invalidity caused by work accidents. During ancient times, it was mainly men going to war who were covered, because the risk of not being able to support themselves after a war was high, and their war injuries were not their own fault.

Later on, more general approaches emerged, although they were weakly applied. The Poor Law Act of 1601, in the United Kingdom, seems to have been the first law implementing support for specific groups in society aside from soldiers. There had been some earlier laws—for example, the Poor Law Act of 1388—the main aim of which had been to cope with possible labor shortage in the years after the Black Death; however, the 1601 act was the first under which a specified group, paupers who were old or sick, would receive support. On the other hand, others needing support would have to be employed in a house of correction. This law worked—on a decentralized basis—for more than 200 years, but communities were economically pressed by growing populations and the beginning of industrialization, which began earlier in the United Kingdom than in most other countries. Due to growing pressure and changes in economic and philosophical thought, including laissez-faire attitudes and a belief in the need for incentives for the poor, a new Poor Law was implemented in 1834. Its main principle was less eligibility and inclusion of a strong test; it provided that most people should be discouraged from receiving poor relief—the beginnings of the stigmatizing effects of social policy. The influence of Adam Smith and the free-market mechanism was clear during this period. In other countries, other poor laws with the same ideological emphasis as those in the United Kingdom were gradually introduced.

The church also played a central role in coping with the legal and administrative problems of society in many countries; however, this impact was quite different from country to country, mainly because of variations in religion. The Catholic Church emphasized its responsibility and also (even if first written down in the *Quadragesimo Anno*, 1931) the principle of subsidiarity, which implied a higher responsibility for the individual and the family. This has been an important factor in the diversity of welfare states in Europe. The Protestant church, on the other hand, has been more inclined to argue for state intervention and a smaller role for the church in relation to welfare state development.

In most European countries, development of the welfare state in the 19th century was brought about by growing industrialization and changes in demographics and societal structure, including increasing pressure on the cities. The welfare-related developments included poor laws, the establishment of mutual societies, and growing voluntary action and private charities. The role of the public sector was still limited.

From 1820 onward, the world economy grew more dramatically than ever before, and a comparison of the gross domestic product growth rates from 1500–1820 with those from 1820–1992 clearly shows the difference. From 1500 to 1820, the growth rate was 0.04 percent, whereas from 1820 to 1992 it was, on average, 1.21 percent. Economic development also seems to have had an effect on the possibility of development of public support. Periods of rapid welfare state development correlate with periods of rapid economic development.

The most rapid economic expansion occurred from 1950–1973, the second most rapid from 1870–1913, and the third from 1973 onward. Excluding the period from 1973 onward, when the debate over retrenchment and crisis was prominent, the two remaining periods are central to understanding the evolution of the welfare state.

Between 1870–1913, many new types of legislation were passed addressing different and, especially new, social risks. Accident insurance, sickness, old-age pension, and invalidity were among the areas covered. Bismarck's reforms in Germany in the 1880s emphasized social insurance. The first reform was a law concerning sickness in 1883, which was followed by industrial injury in 1884 and invalidity in 1889. These types of legislation were passed in many other Western European countries in the period leading up to 1913.

Bismarck's social insurance reform was a response to the industrialization of Germany and fear of uprisings by the working class unless it was covered against new forms of risk. These new risks were caused not only by the new industries, but also by population movements, which indicated that the family's responsibility was weakened. Without public-sector intervention, many families would have been left without support in cases of industrial injury, sickness, and old age.

Reforms in Germany were based on mutual aid and combined the use of state intervention with employer responsibility. In this way, reform continued along the path already traced, with individuals being covered either by employers' liability, personal savings, and private insurance, or a combination of the three. Furthermore, this system used the capitalist production systems combined with state intervention. The tendency toward a more mixed economy was apparent.

In other European countries, in addition to personal savings and private insurance, mutual-aid societies were of central importance. When these types of remedies seemed to lose strength and social problems increased, social security reforms evolved, and the state became more involved. Thus, it can be said that changes in demographics and economic conditions (industrialization and growing class conflicts) were the catalysts for the rising tide of welfare state reforms.

From a more ideological point of view, the liberal mode of thinking influenced the development of reforms in many ways. Collectivist approaches and thinking, especially Marxism, had an impact on various systems in the sense that the development of better living and working conditions was part of the class conflict in many countries. This discord involved more than just struggles between the traditional classes, that is, the workers and the capitalists. Especially in Scandinavian countries, coalitions were formed between workers and farmers with the aim of promoting decisions favoring both groups. As compromises between different groups in society were reached that were not formed along the traditional lines between those owning the means of production and those without, it gradually became apparent in many political democracies that these "coalitions" were driving forces toward a welfare state; therefore, the ideology behind the welfare state is not one-sided, but has many different faces and often a mixture of attitudes. Even though the term *welfare pluralism* first emerged late in the development of the welfare state, traces of it can be found early on in many countries.

The period prior to World War I was influenced by and ran parallel to a gradual reduction of voluntary work as part of social policy. Later on, increased state intervention appeared in many welfare states. When World War I started, reforms naturally came to a halt in many countries. Economic and political resources had to be used to cope with the war. After the war, the possibilities of, and need for, reforms gradually surfaced again. The process of, and wish for, changes and reforms of social security and increasing coverage of different needs, combined with state intervention in the economies, still existed, even though it had been difficult to implement new initiatives during World War I.

Expenditure for social protection and other welfare state activities continued to grow after World War I, although the classical way of thinking about public finance was a hindrance to any active stimulus to the economies. John Maynard Keynes's work first made clear that the public-sector economy could be used as an instrument for creating jobs and stimulating the economy. The economic rationality for growing pressure on the systems existed, partly due to the fact that ever more people were living in the cities in poverty and destitution without proper support.

Reforms were halted by the growing tensions in Europe and the outbreak of World War II in 1939. World War II and the preparations for what was going to happen after the war were important in the development of the postwar welfare state. The war seemed to inspire a more collectivist way of thinking, encompassing many who needed help through no fault of their own. In addition, there was a belief that the best way to reduce the possibility of another war would be to reduce tensions among countries, create jobs, and guarantee decent living standards.

Lord William Beveridge, especially in his 1942 report, *Social Insurance and Allied Services*, laid the foundation for many postwar welfare state systems. He proposed to reduce unemployment, provide a comprehensive health care system, and guarantee a minimum income. This more universal type of welfare system, which in T. H. Marshall's understanding was implicitly built on citizens' rights, laid the groundwork for the systemic development of the welfare state in many countries. In the United Kingdom, Beveridge's ideas combined with a more Keynesian economic approach to foster a slow but steady expansion of the public sector after the war, thus emphasizing the impact of specific people in the development of the national welfare state, as well as future development.

The period from 1950–1973 can be labeled the golden age of welfare state development. It combined high economic growth with rapid expansion of the public sector. Welfare states throughout the world, with some exceptions and differences in pace, expanded rapidly during this time. Economies that developed more rapidly, for example, those in China, Russia, Brazil, India, and South Africa, later developed welfare states. All-encompassing systems and a greater reliance on public-sector provision than on the market and civil society were the cornerstones of development, especially in Europe, the northern United States, and Oceania. These systems included coverage of broader groups in society; better and higher levels of benefits; and new types of services for children, the elderly, and other vulnerable groups in society. Finally, health care systems were expanded in response to a growing need for treatment and new methods for taking care of different types of needs.

Aside from the possibility of expanding the public sector economically, a changed division of responsibility between family and society gradually took hold in many countries. This could be seen in the increasing number of women who entered the labor market, as well as the new types of care for which the public sector became responsible. The function of the family as a core unit for providing welfare diminished in many countries, although it still had an important role, and in some welfare states a very profound role, for example, in the Southern European welfare state.

The golden age of expansion thus experienced a higher level of state involvement and a reduction in the role of the market and civil society—including voluntary organizations. The other side of the coin of this rapid expansion was growing taxation. The higher level of taxes and duties, combined with the economic recession in most of the world after the first and second oil crises in the 1970s, which quadrupled oil prices, brought into question the survival of the welfare state. In combination with the increase in oil prices, unemployment rates grew, inequality increased, and public sector deficits started to rise in many countries. These factors led to a growing disbelief in the Keynesian fine-tuning of the economy and doubts about the welfare state's ability to guarantee decent living standards with so much public-sector debt.

Furthermore, the legitimacy of the welfare state was questioned by both the New Right and the New Left. The New Left criticized the welfare state for not having honored its primary commitment to full employment and for not having brought about an equitable society. The state's role had become too weak compared to the markets, and a reformulation of the state's role in societal development was needed. The unfulfilled expectations increased the New Left's criticism of the welfare state. The New Right criticized the welfare state from the other side. The economic burden on society of a growing public sector crowded out private investment, and generous unemployment benefits reduced the incentive to work, especially at low-income jobs, creating problems in the labor market. Finally, the New Right questioned the role of the bureaucracy and pressure groups, especially within the framework of public choice. The argument was that the bureaucracy and pressure groups were mainly considering their own interests instead of society's, reducing society's overall welfare.

The growing legitimacy crisis and, some argued, already a financial crisis, led to a new orientation of the welfare state in many countries, and the growth of the public sector came to a halt in many locations, the exception being latecomers. Perhaps surprisingly, only a few real cutbacks in benefits or services in the various welfare states were implemented. A continuously high state level of involvement in welfare prevailed, and convergence seemed to be on its way, at the least among the richer Western European countries. Thus, the states' involvement in and financing of many activities can still be seen, although the focus seems to have shifted slightly toward health care and trying even more than in the golden age of the welfare state to target support to the vulnerable groups. Long-term consideration of demographic changes and the impact of globalization on the welfare state have opened new avenues for debate and discussion about the welfare state's future development. Moreover, the historical distinction between the deserving and undeserving was resurrected as a central element in the way the welfare states provide benefits to their citizens.

A more profound method of mixing state, market, and civil society has simultaneously occurred in many countries. Voluntary groups and organizations also seem to have gained importance. In addition, the division of welfare into public, occupational, and fiscal welfare has changed, with many welfare states increasingly relying on occupational welfare, sometimes supported by fiscal welfare; in this way a different role for the state has emerged.

Marketization and privatization were buzzwords for many conservative governments in the 1980s and 1990s. They were combined with a more liberal approach to economic policy and greater reliance on the individual's commitment to society. Market elements were incorporated into public-sector provisions, and the boundaries between state, market, and civil society underwent changes. Retrenchment of the welfare state could be witnessed during this period in several countries, although the real cutbacks were few and mainly hit the unemployed and those living on social assistance; therefore, there was a discrepancy between rhetoric and reality in relation to the welfare states' development.

The welfare state still seems to be a foundation tone in many societies, and more countries are trying to develop societies in such a way that access to care and social benefits will be possible to ensure a decent living standard for those outside the labor market. It can therefore be argued that there is no real crisis of the welfare state, just an adjustment of present ideologies and a less collectivist attitude, made evident by the changes in many countries throughout the world.

THE WAY FORWARD

A single definition of the welfare state still does not exist. Different types of welfare states and suggestions for what a welfare state should be about. To some extent, this has to do with the differences among the nation states' economic, cultural, and political developments. The interaction and mutual interdependence also creates pressure for convergence among the various countries' systems, while trying to maintain respect for national traditions and differences in institutional structures. The welfare state emerged in response to new needs—and it continues to evolve as new needs arise and some of the old ones subside. The insecurity related to globalization and increased free movement of workers and capital also indicates a continued need for a welfare state.

Developments in many countries seem to underline that the citizens want welfare services—and they want more of them as countries become richer. At the same time, the distinction between public and private delivery is less important so long as the quality is good and access is not dependent on income.

Many voters still want increasing welfare benefits and services; however, in many countries, it has become even more difficult to finance the welfare state in the traditional way, with the state being the central actor, especially in the wake of the financial crisis that started in 2008. This emphasizes that the development of welfare states seems to be dependent on the general economic climate and an increase in wealth. Wealthier countries will find it easier to provide their citizens with more welfare than poorer societies. The increased impact of globalization also implies fewer differences among welfare states, although different perceptions of what welfare states can and should deliver have an effect on the welfare states' development. Furthermore, there is a constant change in the boundaries between state, market, and civil society, with change seemingly being a constant challenge to the development in welfare states. The role of civil society and the question of how to deliver welfare have thus become more important than they were 10 or 15 years ago. In many welfare states, the high level of public-sector deficit and debt has also become a central issue given the restrictions that deficit and debt place on the welfare states' future abilities to pursue a path with more spending on welfare.

The focus on the labor market and its importance in societies has also increased, dramatically so given the impact of the last financial crisis, with negative economic growth and only a slow economic recovery. Having a job has become an important factor related to integration into society, and in recent years, the active labor market policy has increasingly focused more on work and less on increases in human capital; therefore, the high level of unemployment in many countries has had a negative impact on welfare states' performance. For example, in Southern Europe, the high level of youth unemployment can be seen as a specific and perhaps long-lasting challenge for the welfare states. Individuals who remain outside the labor market for a lengthy span of time run the risk of only marginally entering the labor market at a later date. These individuals have a more limited earning potential, and they thereby become, to a larger degree, more dependent on welfare benefits than those having stable and permanent jobs.

A central issue in the years to come will be how to cope with the growing inequality, as well as the need for higher economic growth and sustainable public-sector finances in the welfare states, which will aid in job creation and the ability to main the welfare state. Citizens continue to expect more welfare, as it increases their well-being and happiness. Although many welfare states have similarities, there are still differences based on the historical features and traditions. Hence, some countries have a more corporatist approach, some have a more liberal approach, and others have a more universal approach to welfare. For the time being, there is a crisis; however, the crisis may prove short-lived if the welfare state can return to a period of growth and development, making it possible to finance welfare. This also depends on whether citizens look at the welfare state as a burden or a social investment.

Despite the high level of unemployment, many countries are expecting a reduction in labor supply and risk of insufficient labor within the next 20 to 25 years due to the aging of the population. Consequently, many countries have been making changes to their labor market policy to increase the prospect of a continuation of a high labor supply. Demographic changes are thus becoming even more important and have been part of the reason for a number of reforms in pension systems worldwide, with the aim of getting workers to retire later and save more money for pension purposes. These changes have resulted in a shift away from state pay-as-you-go systems toward a higher reliance on occupational welfare and labor market-based pension funds. A lower level of state-financed pensions may put those in the labor market in a more precarious position. Pension reforms, with lower state pensions and a later retirement age, are another way welfare states are reducing pressure on public-sector spending, and thereby the ability to finance welfare now and in the future.

Pension reforms started before the financial crisis, but they have intensified in the wake of the crunch. In addition, in several countries, there have been severe cuts in public-sector spending to reduce the public-sector deficit. There has also been an increase in taxes and duties as a way to try to make the public-sector financing more sustainable with a view to the future. The aforementioned boundaries between state, market, and civil society have therefore been moving toward a market-based approach and an expectation of a growing role for civil society.

In recent years, there has been a tendency to look into not only the economic perspectives of the development of the welfare state, but also how to ensure social cohesion, well-being, and a broader interpretation of what welfare is. This can be seen in the growing interest in happiness for people in different societies and the impact of this focus. It seems that a high level of social security and other related types of security are important measures related to the good life, thus the welfare state will presumably have a central role in this historical development.

A

ABSOLUTE POVERTY. This term refers to a certain "basket of goods" multiplied by the prices of those goods. The basket of goods consists of what is essential for survival or a certain minimum standard of living. Calculated in this way, depending on the wealth of the nation involved, the level could be supplemented by a percentage to cover items not included in the basket (e.g., nonfood items). The calculation results in a line that the individual should be above to not be living in **poverty**.

The absolute poverty line has the advantage of making it possible to compare poverty in different countries in a certain year, at least if purchasing power is taken into consideration. One major disadvantage of using this measure is that it is difficult to use throughout time, as prices change due to **inflation** and production methods are altered. Furthermore, it ignores the problems of being a poor family, that is, it may be difficult to buy goods cheaply by using the different bargains in the **market** when buying many of an item, and it overlooks such nonmonetary considerations as personal security. Finally, it is difficult to decide which items should be included in the basket of goods before calculating the poverty line. Different goods, it is argued, should (or should not) be included, and they may vary among countries.

An absolute poverty line does not provide any information about the type of **welfare state**, nor does it give any indication of policies employed to reduce poverty. Different welfare states, depending on the relative wealth of the countries, will also presumably have different viewpoints about what goods are necessary for survival, not only in a nutritional sense, but in the sense of being socially included in society, for example, to be able to participate in cultural and social life. Today, for instance, it can be asked whether mobile phone and access to the Internet should be included in the necessary basket of goods. In this way absolute poverty is a **normative** concept.

ACCIDENT INSURANCE. Accident insurance is taken out to protect against certain well-defined accidents, for example, a workplace injury. In most **welfare states**, this was the first **contingency**, aside from support to the poor, to be covered by state support or state legislation. This was achieved by making it an obligatory insurance, a state-supported insurance system or a state system in which those who were injured could be paid for a shorter or longer period. A dependent **family** may also be supported by accident insurance.

The reason this area was the first to be covered seems to be that it was a new risk (today they are labeled the old risk, whereas new risk, for example, is family breakups) that emerged as a consequence of industrialization. Many families moved to the city, where relatives no longer supported them when injuries occurred. It was therefore impossible to maintain a decent standard of living. The injury was seen as being no fault of the individual, who therefore deserved support. It can be argued that, if no such support existed, it would have been difficult to attract more labor to the cities, where it was needed in the new factories.

Germany was the first country to introduce accident insurance, between 1881 and 1884, followed by **Austria** in 1887, and **France** in 1898. In Scandinavia, accident insurance was introduced around 1900, and in the **United States** and **Canada** in 1930. In many welfare states today, different kinds of accident insurance still play an important role in covering families and individuals against specific kinds of risks. In addition, obligatory insurance against risk is a way of **financing** the welfare state that reduces the pressure on the more traditional means, for instance, income **taxes** and duties. *See also* RISK SOCIETY.

ACTIVE AGING. The possibility for the elderly to continue having an active social life, including social, economic, cultural, and civil affairs. Active aging also relates to the fact that the elderly will stay in the **labor market** longer and presumably be healthier longer than was the case with previous generations. Both aspects will mean that **public-sector** expenditures on welfare will be less strongly affected by current **demographic** transitions than had been expected. Recent **pension** reforms throughout the world have also reduced possible pressures on the public purse. Active aging policies further aim to remove age **discrimination**, ensure flexible retirement, and support **lifelong learning**.

ACTIVE LABOR MARKET POLICY (ALMP). This is an important element of many countries' welfare policies, as it can be a way of ensuring **social inclusion**; in addition, it is a way of helping the individual to be independent of financial or other types of aid from society. A reduction in people's dependence on society, for example, might also be reducing spending on **unemployment benefits** and **social assistance**. This is an important positive element of ALMP.

ALMPs can have many forms and variations; examples include on-the-job training, vocational training, and general **education**. Such policies can be in the public or private sector and can include various forms of economic support from the **welfare state** to get people back into the **labor market**. In the

Scandinavian welfare states, ALMPs have been central in ensuring full **employment** since the mid-1950s. In many countries' **social-security** systems, activation has been one of the conditions for receiving social help.

ADVERSE SELECTION. When an individual with a significant risk is able to hide this from an insurance company, the problem of adverse selection arises. When analyzing the various ways of providing **social policy**, it is difficult to provide a **market**-based solution in the face of adverse selection, and in areas where this risk is high, public intervention is needed. Insurance companies find it difficult to set a correct premium, one that corresponds, for example, to the individual's risk of falling ill. This could result in a lack of supply, as the possibility of correctly calculating income and expenditures is difficult, implying a high risk of losses for insurance companies when providing this type of insurance. In these cases, either obligatory insurance for all citizens or **universal** state insurance is often seen as the solution.

AFFIRMATIVE ACTION. This American term describes a method for supporting disadvantaged groups. This can be through special treatment or other types of help. Another way of describing it is positive discrimination toward specific groups. Affirmative action has especially been used in relation to **gender** and **ethnicity** issues, but it also arises in treatment of people with disabilities, for example, in access to public buildings. In many **welfare states**, affirmative action has resulted in improvement of various groups' positions, including their **integration** into society. *See also* POSITIVE DISCRIMINATION.

AGING OF SOCIETIES. In the years to come, most mature **welfare states** will witness a change in their **demographic** composition. An increase in the number of elderly people and a decrease in the number of young people are the consequences of a falling birth rate and longer **life expectancy**. This has implications for welfare states, as the elderly in many welfare states receive public **pensions,** use the **health care** system more than others, and need more personal social **care**. In addition, it has implications for the **labor market**, which may be shrinking, thus, it has been argued, making it more difficult to increase wealth. The implications of the impact of aging vary depending on the change in birth rate, and they can also be mitigated by changes in the level of **migration**. An aging population may result in a variety of consequences, depending on such factors as changes in birth rates or variations in the levels of inward and outward migration. There is frequent discussion about how welfare states can cope with these changes. Views on the matter are diverse, ranging from those who believe that radical changes need to be made, to those who believe there is no need for any alterations. In particular, it seems that there will be changes in the labor market, emphasizing the need for an **active labor market policy**. Individuals might live longer, and also healthier, lifestyles, reducing the pressure on **public-sector** spending. New types of welfare technologies can also imply a decreased need for more people to do the **social services** for the elderly, lessening the need for both spending and the use of labor.

ALLOWANCE. A fund given to the individual by the state, the **market**, or **civil society**. The allowance can be based either on contributions or civil **rights**. Different types of allowance exist under different systems, including, for example, **housing** or child allowances. These allowances also have a different value in different countries, that is, some **welfare states** are more generous in certain areas than others. Comparisons of the value of different allowances in welfare states often try to calculate the value based upon purchasing-power parities or, for example, the proportion of cost of having a child paid for by the welfare state.

ANCIENT WELFARE RIGHTS. In ancient times, there was no well-developed form of intervention and support for the needy. Still, in some sense, the **right** and duty to share food with those who were unable to hunt or gather for themselves, mainly the elderly and children, was a form of **social assistance**. In relation to benefits and **services**, taking **care** of those in **need** was based within the **family**.

In classical Athens (6th century BC), a specific type of social assistance for soldiers was developed for those who had been wounded in war and were no longer able to take care of themselves. Support was later extended to citizens who had been determined eligible by a vote of the common assembly. In Rome, the state provided people in need with some grain, but it was not a fully developed system.

In many European countries, the **church** and monasteries later provided places where needy people could get some help, mainly **benefits in-kind**. With the onset of the Reformation in Northern Europe around 1730, the church began losing its property and therefore its ability to provide support for the poor. As a consequence, the state gradually took over this responsibility.

Insurance-based systems have existed in many countries for some time. In Rome, for example, a funeral insurance existed to support those expenses; however, only in 1698 was the world's first life insurance company started. In some countries, "friendly societies" were created with the purpose of supporting one another in cases of severe need. This was mainly done among **trade unions** and other groups with specific needs. The **Poor Law** of 1601 in the **United Kingdom** was the beginning of a more institutionalized state system.

In most countries, the real development of social systems was a response to the Industrial Revolution and the breakdown of traditional bonds between families, as well as inflows into the cities, which caused new risks. Systems like those developed during ancient times are currently in place in several **welfare states**, and the implicit distinction between deserving and undeserving plays a role in many countries' social policies.

APPEAL SYSTEMS. The systems in most **welfare states** through which citizens can complain about misconduct or ill or improper treatment by **street-level bureaucrats**. The appeal systems can have various forms and structures, but the main idea is that they will help to ensure all citizens the same treatment within the legal framework of a given society.

ARGENTINA. The first area of risk to be covered in Argentina, as in many other countries, was **industrial injury**, for which a law was passed in 1915. In the 1920s and 1930s, Argentina was one of the richest countries in the world, and one should therefore have expected a more rapid development of **social security** laws than actually was the case. A law providing **maternity benefits** in 1934 followed the law on industrial injury, and the first **pension** system was created in 1944. The pension system originally targeted only a small group; however, in the late 1960s, it became a more general system. After World War II, Juan Peron governed until 1955, and a lengthy period of economic and political problems followed, including dictatorships. **Unemployment benefits** for construction workers were introduced in 1967; in 1991, they were provided more generally. **Family allowances** were introduced in 1957. The Argentine system mainly relies on covering employed persons and therefore is not **universal**. It can be seen as a **conservative** system, in which only limited public intervention and support are involved. It is also comparable to **Southern European welfare state models** in that it relies more on the **family** than the state.

ARROW'S IMPOSSIBILITY THEOREM. This is the most famous theorem in **welfare economics**, named after Kenneth Arrow's famous contribution in 1951. It states that, given certain conditions (described here), it is impossible to choose a **social welfare function** that will optimize society's welfare and is unambiguous. The criteria are as follows:

1. The **Pareto** criteria should be fulfilled.
2. There should be no dictatorship.
3. There should be independence of irrelevant alternatives.
4. There should be an unrestricted domain.

The first criterion is the traditional one in economics, that changes should be made so long as one person's position can be improved without anyone else being worse off. It could also be more simply stated that the society should produce and distribute along the production function for the society. The second criterion implies that the solution should not just be determined by one person, but should have broad support, and that the welfare function should represent all members of society. The third criterion—independence of irrelevant alternatives—implies that an alternative should be a possible alternative, not, for example, something outside the available production frontier. The fourth criterion, unrestricted domain, implies that a ranking of different possible solutions should be possible. This means that the different combinations of goods and **services** in a society can be ranked and measured against one another.

The main problem with the measurement of welfare is the need to make **interpersonal comparisons**. One individual's use of a good may give that person a specific **utility** that is different from another person's utility of the same good; therefore, it will be difficult to find a solution.

Many have tried to solve the problem by relaxing one or more of the restrictions, but it still seems that it is impossible to objectively determine a society's welfare function and make recommendations about the welfare policy in that country. At the same time, using elements from the criteria may help in prioritizing possible solutions.

ASYMMETRICAL INFORMATION. A situation in which the amount of information is not the same for all involved in a decision. This can be in an agreement or in administrative processes. This may be the case when an insurance company does not know whether an individual is a good or bad risk. Asymmetrical information is related to **moral hazard**. It also relates to the discussion about how to manage and steer different parts of the **welfare state**, for instance, the **health-care** sector, where professionals like doctors have information that the **principal agents** do not. This makes implementation difficult, and it also makes it challenging to ensure a high degree of efficiency. Asymmetrical information can also exist when individuals applying for a **disability pension** do not precisely inform about their abilities to take up a job.

ATTITUDE GROUPS. These are, to a considerable extent, the same as **pressure groups**. The main difference is that in an attitude group, the individuals participating share the same beliefs, for example, a religion or ideology.

ATYPICAL EMPLOYMENT. Increasingly, many workers do not have regular jobs with a permanent contract. Instead, they may work from a distance from home or as teleworkers. Atypical employment can also refer to work that is short-term and based on a specific contract, or shifting between being employed and self-employed. With new forms of work, new problems arise for **social security** systems, for example, how to provide **unemployment** insurance for those not working in the typical way with a fixed number of work hours. Atypical employment has also raised new issues on how to balance work and **family** life.

AUSTRALIA. Australia introduced **social security** later than did many Western European countries. **Industrial injury** was the first area covered, but it was not implemented throughout Australia at the same time—it took from 1902 to 1946. Old age and **disability pensions** were introduced in 1908, and widows' pensions in 1942. Then came **family allowances** in 1941; **sickness, maternity,** and **unemployment benefits** followed in 1944. As a member of the British Commonwealth, Australia has been inspired by the **United Kingdom,** and its more **universal** approach is in line with Lord William Beveridge's suggestions. Furthermore, the labour movement in Australia was strong and held office as a minority **government** in 1904 and 1908. By 1914, it had gained a majority. The strong impact of the **trade unions** seems to be one of the reasons for a more egalitarian approach in Australia than in many other **welfare states.**

Old-age, disability, and unemployment benefits, as well as family allowances, are, as a rule, paid by the government. Thus, in combination with the general criterion that it is covering residents in many areas, this system in these specific areas resembles the **Scandinavian welfare state universal model.** Some would describe Australia as a fourth world of welfare capitalism because of its combination of the **means-tested** and **residual** welfare state types on the one hand and the more universal types of benefits on the other.

As have other countries, Australia has increased the age of retirement in recent years, including giving economic **incentives** to work until a later age. It has also made reforms to the **labor market** system, making the Australian welfare state leaner and closer to a **liberal** type of welfare state. Focus on activation and work-first has also been on the agenda. At the same time, Australia has been somewhat shielded from the **financial crisis** given its natural resources and a high level of trade, especially with **China.**

AUSTRIA. After 1867, the former Austrian empire became the dual monarchy of Austria-Hungary. The first Austrian republic was established in 1918. In 1854, an **invalidity pension** for mineworkers was introduced. The first **social security** law in Austria, the **industrial injury** law, was passed in 1887. It was followed by **sickness** and **maternity** coverage in 1888, and then by pensions for salaried employees in 1906, and wage earners in 1935. **Unemployment benefits** were first introduced in 1920, and **family allowances** began in 1948.

Austria was inspired by **Germany** and the **Bismarckian model**, which is also reflected in the Austrian system's strong reliance on participation in the **labor market** and contributions from the labor market. The system is, thus, mainly insurance-based, although the family allowance system is **universal**. In certain areas, for instance, dental and medicine, user charges are applied. Austria can be mainly described as a Bismarckian welfare state due to the strong emphasis on and use of insurance funds in the system.

Despite **financial crisis**, there has been some improvement in the system, including coverage of self-employed people and better ability to save for **supplementary pensions**. There has also been a focus on changes in the pension system, with a later retirement age being expected.

AVERAGE PRODUCTION WORKER (APW). This term is especially used by the Organization for Economic Cooperation and Development when comparing the level of benefits in different countries. This is done by referring to the level of benefits acquired by a person who has the same income as an average production worker. It is, thus, a standardized way of measuring the level of benefits. It is therefore also used as one element when calculating the **replacement rate**.

B

BASIC INCOME. The level of economic resources that a **welfare state** will guarantee an individual. It is most commonly understood as the minimum income that all citizens are guaranteed by the state. The level of **social assistance** can often be an indicator of the level of basic income, but it is only an indicator, because, for example, student benefits will be at a lower level, as they are expected to earn income later in life. Furthermore, the self-employed may, for short periods of time, have lower income levels due to variations in their ability to generate profits. Basic income can vary in amount depending on the type of benefits, for instance, a basic **pension**. Some see basic income as a way of setting a level so that no citizen will be living in **poverty**.

BASIC NEEDS. The goods that an individual and/or **family** need to survive and have a decent standard of living. The **International Labour Organization** has defined it as including two specific areas: (1) adequate food and clothing and some household goods; and (2) access to such essential **services** as water, transportation, **health care**, **education**, and culture. It is emphasized that basic needs should be understood within a country's historical and cultural tradition. This makes it difficult to measure and be precise about the concept, but it stresses that not only a minimum requirement, a certain basket of goods, should be reached.

The concept of basic needs has been used in the debates on **poverty**, especially **absolute poverty**, but also on living standards more generally, for example, in Erik Allard's discussion of having, loving, and being. It is argued that basic needs should be fulfilled before an individual is able to move on to fulfill other needs. At the same time, there is no unanimous agreement on what the basic needs are in more concrete terms; therefore, it has been difficult to use in relation to policy recommendations for the development of the **welfare state**.

The term is also related to the understanding of **deprivation**. The **European Union (EU)** has found that a person is living in material deprivation if they cannot afford three out of the following nine items:

1. Coping with unexpected expenses
2. One week annual holiday away from home

3. Avoiding arrears (in mortgage or rent, utility bills, or higher purchase installments)
4. A meal with meat, chicken, fish, or the vegetarian equivalent every second day
5. Keeping the home adequately warm
6. A washing machine
7. A color TV
8. A telephone
9. A personal car

It is naturally open for interpretation whether this reflects basic needs, but it does emphasize that what is seen as basic needs will change throughout time in accordance with changes in living standards in given countries, or, in this case, in the EU.

BELGIUM. The first welfare areas to be covered in Belgium were **sickness** and **maternity**; these benefits were provided through a mutual benefit society. In 1844, the country brought into law an obligatory **invalidity** and old-age **pension** for seamen. In 1903, coverage against **industrial injury** was introduced. This was followed by **unemployment benefits** in 1920, and, in 1924, a law covering the pension system was passed. Finally, in 1930, **family allowances** were introduced.

The Belgian system is chiefly a **continental** and **conservative** type, with a high reliance on the **labor market**, only relying on the state as the main provider to a limited degree. Belgium's historically close connections with **Germany** seem to explain the development of its system. A major problem in Belgium has been its division into two separatist areas divided mainly by language, which has influenced the system and will likely continue to do so. While Belgium has also been negatively influenced by the **financial crisis**, at the same time, for example, in 2012, it implemented longer parental leave.

BENEFIT PRINCIPLE. This principle states that those who enjoy public-service benefits should pay the **taxes** to **finance** them according to the degree of **utility** from the **services** received. It is mainly used when delivering public services, where it is possible to make a connection between users and the supply. Common examples are roads, bridges, public transportation, water, and electricity. In some countries, the principle is partly used in relation to the payment for specific **care** facilities for children and the elderly. In recent years, there has been an increase in **welfare states** attempting to combine financing, especially in **health care**, with increased user charges, although they do not always adhere to the general benefit principle.

BENEFITS IN CASH. This is money given to individuals who qualify for an income transfer when a specific risk occurs. It can be in the form of **unemployment benefits, maternity benefits, social assistance**, and so forth. In different **welfare states**, various criteria govern receiving these benefits. The main ones are eligibility, a **means test**, and whether one is covered as a citizen or as a member of an insurance fund. Receiving a benefit can also imply a demand for activation, or, in some developing countries, children's participation in **education**. In most welfare states, the criteria must be analyzed in the historical, cultural, and national context in which they have developed. It seems that there is a tendency for countries to learn from one another, resulting in a tendency toward **convergence**, that is, the systems resemble one another, although not necessarily the entire structure and level of benefits. Finally, the level of the benefits depends on the economic conditions in the country and the willingness of those not eligible for benefits to contribute if they are paid out of general **taxation**.

BENEFITS IN-KIND. These benefits are provided in the form of such goods as bread and **housing**. In many **welfare states**, this was one of the first ways of delivering benefits, the argument being that those in **need** should have bread and a place to live and not have a chance to spend the money on something else. It is also argued that by giving benefits in-kind instead of in cash, the voters' or citizens' willingness to pay for these forms of welfare will be greater than otherwise.

Today, these benefits are still used in some countries, primarily in two specific areas. The first is among certain groups that are unable to take **care** of themselves. The second is as assistance for those with particular handicaps or illnesses. The first group may include, for example, alcoholics and drug addicts. The fear is that if the benefits are not in-kind, the support would be used to buy alcohol or narcotics.

The second area in which benefits in-kind are used is where the state can buy products (e.g., wheelchairs and help remedies for different disabled groups) at less cost than an individual could. This can also apply to certain types of goods, for example, medicine for those with lifelong diseases, where instead of doing an income transfer, medicine may be given directly. For instance, it could be argued that homes for the elderly and **child care** are benefits in-kind, but these lie outside the definition given here, as they are mainly seen as **social services**. The criteria for receiving these benefits are outside the scope of benefits given directly, relating to certain characteristics of the groups receiving the benefit. Some countries use benefits in-kind to provide places where the poor can get a meal. In other countries, benefits in-kind are issued as **vouchers** that entitle the individual to certain goods or

services. The food stamp program in the **United States** is an example of this type of benefit in-kind.

BEVERIDGIAN MODEL. The Beveridgian model is named after Lord William Beveridge and his now-famous report, *Social Insurance and Allied Services*, issued in 1942. This report gives the name to a **welfare state** model characterized by **universal** provision of welfare and the intention of providing full **employment**. The basic idea is to provide comprehensive **health services** and specific **allowances** to children. Proper **housing** conditions were also part of what was considered necessary to ensure a good and decent living standard. The report argues (in paragraph 302) that a **social security** system should be built on three bases: (1) **social insurance** for **basic needs**, (2) national assistance for special cases, and (3) voluntary insurance for economic support on top of the basic level. The report assumes that the social insurance for basic needs would be "as comprehensive as possible," and, in that respect, it does not resemble the way we now think about insurance systems. It was not only those employed who were expected to pay into the insurance; *Social Insurance and Allied Services* claims that the state should also contribute. This implies that some individuals should be obliged to pay more through the **tax** system, even when the direct contribution is assumed to be a flat rate. The report focuses on want, disease, ignorance, squalor, and idleness. In this sense, it also reflects the ongoing debate about only giving support to those most in **need**, not to people who are merely idle or want to live off the benefits of the welfare state. The distinction between **deserving** and undeserving recipients of welfare benefits has been an element running through the welfare state's principles for many years.

The Beveridge report, and its implementation in the **United Kingdom** after World War II, must be understood in light of the historical circumstances. Following the war, there was a need for security and stability. This illustrates that the model of welfare will not be the same throughout time. It will change as economic and political circumstances vary.

The Beveridgian model can be described as an attempt to guarantee full employment, that is, a **right** to work. Its policy is aimed at providing jobs, a minimum level of subsistence, and a guaranteed standard of living. It proposes a universal welfare state, implying that people will mainly be covered as citizens, and the transfer should consist of low-level **flat-rate benefits**, **financed** through general taxation.

This model has been implemented primarily in the northern parts of Europe, and it must be stressed that no country can be expected to follow the Beveridgian lines completely, making it more a typology than a concrete description of countries' systems. Still, the concepts behind it have had a profound impact on **social policy** and welfare-state thinking in numerous countries.

BIG SOCIETY. The idea launched in the **United Kingdom** in 2010, by the then Conservative Party prime minister, David Cameron. The principal idea is to help people to come together in their neighborhoods to do good by engaging in more **voluntary work** and increasing **civil society's** involvement in the way the **welfare state's** work is undertaken. In this way, it reflects historical debates and issues concerning who should deliver welfare and the extent of civil society's role.

BISMARCKIAN MODEL. Named after German chancellor Otto von Bismarck (1815–1898), who established a compulsory insurance scheme in the 1880s, this system covered sickness, industrial accidents, and old age. The models were introduced to reduce political pressure from the growing working **classes** in cities and because of the fear of social uprisings. It was a new, but soon well-developed, structure that emerged to offer high coverage of the new risks stemming from the Industrial Revolution, for instance, **industrial injuries**. Furthermore, it helped to reduce social unrest and build a system in which mainly those in the **labor market** were covered.

Even today, the Bismarckian model can be characterized as relying on the labor market as the core provider of welfare and basing the **right** to transfers and their size on being in the labor market and having paid contributions. In this system, the degree of redistribution is small—going primarily from those not experiencing a social event to those needing help after being in the labor market. It builds on contributions from employers and employees, and the state's involvement is rather arbitrary. There is also some support for those outside the labor market.

The model was chiefly used in Continental Europe, with **Germany** as the prime example. It still prevails in Central Europe. It must naturally be borne in mind that the Bismarckian model is described here as an ideal type of welfare. National variations stemming from various historical, cultural, and economic conditions in the different countries involved will thus exist. The Bismarckian model has also been labeled the **continental model**, referring to the countries from which it originated.

BLOCK GRANT. A payment that typically comes from the central **government** to a regional or local part of the **public sector** that can then be used for a number of previously specified purposes at the lower level. This makes it possible, often within specified limits, to make local priorities of which areas of the **welfare state** to develop and/or reduce. Block grants thus permit local influence on the development of the local part of the welfare state. The size of the grants can be based upon objective or subjective criteria. An example of objective criteria is the number of people living in an area. An illustration of subjective criteria is a wish to develop certain rural areas. Finally, it is a way of **financing** a decentralized welfare state.

BRAZIL. Brazil was under Portuguese rule until 1899, when a republic was created. This may explain the late development of the **social security** system. In addition, for many years, Brazil has been ruled by dictatorships. During the 1920s, social unrest created pressure for social development.

Industrial injury began being covered in 1919. This was followed in 1923 by **pension** and **sickness** schemes for railroad workers. In 1934, individuals working in commerce were also covered, and, in 1936, this coverage was widened to include those working in industry. **Family allowances** followed in 1941, and, finally, **unemployment** was covered in 1965.

The system is mainly based on being an employed person, but it also requires some **public-sector finance** to support the different funds should there be a deficit in funding pensions, sickness, and **maternity**, as well as the main part of the unemployment system. Supplementary private pension systems also exist, and civil servants are covered under their own system.

The main criterion for eligibility is being part of the **labor market**, and, in this sense, this is a traditional **Bismarckian** system. There is still a high degree of **inequality**, and there are many poor people in the country. Brazil has had one of the most rapid economic development rates in the last 10 to 15 years, also generally implying a higher living standard; however, many people still live in **poverty** and without strong support from the social security system.

BREADWINNER. The person who earns the money to support the other members of the household. In many countries and social systems, this has traditionally been the man, which has given rise to the "male-breadwinner model" in **gender** analysis of the **welfare state**. Welfare states in Europe have increasingly had a dual-breadwinner system, suggesting that both men and women are in the **labor market**; therefore, the household income comes from two income earners.

BRIGGS, ASA (1921–). Briggs is a British sociologist and historian primarily known for his writings about the **welfare state** from the historical perspective. His definition of the welfare state, found in that entry, is often used as a starting point for further discussion of what a welfare state is or should be.

"The Welfare State in a Historical Perspective," in *The Welfare State* (1969), edited by C. Schottland, is a useful starting point for discussion on this topic.

BULGARIA. An Eastern European country with 7.5 million inhabitants and a modest **welfare state** often **financed** by a combination of employer and employee contributions, but also through general **taxes** in relation to **health care** and hospitals. The first law regarding **sickness** and **maternity** dates from 1918; laws on old age, **disability**, and **industrial injury** came in 1924; **unemployment** laws were first enacted in 1925; and **family** benefits were first introduced in 1942. Thus, Bulgaria is, in general, a latecomer to developing its welfare state and still has a rudimentary welfare system. The **pension** age is 63 for men and 60 for women; however, this is being changed so that men and women will receive equal treatment. An increase in the pension age to 65 for both **genders** was decided on in 2012. Bulgaria's pension system has a first-pillar earnings-related **pay-as-you-go** pension, a second pillar that involves mandatory individual accounts for all workers born after 1960, and finally a voluntary third pillar.

The country became a member of the **European Union (EU)** on 1 January 2007. Since 1 January 2014, when the rules on the free movement of workers were enacted, there has been an increase in the movement of workers from Bulgaria to other EU member states.

BUREAUCRACY. Although they date back some time, bureaucracies were originally poorly developed; their main purpose was to support the ruling king or emperor. In social science, the debate about bureaucracy is often related to **Max Weber** and the discussion about how to effectively organize production (including administration in both the public and private sectors) and use people's different skills most efficiently. In its original form, bureaucracy should be capable of "attaining the highest degree of efficiency and is in this sense formally the most rational known means of carrying out imperative control over human beings. It is superior to any other form in precision, in stability, in the stringency of its discipline, and in its reliability" (Weber, *The Theory of Social and Economic Organizations*, 1947). Another way of stating this is that the "bureaucratic administration is, other things being equal, always, from a formal, technical point of view, the most rational type. . . . The choice is only that between bureaucracy and dilettantism in the field of administration" (Weber, 1947).

The argument for the superiority of bureaucracy has been that those employed in the bureaucracy would know the precise rules for working and making decisions. This would reduce the time spent on finding solutions, and therefore the time used on the production line. Historically, bureaucracy has been a response to the growing complexity of organizations and the need for delegation and control. The expectation was that it would make production more rational and produce fewer failures. The techniques it used were fewer personal relationships, rules for behavior, and a hierarchical decision-making process. It was expected that a detailed description of how to behave would make all functions more efficient.

But this is only one of many different views of bureaucracy. Another is that bureaucracy is inefficient and a waste of resources, and that its operations have been conducted more in the self-interest of the producers than in an effort to give the consumers better possibilities. As the **welfare state** has grown, bureaucracy has also had to administer, steer, and plan the benefits and **services** provided by the welfare state. This has led to a debate about whether bureaucrats overburden the welfare state and how the bureaucracy could have a negative impact on society's functioning. According to William Niskanen, bureaucrats primarily act in their own interests. It has been argued that this action of the bureaucrats has had a strong impact on the growth of the **public sector.**

Some theorists, mainly adherents of the **public choice** tradition, have contended that the main reason for the growth of the welfare state is that the bureaucracy wishes to fulfill its own aims and not the clients' interests. The argument is that the status, power, and income of a bureaucrat depends on the size of the bureaucracy; therefore, only an increase in the bureaucracy will improve an individual bureaucrat's position.

Several arguments can be raised against this claim. First of all, the bureaucracy does not act alone. Many countries have elections, and there is usually a Ministry of Finance that wants to reduce spending. Furthermore, from a historical point of view, given the development of the welfare state, it is unreasonable to assume that bureaucracies should have started to push for growth during and after World War II, and to a greater extent in the 1960s and 1970s. Hence, it is also unreasonable to assume that they—at least alone—should be able to get the public sector to flourish. But this is not to say that it cannot be argued that in some areas and some cases, bureaucracies have had an impact on the growth of the welfare state.

In addition, it should be noted that bureaucracies are a combination of the administrative bureaucracy, professional bureaucracy, and **street-level bureaucrats.** The administrative bureaucracy in the welfare state organizes and plans welfare-state activities. The professional bureaucracy mainly focuses and concentrates on professional jobs, for example, doctors, nurses, and so forth. Professionals may have a special interest in and reason for wanting growth in their own specific area. The street-level bureaucrat is the one whom the individual client meets and who is empowered to make decisions—including discretionary decisions. This means that the individual may be dependent on the person he or she talks to. This often happens with **social assistance** and other social benefits and services that are not bound by previous contributions or do not rely on discretionary decisions. This may pose problems for policy makers and clients, as it can result in different treatment of equal cases. On the other hand, street-level bureaucrats take the individual case into consideration and can be more helpful.

Ongoing methods of measuring the efficiency of the welfare state's activities also need bureaucrats to do the measuring. The evaluation of efficiency may, thus, in itself, increase the need for more bureaucrats. In this way, welfare states are often confronted with a need to balance the need to know what is going on against the cost of administration. Moreover, administration is more expensive when the systems need to be targeted and just. Consequently, achieving a balance between justice and administrative costs is another challenge for most welfare states.

C

CANADA. Despite its historical connections with Europe, Canada developed its **social security** system at a relatively late stage. This may be explained in part by the autonomy of the provinces and the British North American Act of 1867, which united Canada as one country. **Industrial injury** coverage was first introduced in Quebec and Newfoundland in 1908, and then gradually in the other provinces during the next 10 years. A **pension** for the old was established in 1927, and **disability** coverage was added in 1954. In 1940, an **unemployment benefit** program was introduced. In the 1980s and early 1990s, systems relating to **sickness, maternity,** and **family allowances,** covering the whole of Canada, were introduced. Until then there had been only a patchwork of systems in the various provinces and territories.

The Canadian system is a mixture of a **universal** system for residents (pension, sickness benefits, maternity benefits, and family allowances) and systems depending mainly on **labor market** contributions and **finance**; therefore, it lies somewhere between the more **conservative** type of **welfare state** and the **Beveridgian** type of welfare state.

CAPABILITIES. An individual's basic possibilities and his or her capacity to do something. The contemporary theoretical focus is on how individuals or groups can achieve or do certain things. **Amartya Sen** has defined this theoretical approach by saying, "The approach concentrates on our capability to achieve valuable functionings that make up our lives, and more generally, our **freedom** to promote objectives we have reasons to value." Furthermore, it "represents the various combinations of functioning's (being and doings) that the person can achieve" (*Inequality Reexamined*, 1992).

This way of looking at the concept reflects individual choices about different approaches to deciding on a specific living standard (given the limits) by choosing between different elements in life. It also posits that capabilities are within a given set of possibilities and the structure of society. The concept can be used to stress that individuals lack things. If individuals want to use or have a specific type of good, then the problem of not having access to it is a restriction and lack of capability. The concept can also be used to analyze **marginalization, social exclusion,** and **equality.**

CARDINAL UTILITY. The ability to compare the **utility** derived from consumption both between and among individuals. It means that we can state how much more utility, for example, a person gets from an extra unit of a product, and that we can compare the utility that person A and person B derive from a certain good. In practice, the concept is difficult to apply, but, in theory, it is a useful assumption, as it allows for the comparison of different levels of welfare in or between societies and discussion about different solutions to specific problems.

CARE. Doing something for either oneself or for another person, to include help within the family, or it can be something the **welfare state** does in relation to, for example, children and elderly people. Care is important in many welfare states, as many people, including children and the frail elderly, are often unable to care for themselves. Historically, most care has been undertaken by the **family**; however, with the increased participation in the **labor market** of both men and women, there has been an increased need for care. In principle, care could be provided by the **market** through user charges in several areas. Private-sector-based care can have the disadvantage that it will not be possible for low-income earners to pay for the care, and they thereby risk not receiving it. *See also* COMMUNITY CARE.

CASH BENEFITS. *See* BENEFITS IN CASH.

CHARITY. The historical development of **welfare states** has also been filled with charity, where some people, organizations, or institutions (for example, religious) have donated money in voluntary form for welfare purposes. It is still the case today that friends and **families**, as well as **civil society**, donate money or pay for certain activities for individuals in **need**. The Bill and Melinda Gates Foundation is a modern example of how wealthy individuals donate money to charity.

Whether the form has been with or without obligations to receive the charity has been one matter for discussion. Another is whether charity, like voluntary activities, implies that the **right** to receiving support is no longer based upon objective criteria, but on the viewpoint of those donating regarding who deserves and who does not deserve to receive the support. At the same time, the **financial crisis** in many welfare states has implied that many vulnerable people or people at risk of **poverty** are dependent on support through charitable activities. *See also* CHURCH.

CHILD BENEFIT. **Social security** systems include specific child benefits, and the criterion for receiving such benefits is that there is a child in the **family**. It was late in the development of **welfare states** that these benefits were enacted in most countries. A benefit can be **means-tested** but does not have to be. It can also be of a different size depending on the age of the children. Most countries providing child benefits offer them as **universal** systems to support families with children that frequently have a lower average income than other groups in society. In this way, child benefits involve a redistribution of resources to families with children from families without children. In some systems, access to child benefits is therefore also dependent on the households' overall level of income and/or wealth. *See also* FAMILY ALLOWANCE.

CHILD CARE. Arrangements for taking **care** of children when parents are working. Child care can either be publicly or privately supplied. Furthermore, it can either be free of charge or paid for by user charges, or by a combination of payment from the users and public payment. In some countries, employers offer child care as a way to attract labor. In some countries, the development of child care has been seen as a way of making it possible to expand the **labor force** by giving mothers the option of both having a job and taking care of a child. Reconciling work and **family** can be achieved by, among other things, a well-functioning child-care system, as it enables both parents to be in the **labor market** and participating in the family's daily life at the same time.

The way a child-care system is organized largely follows the patterns of the various **welfare-state** models, although in recent years, there has been a rapid expansion of day care in most welfare states in Europe. A well-developed day-care system can also help ensure a more **gender**-equal development of societies. The **European Union** thus argues that affordable and high-quality day care should be available as part of the **employment** strategy. Finally, in Europe, day care systems are seen as part of the scheme to increase the **labor force**.

CHILD MAINTENANCE. The amount of money one parent (after a **divorce**) will have to pay to the other parent. The size of the payment differs among welfare regimes, and sometimes it can be voluntarily agreed upon, while at other times it is set by the administration or court. The aim has been to ensure the proper upbringing of children and reduce the risk of child **poverty**.

CHILE. Chile was liberated from Spain and became an independent state in 1818, but it was also one of the latecomers in developing **social security** and **welfare-state** arrangements. **Industrial injury** was the first welfare-related law to be implemented, in 1916. Laws covering old age, **disability**, sickness, and **maternity** were passed in 1924. It was not until 1937 that laws concerning **unemployment** and **family allowances** were introduced. In the area of **pensions**, a mandatory private and **social insurance** system was introduced in 1981; however, it was still mainly based on and paid for by the employer and insured individuals, although with some state guarantee for minimum pensions.

The system's main criterion for social-security coverage is to be in the **labor market**. It is therefore a highly **conservative** model, in which the coverage is only for the few, leaving those who are unable to join the labor market dependent on private **charity** and **family** help. Chile is a country with a relatively low income level, which may explain why the system is not more **universal** and also the relatively low level of benefits. **Privatization** and more **market** and less state involvement have been part of recent developments in Chile, which also helps explain the more rudimentary development of social-security systems compared to other countries.

CHINA. The People's Republic of China belongs to the **communist** type of **welfare state**, in which the state has overall responsibility for the citizens, including guaranteeing jobs, which then gives rise to coverage under certain conditions; however, in recent years, China has been introducing more **market** elements into society's development. The first laws covering old age, **disability, sickness, maternity,** and **industrial injury** were introduced in 1951. The late development of a welfare system must be viewed in relation to the lengthy period before and after World War II, the civil war with Japan, which occupied parts of China for extended periods of time. In 1986, a law on **unemployment benefits** was introduced, which covered all workers in state enterprises. The introduction must be seen in the light of the possibility of company bankruptcy stemming from this period, which implied that workers could become unemployed, whereas before they were guaranteed a job by the state.

The system is, in a sense, **universal**, offering everyone access to **health care**, and so forth, but it also involves the duty to take up a job, which thereafter generates one's **social-security rights**. The present system, which has more market elements, and the new risks this implies, seems to be moving toward a more residual welfare system in which the **government** provides a safety net when other means have been exhausted to ensure some minimum standard of living. China is increasingly using the safety-net approach to supplement the insurance systems developed in several areas. This can be seen as a response to changes in the economy, but also the restructuring of society, with more people living in big cities.

CHURCH. The church is a religious organization that, in many countries, has played a pivotal role in the development of **welfare-state** systems. In some countries, the church has been the first to help the poor and needy, but it has also emphasized the distinction between the **deserving** and undeserving. It still has an influence on the thinking of different parties and people, and thereby indirectly on the welfare-state system. For example, the emphasis in some countries on the **family** can be attributed to the role of the church. In certain countries, the church also plays a role in formulating social policies and can be seen as a **pressure group**, especially for the most vulnerable. *See also* CHARITY.

CITIZENSHIP. An individual's legal connection with a country. Most people are citizens of the country in which they were born. Others may change their citizenship due to either voluntary **migration** or involuntary migration (refugees). Citizenship is often connected to civil, political, and **social rights** (*see also* MARSHALL, T. H.). The possibility of individuals being granted different citizenship depends on the law in the given country. Most countries have rules about how to be naturalized. These rules often involve the person's connection to the country and the number of years that individual has stayed in the country. In some countries, double citizenship is allowed.

The concept of citizenship is important in the **social-policy** debate because part of the distinction between different social-policy systems depends on whether an individual has citizenship. Rights to **social security** may depend on citizenship, although in some parts of the world, regional and local agreements provide that rights can be transferred to other individuals without them becoming citizens. This is the case in the **European Union (EU)** and among the Scandinavian countries. A citizen who has been working in another country collects rights to, for example, a **pension**. International agreements of this kind make the concept of citizenship more blurred, and in the EU, for example, the idea of having European citizenship, as well as national citizenship, has been discussed.

CIVIL SOCIETY. The area and functions of private individuals, **families**, or organizations that are not subject to state intervention or regulation. It is a way of describing institutions and organizing activities that are not inherently built into the more formalized structures of society. The concept has been defined as a "set of social practices outside the state and outside the relations and forces of production" (Urry, *The Anatomy of Capitalist Societies: The Economy, Civil Society, and the State*, 1981). Civil society is, thus, not a single entity, but a broad variety of individuals and groups who, for different reasons, ranging from altruism to family bonds, often help one another in various ways and thereby form part of the **solidarity** of society. It is presumed, although not always certain, that family members help one another.

Historically, civil society has been seen as a way of living in a civilized political **community** and was, therefore, more of a term for civilized society. Around 1750, the perspective on civil society changed, and observers started to look upon it as being the dichotomy of the state. The distinctions among state, **market**, and civil society gradually emerged.

In the past 20 to 25 years, civil society has been brought back into the analysis of the **welfare state**. Highlighting the problems and reasons why something happens outside the state and the market has made this possible. Furthermore, it is obvious that some social problems tend to be solved and clarified outside these two areas and without any need for public intervention or market-based solutions. The debate about civil society also covers the question of whether individual or collective solutions with a higher emphasis on civil society will involve less **need** for collective solutions and more **individualistic** solutions. It can be said that civil society is a sphere in which self-interest and egoistic, rational behavior will and can occur.

The relations among **state, market, and civil society** can also be labeled the welfare triangle, the welfare mix, or the mixed economy. Within civil society, voluntary organizations and self-help groups have been forming, which may result in different, and therefore unequal, treatment of groups in need. In this case, a higher reliance on civil society may impose greater **inequality** and injustice. Finally, institutions in civil society are not necessarily open to information from and control by independent authorities.

CLAIM. A demand to receive certain benefits or **services** from the system, which can be, for example, the state, a fund, or an insurance company. A claimant is therefore a person claiming certain **rights** in the **social-security** system.

CLASS. The division of the population into different groups in society. The main criterion to distinguish among classes is their position in the economic hierarchy. One such division is the **Marxist** distinction between those who own the means of production and those who are employed by the owners of these means. In this view, it is to be expected that the inherent conflict between the two classes will end in open conflict and give rise to revolution.

Others argue for a broader concept of class, which could include the working class, the middle class, and the upper class. Contemporary analysis tends to avoid using such a simple description because production methods have changed so much that one cannot separate workers into a specific group.

There are many different types of work, and there are many different ways to acquire income and wealth. Furthermore, the distinctions between the different classes may have vanished in some countries. This is not the same as arguing that no differences exist, or that the **stratification** of societies and analyzing different classes' position in society is of no use in social-science analysis. This type of research emphasizes the relative position of the individual in society and tries to analyze how different policies have an impact on various groups. The strata may be defined by looking at **employment**, single households versus **families, ethnic** minorities, migrant workers, or different income groups and the **distribution** of individuals/families among them.

Class analyses have often been used to describe the historical development of the various **welfare states** by examining the way in which the working class and middle class may have had an interest in that development. An example of a service those classes might have an interest in is providing (or guaranteeing) and delivering certain **basic needs** to the citizens.

The term *class* has recently also been applied indirectly, by using the word underclass as a concept for those at the bottom of the social ladder, and also those who are receiving **social-security** benefits from society. If the concept emphasizes specific groups as being members of the underclass (single parents, the elderly, the unemployed, the disabled, the chronically ill, and so forth), the term describes certain special, vulnerable groups, without indicating that they will be there permanently. **Gender** analysis often has a dimension that replaces the original class-based analysis, as women in many welfare states have been an underprivileged group.

The use of the word *underclass* has been criticized as representing a concept that gives the political decision makers a moral **right** to reduce that underclass's benefits and make demands on the way its members contribute to society's development.

The concept of class has therefore not vanished from the analysis of the welfare state. Instead, it seems to have changed its focus to specific vulnerable groups and their position in society.

CLASSICAL ECONOMICS. A specific school of economic thought in which the individual's self-interest is seen to be the main driving force, which should create growth and prosperity. Classical economists argue for little public intervention—as little as possible—although some would be necessary to have stability and reduce conflicts between different people's interests. Classical economists believe in the **market** as the main regulator of the economy and that growth would be ensured through a combination of accumulation of capital and division of labor. Furthermore, classical economists maintain that the various markets would clear in the long run. For example, the balance of payments would be in equilibrium due to changes in the gold balance. If there was a deficit, gold would flow out and export prices would rise, while import prices would fall. This would then restore the balance of payments. Monetary policy and control are therefore essential for the classical economics model. In this model, there will also only be voluntary **unemployment**. The main theorists in this tradition were **Adam Smith**, David Hume, John Stuart Mill, and David Ricardo.

COEFFICIENT OF VARIATION. A way of describing how close or far one **distribution**, which can be spending, income, wealth, or any number of specified items, is from another. For example, it can be used to measure whether **welfare states** are moving in the same or different directions. The **convergence** or divergence of welfare states has especially been analyzed within the **European Union** countries. The coefficient of variation is calculated by dividing the standard deviation by the mean. The smaller the value, the closer to one another the welfare states are. This can be in overall level of spending, level of **taxation**, and so forth; however, it is less useful when trying to compare changes in institutional settings.

COHABITATION. A term that refers to people, usually a couple, who are living together without being married. This can be seen as change in **family** life when, as happens in some countries, more people live together without being married. This also challenges the way the **welfare states** are organized and the rules related to being eligible for welfare benefits. A question that arises here, for example, is whether cohabitation also implies a demand that cohabitees should support one another and how to calculate **housing benefits** and so forth.

COLLECTIVE AGREEMENTS. Agreements between employer and employee organizations. In some countries, they are an important way of setting the wage level, while they have a weaker impact on other counties. In counties where the effect is diminished, there is a larger role for individual wage bargaining. Industrial relations have been weakened in recent years, especially due to a weaker position of the **trade unions**, which have seen a reduction in membership in some countries. Collective agreements can help ensure stability in the **labor market** and set rules about how to avoid strikes. They can also to help guarantee the understanding of such issues as training, working time, holidays, and so forth; therefore, agreements between employer and employees are still important in many countries, as this can also result in better working conditions and wages for those organized in a trade union compared to those not organized. *See also* COLLECTIVE BARGAINING.

COLLECTIVE BARGAINING. The process of collectively negotiating working conditions (including wages) between the employer and employees' organizations. In many **welfare states**, collective bargaining includes elements of **social policy** and what has been labeled **occupational welfare**. For example, in many countries, **pensions** are partly organized and **financed** in the **labor market**. Agreement among the partners might help in ensuring a high degree of stability in the labor market. The outcome of the bargaining depends on the strengths of both employers and employees, which can vary depending on, for example, the level of **unemployment**.

COLLECTIVISM. A specific way of thinking about societal development. In collectivist terms, such issues as **equality** and equal treatment have high priority. Examples of collectivist thought can be found in **Marxism**. In relation to the **welfare state**, the collectivist approach would prefer state intervention to ensure that all citizens have a decent standard of living. For instance, in the collectivist view, insurance-based **health care** would be unacceptable, as two individuals with the same needs would be treated differently. Collectivists would also try to redistribute society's profits to promote greater equality.

COMMUNISM. An ideological way of thinking about societal development and functioning. Countries like **China** and **Russia** have been—and China still is—influenced by communism. In former communist countries, especially those in Eastern Europe, a central issue has been to ensure full **employment**, as all citizens were obliged to work. As a consequence of that requirement, the other sectors of the **social security** systems were poorly developed, for example, there was no **unemployment benefit** system or **social assistance**. Most countries that once had a communist ideology have moved toward a more Western type of **democracy**. *See also* CONFLICT THEORY.

COMMUNITARIANISM. An American-inspired viewpoint that criticizes the modern **welfare societies** for being unable to fulfill the requirements of both **freedom** and **equality**. Communitarians argue for more **solidarity**, including the use of such local institutions as the **family** or local communities, which can ensure liberty. They therefore also argue in favor of the development of **civil society**. In addition, there is a focus on **social capital**, and a further emphasis on positive **rights**. *See also* COMMUNITY.

COMMUNITY. Sociologically, this is a group of individuals who are linked together by some common characteristics, for example, culture or religion. Living in a certain geographical area can also link people by creating specific social relationships or a common interest. A community can also be understood to have the same feelings or thoughts; therefore, a community can include members of a nation, immigrants, religious groups, or people who have the same interest. The historical archetype of a community is the **family**. In **welfare-state** analysis, the idea of community is more often used as a way of interpreting a specific distinctive geographical area in which **social services** can be delivered. *See also* COMMUNITARIANISM; COMMUNITY CARE; COMMUNITY WORK.

COMMUNITY CARE. Local or **decentralized** units in the **welfare state** supply community care. In sociology, the term *community care* may be broadly interpreted as the **care** provided by a group of people in a local area. When looked at in this way, community care can be difficult to measure and analyze. In most welfare-state analyses, community care is interpreted as the local provision of a part of the welfare state's delivery of goods and **services**. The care delivered is mostly for the elderly and children, but care for the vulnerable and disabled can also be part of community care. To what degree the care is delivered by the **community, civil society**, or the **market** largely depends on the specific type of welfare state.

COMMUNITY WORK. This term describes how a collective (the **community**) solves the problems of the specific community. It can include work within the **family**, as well as neighborhood work and other local initiatives that try to solve local problems.

COMPARATIVE ANALYSIS. This type of analysis refers to the comparison of countries, types of **welfare states**, or systems. The use of comparative analysis has grown within the last 20 to 30 years so that analysts are able to get a better grasp on both the development of the welfare state in individual countries and comparisons between and among countries. In addition, it places welfare states in a broader context and clarifies similarities and differences between countries. These studies often compare the different types of welfare states (**Bismarckian, Beveridgian, Scandinavian**, etc.) in specific countries or among broader sets of countries.

These analyses are often quantitative, that is, they compare the amount of money spent on different areas in **social policy** or in total **public-sector** expenditures. Comparing the level of **benefits**, economic living standards, the number of people living in **poverty**, and so forth, are common studies. Studies comparing the systems and different criteria for receiving benefits have also emerged within the last 10 to 15 years. The **European Union**, for example, now regularly publishes an overview called *Social Protection in the*

Member States of the Community, from the Mutual Information System on Social Security, which is a European information system on social protection in the member states. It includes comparative tables on organization, **financing**, **health care**, **sickness**, **benefits in cash**, **maternity**, **invalidity**, old age, survivors, **industrial injuries** and occupational diseases, **family** benefits, **unemployment**, and guaranteeing sufficient resources. Comparative analysis is often difficult, as the available data are often not comparable, and if they are comparable, it is only at an aggregate level, which makes detailed conclusions difficult to reach.

In the last 15 to 20 years, comparative analyses have also been supplemented by qualitative analyses, which examine the administration of the systems and how the individual perceives and gets support from the public sector. These analyses take into account the administrative impact of the **bureaucracy** and the **street level-bureaucrat**.

In fact, some of the analyses have pointed out that there is no country that fits exactly into any one type of welfare state. This is due to differences in national systems, which is why they are treated as ideal types in this dictionary. Ideal types make it possible to make at least some comparisons and draw some broad conclusions about different types of countries and their differences and similarities. Individual countries also often use comparative analysis as a mirror for their own development, and it is also used by **pressure groups** as support for why a system should be improved.

COMPLIANCE. This is used to describe the degree to which individuals or groups of individuals obey rules, for example, with regard to paying **taxes** and **child maintenance**. Lack of **tax compliance** has increased the **public-sector** deficit in many **welfare states**, worsening the **fiscal crisis** by reducing the public sector's income. A focus on compliance could thereby reduce the financial pressure on the welfare states. Without intervention to ensure that child maintenance takes place, lack of compliance can imply difficult times, especially for single parents with low incomes or who are outside the **labor market**.

CONFLICT THEORY. This theory points out that as resources become scarce, there will be conflicts about how to distribute them among different groups in society. In conflict theory, the outcome of the **welfare state** is a result of the conflict (or, more mildly, competition) between different groups or **classes** in society. **Karl Marx's** analysis of the state was based on a conflict between labor and capital. Modern conflict theory distinguishes between systemic and social conflicts. The systemic conflicts are between institutions, whereas social conflicts are between individuals. They can be within **families**

or at a place of **employment**. Among proponents of this theory, there is no agreement about whether conflict is positive or negative. It may be positive in resolving problems; it may be negative in that it creates opposite interests that can only be resolved by use of physical power.

CONFUCIAN MODEL. A **welfare-state** model developed mainly in the Far East, in such countries as **Japan**, Singapore, South Korea, **China**, Thailand, and Malaysia. It is not a very specific model and includes several elements from different European types, but it maintains its own historical flavor and status. One of the primary distinctions between the European and Confucian models has been a historic tradition of relying much more on **families** in the Asian countries than in Europe, perhaps with the exception of some Southern European countries.

Countries in East Asia have combined conservative **corporatism** with **subsidiarity**, but the corporatist structure lacks the workers' involvement, which is present in traditional European countries. The use of the subsidiarity principle lacks the strong role of the **church**, as in Europe. The family and extended commitments of individuals toward certain groups are the main means of delivering **social welfare**. This also explains why the role of the state has been minimal in comparison to other welfare-state types, and why **charity** and voluntary action have been prominent.

Many of the countries that exemplify the Confucian model initially developed their welfare states in the late 1960s and 1970s, in response to political and economic problems that arose in the aftermath of World War II, for example, Korea and Japan. But economic growth has made it possible to develop new forms of social welfare, although at a much slower pace and lower level than in Europe.

Confucian systems are top-down, rather than bottom-up. This is in contrast to many European countries, where the struggle between the working **class** and capitalist ruling class was one reason for developing a welfare system. So, even if the Confucian model resembles some European types of welfare-state systems, it has its own features and stands out as a model combining different European types with Confucian learning.

CONSERVATIVE MODEL. This model emphasizes the **market** as the institutional provider of **social welfare**. It stresses that the **public sector** should only intervene when all other possibilities have been exhausted. The conservative model further stresses that the market is the main provider and financer of the **welfare state**. This implies a strong emphasis on the **labor market**, especially local labor markets, as they can develop systems and welfare for those who need it. Support for those covered by the systems is high, whereas those outside and supported by the public sector will receive far less.

In some ways, the conservative model resembles the **Bismarckian** model, with its strong emphasis on the labor market and low support to those outside it. Examples of countries characterized as conservative are **Germany**, **France**, and **Austria**. There is no real commitment in the welfare systems to develop and maintain full **employment**.

Redistribution in countries following this model is minimal. Such a country is sometimes referred to as a "night-watchman" state, as it only intervenes to a limited degree and leaves most activities outside its scope.

CONSTITUTIONAL LAW. This law is made up of the rules by which a given society will have to act. In some countries, constitutional law states the **right** to have a job, but not necessarily how to achieve that goal.

CONTINENTAL MODEL. This refers to a **welfare-state** model geographically placed in the center of the European continent. It resembles the **conservative model** and has many elements of the **Bismarckian model**. Thus, this model is typically argued to be in place in such countries as **Germany**, **France**, **Austria**, and the **Netherlands**.

CONTINGENCY. This is a risk, often specified beforehand, that may occur. For example, a contingency can be **sickness**, **unemployment**, or **disability**. When a contingency occurs, depending on the type of **welfare state**, this gives access to benefits and **services**, although the level may vary from country to country.

CONTRIBUTORY BENEFIT. This benefit is only available to those who have contributed to **financing** it. In many countries, such things as **unemployment benefits**, **sickness benefits**, and **pensions** are contributory. The size of the contribution and how it is calculated can vary among countries, different **welfare-state** models, and the type of system. A contributory system, especially when it relates to benefits based on the size of previous payment, as, for example, in the pension system, can be a disadvantage for individuals working on temporary contracts, and it is often a disadvantage for women, since they may bear and raise children and thus spend less time in the **labor market** or accept part-time **employment**. In this sense, the contributory benefit is not **gender** neutral. Furthermore, individuals with low incomes tend to get lower pensions than those with higher incomes. Hence, such a system also reproduces the **inequalities** in a society.

CONTROL GROUP. In research, a control group is a group of people who are not given the same treatment as those in another group. The control group offers the possibility of testing whether the outcome of the activity is due to the initiative taken or just a random outcome. A control group can help in measuring the effectiveness of an initiative. In social science, including **welfare-state** analysis, these groups are seldom used because they are looked upon as being unethical; however, in recent years, the need to know the effectiveness of an intervention has increased the use thereof, for example, by giving a group in one area another type of **services** than those receiving services in another area. In health policy and **health care**, including the development of new medicines, control groups are often used.

CONVERGENCE. This concept relates to a debate about whether countries, at least in the same regional economic area, for instance, Europe or Southeast Asia, will move toward some common type of welfare model, or at least are moving in a direction where the differences between institutional structure and level of spending of the countries are decreasing.

Convergence can be considered from various angles. Harold Wilensky (1975) was the first to argue that convergence was part of natural, long-term economic development. The power resource school criticized this standpoint, arguing that politics matters. **Globalization** has been the basis for another contention that convergence would occur in **welfare-state** policies, given that globalization would make it more difficult for individual countries, especially the smaller ones, to pursue independent policies. Convergence can be measured in different ways. The most commonly used measurement is the coefficient of variation, which indicates whether a movement in the same or different directions can be seen. Convergence is also looked upon with regard to a change in systems, for example, whether activation is used more or less.

Data from Europe seem to indicate that convergence may occur or already be occurring on the level of overall spending, but that, at the same time, it is possible to maintain a variety of institutional structures and approaches at the national level. Thus, this view maintains that convergence will occur, but that it need not be through either a race to the bottom (i.e., the lowest level of spending and/or level of benefits) or by catching up to the highest level in a region. It may be, for instance, the result of different historical patterns of welfare-state development. If convergence develops, this might imply that the difference among welfare states in Europe will be reduced, perhaps suggesting that a **European social model** will develop.

CORPORATE SOCIAL RESPONSIBILITY (CSR). The social role a company can have or take. CSR consists of policies at the company level that have to do with how to ensure continued **employment**, but also how to help, for example, people with disabilities to continue in their job or get a job. Furthermore, it can address how to help **families** reconcile work and family life. It can be questioned how and whether the companies' policies on CSR are actually implemented, especially when companies face financial constraints.

CORPORATISM. Corporatism involves the **integration** of **labor market** partners in the decision-making process. It is interpreted in different ways, ranging from full co-optation of the partners in the states' decision-making process to a more partial inclusion in the process. Corporatist states can grant a varying degree of autonomy to the partners involved in the process. The Italian period of corporatism, for example, resembled a dictatorship, where the partners were only formally included and had no autonomy. In other countries, the corporatist strategy has been used to build a consensus about societal development, especially in **labor market policy**. In these countries, the partners have frequently been involved in the administration of labor market policy as well.

Corporate structures can be found in many **welfare states**, especially in relation to integrating labor market partners in decision making. This is also the case within the **European Union (EU)**, where the partners play a pivotal role in formulating and discussing new initiatives in these areas. In the EU, integration of the partners is seen as essential for the **open method of coordination** on **employment** and **social exclusion**; however, the weakness of **trade unions** has reduced their influence in recent years, along with the option and possibility of steering welfare-state developments through corporatism.

COST–BENEFIT ANALYSIS. This process considers both the costs and benefits of a specific project. A project can then only be recommended if the benefits exceed the costs. If more than one project is evaluated, the analysis will compare the surplus of the various projects and choose the one for which the general positive value is highest. This, of course, assumes that the projects are comparable.

Although it is reasonably simple to calculate the costs of a given project, it is difficult to calculate the benefits of a given project. Naturally, there are some problems related to cost calculations, including insecurity in the longer term for project costs, how the venture will develop, and the cost involved in maintaining and running the project, but the problem of benefits is even greater, because benefits in different projects include, for example, the well-being of individuals, or longer life, shortening of traffic time, and so forth. Included are the benefits that involve the individual's **utility**, and **welfare economics** does not give us any specific and well-known way of aggregating them.

For both costs and benefits, there are further problems in deciding which discount factors to use. A high factor will reduce the value of future income at current prices, and a low factor will mean a relatively higher value for the future income compared to a situation with a high factor. As costs and benefits arise at different times—in big projects, often with expenditure first and income afterward—the size of the discount factor can be important when calculating whether a project will end with a surplus or deficit at current prices.

The reason for using an analysis like cost–benefit is that it enables the decision-making process to take other criteria—not just purely economic criteria—into consideration. This means that broader social aspects can be considered when making decisions; however, this raises the problem of and need for making **interpersonal comparisons**, which is difficult because it is impossible to know all the affected individuals' personal preferences. For example, individuals' valuation of spare time will vary. The same is the case for a cleaner environment, and so forth. Therefore, a cost-effectiveness analysis is often carried out because it only compares costs of different projects and does not use information about benefits.

Finally, an ethical issue is that benefits might be lower to the elderly in principle, due to their lower life expectancy in comparison to that of younger people. *See also* COMPARATIVE ANALYSIS.

CREAM-SKIMMING. This refers to situations in which providers of **services** or benefits, including welfare services, try to attract those with the lowest risk or those who are easiest to help, for example, in relation to **care**, increasing a provider's income; therefore, it might be a claim by those **financing** an activity that providers shall take everyone who is an eligible user, who, for instance, have an objective **right** to be provided with the service. Cream-skimming is especially argued to be possible within the provision of services within **health care** and activation of the unemployed where those private providers receiving payment from the **public sector** get a higher income if they can help the sick or **unemployed**. This is, for example, a higher payment if an unemployed individual returns to the **labor market**.

CROATIA. This country was part of the former Yugoslavia, with a legacy of having a **communist** type of welfare system. Croatia entered the **European Union** as the 28th member on 1 July 2013, and it has a population of approximately 4.5 million. The first law regarding old age was enacted in 1922, whereas the current law, after independence, is a **pension** insurance law (1998). This is a **social insurance** and mandatory individual account system. Since 2011, it has been possible to opt out of the system if the pension from the social insurance system would be more favorable than the two-pillar system. Coverage of **unemployment** dates back to 1952, **sickness benefits** 1954, and **industrial injury** 2006. The system is generally based on social insurance, thus resembling the **continental** welfare system.

CZECH REPUBLIC. In the geographic area of the Czech Republic, many different types of **social security** programs were originally introduced, following the **German** example. The first elements were introduced when the Czech area was part of the dual monarchy of Austria-Hungary. In 1919, Czechoslovakia became an independent state. Coverage against **industrial injury** was established in 1887, against **sickness** and **maternity** in 1888, and for old age and **disability** in 1906. **Family allowances** followed in 1945, and **unemployment benefits** were introduced after the fall of the Berlin Wall in 1991. Prior to this, the Czech Republic had a **communist** type of welfare system.

The Czech system is partly based on being in the **labor market** and partly on being a citizen. It therefore has a combination of **universal rights** with specific benefits relating to being in the labor market. The system has been changing since the breakup of Eastern Europe, and it seems to be moving toward a more **Scandinavian welfare state** approach, with general coverage in many areas, but, at the same time, labor market participation seems central; however, in recent years, the **fiscal crisis** has implied a lack of funds and options to invest in welfare policies, although the Czech Republic still has a high degree of **equality** compared to many other European countries.

D

DAY CARE. *See* CHILD CARE.

DECENTRALIZATION. This refers to both the process of dividing and the actual division of competencies in different countries. In several **welfare states**, a decentralization of responsibilities to lower administrative levels has taken place. The degree of decentralization of tasks and the ability to **finance** also varies among countries. One example is the **United Kingdom**, which has witnessed devolution of welfare delivery to England, Wales, Northern Ireland, and Scotland. A core issue is often how to finance welfare at a decentralized level with this being within the overall macroeconomic options for a country's development. *See also* BUREAUCRACY.

DECOMMODIFICATION. This relates to the degree to which individuals or **families** can maintain a decent standard of living without being dependent on **labor market** participation. In recent times, this concept has been used especially by Gøsta Esping-Andersen (*The Three Worlds of Welfare Capitalism*, 1990) in his attempt to classify types of **welfare states**. Others have questioned the use of decommodification as a starting point for welfare-state analysis, pointing out that history and culture play an important role. Furthermore, some systems provide a high degree of coverage by using the concept of **citizenship** as the main criterion when delivering welfare, thus avoiding the idea that the individual's protection is dependent on the ability to be in the labor market. In these systems, decommodification has been important in the development of the welfare state.

DEFAMILIZATION. This refers to how **welfare states** help, particularly women, to be independent of the **family**, especially in terms of economic independence. This can be accomplished in various ways, including **child care** and **family allowances**. In welfare-state literature, the concept is often connected to the concept of **citizenship**. The ability to combine **work and family life** has been of increasing importance in many welfare states, as this helps ensure **gender equality** and increase production and labor supply.

DEFINED BENEFIT PLAN. This mainly refers to the level of **pension** in a pension system in which the pension is dependent on the number of years with paid contributions in the **labor market**, the size of the contributions, and often the final year's salary or the average salary.

DEFINED-CONTRIBUTION PLAN. A **pension** plan in which the benefit is dependent on the contributions and capital income earned on those contributions. Pension systems in the **welfare state** have increasingly moved toward this type, instead of defined–benefit plans, as it reduces the risk of not being able to pay out benefits, especially in **pay-as-you-go** pension systems. The pension will thus depend on the ability to invest the benefits during the time period when the savings for pension purposes are done.

DEMOCRACY. The word *democracy* comes from the Greek "demos," which means the poorer people. When discussions about democracy started in Greece, the poorer people were those without any influence on the decision-making process. In this form of **government**, the majority of the people in a society make decisions about their leaders and laws through either direct or indirect voting. It includes elections in which different groups or groupings can participate, and nowadays also access to the media. An election with one candidate may, therefore, not be considered democratic, unless it is clear that no others want to be elected and have had a fair chance to participate in the election.

Some of the main questions in relation to democracy are which decisions should be made at which level, whom to elect as representatives of the different groups in society, and how the system should take **care** of or accept the political minority. For instance, should democracy give a small majority the possibility of not respecting a minority's specific interests? In many countries, democracy has historically been followed by a period of dictatorship and then, after a certain period, a return to democracy. Examples of such countries include **Germany**, **Italy**, **Greece**, **Spain**, **Japan**, and **Russia**.

One of the questions that arise when discussing democracy is how to elect representatives. Should all the small groups be represented in the parliament, with the risk that it may not be possible to form a majority coalition, thus making it impossible to steer the country effectively? The expression a "Polish parliament" originates from the situation in **Poland** in the 1920s, when there were so many parties in parliament that it was not possible to form a coalition, and no decisions could be made.

On the other hand, some types of electoral system have been criticized for not being sufficiently democratic. For example, in the British system, one party can govern with only about 35 percent of the population supporting it.

This is because of the first-past-the-post system (i.e., only one representative from each constituency). Furthermore, it is nearly impossible for new parties to emerge, which tends to result in a dual-party system. The electoral college in the **United States**, through which a minority of the voters can elect a president, has also been criticized. The relationship between the media and elected officials and candidates has come more into focus because of the media's increased influence in democratic elections. In **social policy**, democracy has been particularly tied to how to **integrate** the more vulnerable in society, that is, to **prevent** them from social exclusion from decision making.

Finally, the question has been raised within social policy in the past 10 to 15 years of how to involve people in the decision-making process of the various institutions and at the local level in general; therefore, democracy is an issue not only at the macro level, but also at the local level. *See also* PLURALISM.

DEMOGRANT. This **social security** scheme is financed with public money and, when a specific social **contingency** occurs, there is a **right** to a benefit. This implies that no **means test** is taken into consideration. The aim of the demogrant has been to supply a minimum, flat-rate level of benefit for groups that are, without doubt, **deserving**, therefore requiring no means test. Typical examples are **child benefits** and **invalidity pensions**.

DEMOGRAPHY. An analysis and description of a given population, describing the population in different age groups, the number of births, number of deaths, and **migration**. It provides information about the population at a specific time (stock) and the movement during, normally, one year (flow). Demographic figures are calculated in various ways, because the number of deaths and births is not enough in itself to describe a population and its trends. The number of elderly, for example, affects the absolute number of deaths. The overall change in population is influenced by deaths, births, and migration. The absolute figures present only part of the picture; therefore, relative numbers are calculated, including, for example, the number of children a generation of women is expected to give birth to. This makes it necessary to know the number of fertile women, that is, women between 15 and 49. This information can then form the basis for a calculation of expected trends in population in the years to come.

Demographic information about changes in different groups of the population is used in a number of disciplines and for various purposes. For instance, it is used to forecast the consequences of the demand for **health care** and **child care** for children and schools. Furthermore, the **dependency ratio**, and changes in it, can be used to estimate either a **need** for retaining money for these purposes in the future or finding ways to reduce **dependency** and related costs.

In relation to the private **pension market**, changes in demography, and especially **life expectancy**, have played a vital role in developing adequate solutions to the risk insurance companies incur when covering specific groups. How high should the group's premium be if an individual is entitled to receive a pension when retiring, and what is the risk of paying out life insurance if the individual dies before reaching the age of retirement? Knowledge about mortality and the causes of death have a high value for those offering this type of insurance.

Finally, knowledge about demographic changes may play an important role in how **public-sector** expenditure will change and how private producers may also need to change their production. In most countries, demographic statistics are readily available. Certain demographic information is sometimes seen as an indicator of the level of welfare in a given society. This is the case, for example, with the average life expectancy and infant mortality. A long average life expectancy is seen as proof that, among other things, the **welfare state** is providing a good **health** system, good nutrition, and so forth.

In recent years, demographic analysis has especially been used to predict and analyze the consequences of the **aging of societies**, which will take place in most Western countries through the year 2050. There has been a growing concern about the impact on public-sector spending and the ability to have a sustainable welfare state, and this question has been raised in the discussions in many countries. Demographic information is, thus, also important in analyzing and making decisions about the long-term development of welfare states. The possible change in demography has, therefore, been an argument for making changes in welfare states, particularly later retirement from the **labor market** and a higher pension age, as well as other modifications to the pension system. Use of welfare technology to make it possible for individuals to take **care** of themselves longer has also played a role.

DENMARK. Denmark follows the **Scandinavian welfare state** type. The origin of the Danish **welfare state** dates back to the Poor Relief Acts of 1798; however, in the first Danish constitution of 1848, poor people were deprived of their political **rights** when receiving poor relief. In the period before the Industrial Revolution, some voluntary **sickness insurance** funds where established, but it was only in the late 1880s that new laws were introduced. In 1888, a law on **child maintenance** for children born outside of wedlock was enacted. In 1891, a new poor relief law was enacted; in 1892, a sickness insurance reform was passed; and 1898 saw the introduction of **accident insurance** reform. **Unemployment** insurance reform followed in 1907.

Otto von Bismarck inspired the changes, but from the beginning, the Danes tended to adopt a more **universal** approach. In 1933, a coalition between workers and farmers (which also had a majority in parliament) introduced a new set of laws, which were passed. These included the Public Assistance Act, the National Insurance Act, the Employment Exchange and Unemployment Insurance Act, and the Accident Insurance Act. These new laws can be seen as a first attempt to create a welfare state based on universal coverage, paid for by general **taxation**. These alterations were combined with a wish to fine tune the economy through public intervention.

After World War II, new areas were covered. The most important was the old-age **pension** without a **means test**, introduced in 1956. Reforms were made in sickness insurance and public assistance. Unlike what had happened when the first constitution was adopted, there was no loss of civil rights as a consequence of receiving public assistance. As an example of the move toward a general welfare state, the **government** assumed marginal responsibility for unemployment funds in 1967. Furthermore, the state's overall spending in the field of **social policy** grew rapidly—from around 10 percent of the **gross domestic product** in the late 1940s to approximately 17 to 18 percent in the late 1960s.

The reforms continued, albeit more slowly, in the 1970s, and they gradually stopped in the 1980s. Still, the Danish welfare state can be characterized as a model of the universal approach, also based on broad societal agreement among different groups and a **corporatist** way of dealing with many problems. This is especially so in relation to **labor market policy**. The trend in the 1980s included a more highly **decentralized** welfare-state model. During the 21st century, increased focus on activation, work first, and later retirement has been central in the development. It can be said that the Danish welfare state has matured, and therefore is only making gradual changes in light of pressure for both reforms and cuts in expenditures; however, at the same time, a system with relatively high public support continues to exist.

DEPENDENCY. The economic, physical, or psychological **need** of an individual person for the delivery of **services** in-kind or in cash that the person relies on receiving. Dependency can be either material or nonmaterial, as the dependent person may, for example, have the necessary economic means but still feel lonely. Often dependencies focus on various kinds of support from the **welfare state**. *See also* DEPENDENCY RATIO.

DEPENDENCY RATIO. This ratio calculates the relationship between those who are dependent on welfare **services** and those who are not. It is a way of describing the burden of those who have to pay for those receiving benefits from the **public sector**. Those paying may naturally, at other times in their life cycle, be receiving benefits. The dependency ratio is frequently defined as the ratio between those aged 15 to 65 and those younger and older. A dependency ratio of one indicates that there is a balance between the number of those able to participate in production and the number of those not able to. It is impossible to state just from the dependency ratio anything specific about the possibility of **financing** a **welfare state**, as this also depends on the total level of production and internal decisions about how to finance the welfare state, including the level of savings of those people retiring. however, the dependency ratio may provide valuable information about the future consequences of changes in **demography**.

Dependency ratios may also be calculated to compare those having a job with the rest of the population and may use groups other than ages 15 to 65 when making comparisons. In recent years, dependency ratios have mainly been used to analyze how the change in the number of elderly may affect either total public-sector expenditure or **pension** funds. Furthermore, the figures have been used to discuss possible future problems of the **social security** systems of an **aging of society**. *See also* COMPARATIVE ANALYSIS.

DEPRIVATION. When a person or group does not have the possibilities considered "normal" in a given society, that person or group is considered to be deprived. Such people or groups usually have a low standard of living compared to the average for that society. Deprivation is closely related to the concepts of **inequality**, **poverty**, **social exclusion**, and **justice**. Deprivation can be in one specific area or occur in several areas. It can also be interpreted in both absolute and relative terms. *Absolute deprivation* refers to a situation in which the individual is denied certain **rights**, whereas *relative deprivation* mainly refers to a situation in which the individual does not have full or sufficient access to a set of specified goods and **services**.

DESERVING AND UNDESERVING. Those who, through no fault of their own, have a **right** (deserve) to receive benefits from the **public sector** are considered "deserving." Historically, the use of the concept of deserving and undeserving poor has had different connotations. In some countries, the undeserving poor lost their right to vote when receiving **social assistance**. The level of benefits to the undeserving poor has always been lower than to the deserving poor. In some systems, only the deserving poor could receive benefits; the undeserving poor were left to beg on the streets and live off the **charity** of other people.

The notion of deserving versus undeserving can still be found in discussions about **social policy**. While the deserving poor (for example, the elderly, the disabled, and the chronically ill) receive benefits without any counter-claims being made from the public sector, the undeserving poor have to prove that they need assistance and should often be prepared to do something to receive a benefit. It is not always possible to differentiate the deserving from the usually undeserving; only in a few objective cases is it possible to clearly distinguish between the two.

The unemployed may be both deserving and undeserving. They are considered deserving in most countries if they have been actively searching for jobs, or were laid off because their previous employers closed down or reduced the number of people employed. If, on the other hand, they quit their jobs, only searched briefly for new jobs, and had been unwilling to move for work, then they could be thought of as undeserving. In recent years, in many Western countries, migrants from the Third World have often been looked upon as undeserving, and issues of **ethnicity** and **welfare-state** benefits have thus often arisen. Between the two categories are many gradations, and it also seems that the distinction is closely bound to a moral standpoint, which may change in time and within different cultures. *See also* UNEMPLOYMENT.

DIAGNOSIS-RELATED GROUPS (DRG). Standardized sets of treatment for specific diseases. In **health care**, a DRG fee will be paid to the provider for the **services** delivered. Health care systems in different countries use different sets of DRGs. DRGs relate to differences in the costs of different types of treatment and also to different priorities in the management of the health care system. They provide a possible tool for managing and steering the total level of production in line with total available resources.

DISABILITY. The inability to do something that one could do before. Disabilities can be either physical or psychological, that is, that the disabled individual faces a certain disadvantage. This disadvantage can take the form of a direct physical handicap or be the inability to be part of a group or to interact with other people in a given society. *See also* DISABILITY BENEFIT.

DISABILITY BENEFIT. This benefit is provided by the **welfare state** to people with certain physical or psychological handicaps, as determined by medical examination. The criteria for receiving a disability benefit can vary among countries, and the provision can be either public or insurance based. In most countries, the criteria are primarily focused on physical handicaps as decided by medical examination of the individual, but psychological disabilities are covered, although to a lesser degree. With the changes in types of production away from hard, manual work, stress-related diseases have become more central as a diagnosis related to and being accepted when applying for disability benefits. *See also* DISABILITY.

DISCRETION. Discretion is the ability of those administering social systems to make an independent assessment of the needs of the applicant when making decisions. This issue is often debated in relation to **street-level bureaucrats**, as it is possible that the individual client's level of benefit will be dependent on which bureaucrat he or she has contact with. This discretion can imply a clearer focus on what is needed to **prevent** further contingencies from occurring. At the same time, the risk is that the benefit can be more difficult to obtain for those most in need.

DISCRIMINATION. This takes place when a specific group, due to, for example, **gender, ethnicity,** age, or **disability,** is disadvantaged because of membership of that particular group and therefore has a worse outcome in relation to income, **housing,** and so forth. In principle, many international agreements prohibit discrimination, and in many countries discrimination is not allowed; however, discrimination can also be indirect. Thus, it may still take place, as its occurrence is difficult to document. This can happen when men get the best paid job, when older employees are sacked, when people with disabilities have a higher level of **unemployment** than others, and so on. To reduce discrimination, policies like **affirmative action** have been promoted in some countries. Complaint boards have also been established to deal with such issues.

DISINCENTIVE. A **benefit in cash** or a **benefit in-kind** (or a service) that reduces the individual's willingness to do something, primarily either save or work. The disincentive can be a high level of benefits, high **taxes** and duties, a low wage level, or a combination of factors. A high combined marginal tax rate and reduction in **social security** benefits can result in a situation where an individual who becomes employed will have no increase in disposable income. This is described as a disincentive to take up a job, and it can also be labeled the **poverty** trap. Changing the level of benefit can reduce disincentives, as can changing the period during which an individual can receive the benefit or benefit by the marginal income tax. Finally, reducing disincentives can be done by training to improve the individual's position in the **labor market** or by a general **active labor market policy.** A low level of economic **incentives** has been argued to imply a need for a reduction in the level of welfare benefits. This argument seems to overlook that other economic incentives are at play for many individuals.

DISTRIBUTION. Distribution refers to how income and wealth are divided among different groups in a society. Besides describing the division of money, it may also include a description of how other goods are distributed, as well as the nature of access to different types of **services** (mainly public) in a society. Distribution can be analyzed in two ways. **Functional distribution** shows how income has been divided among those production factors participating in the production process, whereas personal **income distribution** focuses on different people's shares of the total annual income in a given society. The personal income distribution can sometimes be considered for individuals, **families,** and various occupational groups. The emphasis is on people instead of factors of production.

The theory of how income is distributed in a society often takes as its starting point demand and supply, **human capital**, productivity of different individuals, and production factors; however, it can also analyze the strengths of different groups involved in the production process and in society in general. Distribution is often measured as deviations from a strictly equal division. This may have different origins by emphasizing different perspectives in a distribution, for example, those who are furthest away from the average or median income in a society. The distribution can be measured by the **Gini coefficient**. Most analyses take as their base the statistics for income and wealth; however, they also acknowledge that this is not a good and precise measurement because some income is not declared, and the **hidden economy** may produce different results.

Distribution and the description of distribution are also used to analyze the number of people living in **poverty** and how many are living below a certain poverty line. The change in the degree of **equality** is either measured by the Gini coefficient and the number living in poverty when looking at the **market** outcome or the distribution when taking the impact of the **tax** system and welfare benefits into consideration as a measure of the **welfare states'** effectiveness.

Finally, distribution and information about it are used in comparing various countries and within individual countries throughout time. These figures supplement the information given by the per capita production presented in national statistics, that is, the gross national product per inhabitant.

DIVORCE. The dissolution of a marriage between a married couple. In some welfare systems, divorce can have an impact on the benefits available for one or both spouses, but it may also mean that a person will be obliged to pay **child maintenance.** *See also* FAMILY.

DOMICILIARY CARE. In **social services**, this is the **care** delivered in people's own homes. This type of care has become increasingly important as a way of helping the elderly stay in their own homes for a longer period of time.

DUAL LABOR MARKET. A specific way of describing the **labor market** that emphasizes that there is a core and a periphery. In the core, the stable and well-paid jobs are available to the core **labor force**, which often, but not always, are those with the highest level of **education** or long-term **employment** for the same employer. On the periphery, only low, insecure jobs are available. Those jobs often require a lower level of education or no education at all, and working conditions are rather poor. The periphery has generally been in sectors of a society's industrial production, but it has recently been moving into the industrialized world in the service sector, where many jobs offer little security and low pay.

The theory of the dual labor market has been used to explain why certain groups have a higher risk of living in **poverty**, why wages are stagnant, and why labor markets are not clearing to let the unemployed back in. The argument is that those at the core of the labor market—which is most of the labor force—are not willing to give up their demands for higher wages to allow those who are perhaps less able to gain a place in the labor market, which they will only have access to if minimum-wage levels are lowered.

This concept should not be taken too literally, but rather as a way of thinking about how the labor market functions, because most countries have many different segments in the labor market, and it would be difficult to describe each of these with any degree of precision, and even more difficult to analyze the position of many different groups.

E

EARLY RETIREMENT. When someone leaves the **labor market** before reaching the normal **pension** age. Early retirement schemes have been developed in some countries. The intention of these schemes is to allow those who are unable to continue in the labor market for a lengthy period of time to leave it with specific benefits before reaching the pension age. These benefits have also been used as part of **active labor market policy**, as a way of reducing the supply of labor and thereby reducing **unemployment**. Facing changes in **demography** and the need for more labor in the future, several countries have tightened the eligibility conditions for receiving early retirement benefits, including a higher age. Still, with countries becoming richer, more people tend to leave the labor market early to enjoy a "third age," with time to do other things, including traveling, reading, and enjoying other cultural activities. This is an example of how a noneconomic **incentive** can have an impact on the individual's behavior.

EARNINGS-RELATED BENEFITS. Benefits that are dependent on one's previous income. In many cases, the benefit is a percentage of the previous earned income that qualifies for that benefit. This percentage may be combined with an upper ceiling. In many countries, this has been the case for benefits in relation to **unemployment** and **sickness**, and in several countries, more often than before, in relation to **pensions**. This is because in some pension systems, the connection to earnings has been built on the contributions paid during the years in the **labor market**.

EASTERN EUROPEAN WELFARE STATE MODEL. This describes the state and **social policy** systems in Eastern European countries until they were changed in the late 1980s, moving away from **communism**. Before this model, the systems mainly relied on state provision, delivery, and **financing** of social policy. Some of the countries in Eastern Europe have had a history of being involved in social policy in ways similar to other Central European countries and through **church** provision; therefore, in addition to the state benefits, some have been provided by **families** or churches and have been based on the **labor market**, with the system's commitment to full **employment**.

The systems that existed before the late 1980s could be characterized as having job security and **universal** free **health care services**. In addition, they subsidized food and **housing**, which greatly reduced insecurity. Also included were well-developed maternity systems. But due to job guarantees, there was no **unemployment benefit** system, no **social assistance**, and only a rudimentary way of dealing with more specific problems in the fields of social policy. As a citizen, the individual had a **right** to a job, and support was based on this, even if part of the employment was "hidden unemployment."

The main advantage of these systems was this set of guarantees. The main disadvantages were the lack of development of a real **social security** system and the lack of support for those who did not really fit into the labor market or who had other social needs. **Pensions** were often low, and the state apparatus granted privileges to certain groups, making society unequal. **Inequality** was therefore not—as in the rest of Europe and the **United States**—related to being in the labor market or having capital income, but more on whether it belonged to the "ruling **class**."

The changes of the late 1980s have had far-reaching consequences for these countries' systems. At present, they are developing in a variety of directions. In reaction to the old state **bureaucratic** systems, many countries have relied more on **market** provision and therefore have moved toward a more **liberal** approach to **welfare-state** development. Because some have historical ties with Central Europe, they have developed systems that resemble the **Bismarckian** one, which, however, due to financial pressure, look more like a **Southern European welfare state model**, with high dependence on families as the main providers and only marginal intervention from the state. *See also* BULGARIA; CZECH REPUBLIC; ESTONIA; HUNGARY; LATVIA; LITHUANIA; POLAND; ROMANIA; SLOVAKIA; SLOVENIA.

EDUCATION. Historically, education has not been thought of as an element of the **welfare state's** delivery, but, at the same time, it has always been considered a **merit good** in the sense that if given the choice, individuals may prefer less education than what society may deem the optimal level. In modern welfare states, education has become more centralized as a mechanism for ensuring that all citizens actively participate in society's **democratic** life and that the society has an educated workforce. A highly educated workforce is seen as an instrument for ensuring competitiveness against other countries, but also as a way of reducing pressure on public spending, because in most welfare states, the degree of **unemployment** is related to the level of educational attainment. **Active labor market policies** in many countries therefore include education as one of their essential elements. Education has become increasingly important because resorting to the most traditional economic instruments has become more difficult in individual countries due to economic

globalization. **Lifelong learning** has also become more central in ensuring updated qualifications for the workforce in the years to come.

ELASTICITY. The degree to which a change in one factor will have an impact on another factor. Elasticity of demand and supply refers to how the quantity of a good demanded and supplied will react to a change in the price of the specific good. **Welfare-state** analysis examines **labor market** elasticity, which indicates how a change in wage level or **taxation** could have an impact on the **labor force** supply.

EMPLOYMENT. The time spent by a worker in the production process. It is seen as the individual's participation in the **labor market** to produce goods and **services**, and thereby provide a labor input (there is also input from land and capital) to production. National employment statistics only include that which can be measured and registered; therefore, time spent on production in households is not regarded as employment; the same is the case for **voluntary work** and work in the **hidden economy**. Aside from giving rise to income for a person or **family** in many societies, employment also brings social esteem and **integration** into societal life. In addition to being without income, those without work are also—often to a large degree—deprived of contact with other people and might be socially excluded.

Full employment is defined as all those willing to work and wanting a job being able to get one. In neoclassical economics, full employment is defined as being the point at which all those willing to work at the going wage rate can get a job. In Keynesian economics, it reflects whether there is a full utilization of productive resources, and **unemployment** is therefore minimal.

Unemployment will often exist, but the amount will vary throughout time. Since the **financial crisis** that began in 2008, many **welfare states** have witnessed a high level of unemployment, and especially a high level of youth unemployment. There may also be **underemployment**, which is the case when someone wanting work is not actively searching for it due to conditions in the labor market that make the chance of getting a job relatively low. Furthermore, people may work part-time but really want a full-time job. !n developing countries, many individuals have to live off of agricultural production, which is frequently done on small plots. They are employed, but if possible they would want to have either more land to work or to get a job in another sector.

ENTITLEMENTS. This concept describes what the individual can be expected to receive in case a certain **contingency** occurs. Entitlements can be based upon **citizenship** or contribution (voluntary or obligatory), but this can either be based upon **rights** in contrast to discretionary decisions by the administration.

EQUAL OPPORTUNITY. This is **equality** in the sense that equal groups should be treated equally. Equal opportunity can exist between different groups in societies (e.g., migrant and nonmigrant workers) or between different sexes. Equality of opportunity can also be related to the **educational** system. This means that an individual has the same chances; however, the result may still be **inequality** due to different **capabilities** or individual work, either due to difference in working hours or differences in wages in the different segments of the **labor market**. *See also* GENDER.

EQUALITY. Equality refers to the **distribution** of resources in different societies. It can be interpreted in different ways and is often interwoven with moral judgments. The definition of equality has implications for the political decisions made in a given society. It can take different forms, including **equal opportunity**, equal treatment, and equal outcome.

Equal opportunity refers to society's efforts to ensure that all citizens have the same chances in life. This means that society should intervene when, for instance, monopolies threaten to reduce the individual's opportunities. It can also be used as an argument for state involvement in **education** to ensure that individuals from different social backgrounds have the same chances, and, further, to improve the situation of men or women.

Equal treatment refers to equal cases being treated in the same way. This means that people experiencing the same situation should be treated in the same way as others. This does not necessarily imply an equal distribution of income and wealth, but it is more of a guideline for how to behave in specific situations in society.

Equal outcome focuses on the evaluation of the situation by different individuals in society where the outcome of different activities, for example, in the **labor market**, has an impact on the individual's situation. In cases where different outcomes are measured, for instance, in monetary terms, this means that the **public sector** should intervene to try to make the situation equal for all individuals.

None of these definitions of equality gives any indication of which type of intervention should be used in various situations, nor do they give any **normative** indication of which type of equality will be preferable and which may be in conflict with other societal goals, or the time frame in which it should be measured. They merely point to how equality can be interpreted in different ways and how, in a given society, equality will depend on normative viewpoints. Finally, the concept of equality can be used as a framework for comparing different situations in or between countries. The concept of equality can also be interpreted by comparing it with such concepts as **inequality, functional distribution, income distribution**, and so forth. *See also* GINI COEFFICIENT; LORENZ CURVE; SOCIAL EXCLUSION.

EQUILIBRIUM. In economic theory, equilibrium refers to a balance between supply and demand. In purely **market**-based countries, the expectation is that the market will lead society toward equilibrium, which includes full **employment**, no surplus of certain goods and **services**, and full utilization of production facilities. In real life, equilibrium does not exist, or if it does, it is difficult to measure, and society is normally in transition from one equilibrium to another. As a concept, it is useful as an analytical tool to describe how different types of interventions and disturbances may affect behavior and the market's functioning.

ESTONIA. A small Baltic country with about 1.5 million inhabitants. Estonia became independent again in 1991, after having been part of the **Union of Soviet Socialist Republics (USSR)** since 1940, and thereby had a **communist** type of welfare system until its independence. In 1922, Estonia was one of the first countries to introduce the **family allowance**. This was followed in 1924 by laws concerning **pensions, sickness benefits, maternity benefits**, and **industrial injury**.

The present-day **social security** system mostly resembles a **continental model** built on a **social insurance** system. Employers pay one-third of the costs for old-age, **disability**, sickness, maternity, and industrial injury benefits. The state **finances** family allowances, **unemployment benefits**, and **heath care**.

In 1994, Estonia became a member of the **European Union**. Estonia's economy has grown rapidly since it gained independence from the USSR, although it was also hit hard by the **financial crisis**. The **welfare state** is of a more limited character and more in line with a **liberal** type of welfare state.

ETHNICITY. The shared ethnic background of a group. In **welfare-state** analysis, it has been shown that, in many countries, there is **discrimination** based on ethnicity, for example, higher **unemployment** rates and reduced access to public **services**. Ethnicity has assumed an increasing role in welfare-state analysis because migrants, especially, are often poorly **integrated** into societies and therefore typically have substandard living conditions than those originally coming from the society.

EUROPEAN SOCIAL MODEL. This model was conceived of in the **European Union (EU)** as one **welfare-state** model that could be used to compare the **United States** and Europe; however, it is not yet clear what type of welfare-state model this should be. One reason for this discrepancy may be that it is difficult to reach agreement within the EU in areas concerning social and **labor market policy**. The fact remains that national differences exist, as do various approaches to the welfare state. Nevertheless, some core elements exist, including the guarantee of a decent standard of living for all and an agreement that an inclusive society should be built. Moreover, equal access to the **labor market** is expected, and goals for the participation rate of men and women, young and elderly, have been set. Thus, in many ways, the European social model can be understood as a combination of various traditional welfare-state models.

EUROPEAN UNION (EU). Formerly called the European Economic Community and the European Community, the EU now consists of 28 members (**Italy**, **France**, the **Netherlands**, **Belgium**, Luxembourg, **Germany**, the **United Kingdom**, **Ireland**, **Denmark**, **Spain**, **Portugal**, **Greece**, **Finland**, **Sweden**, **Austria**, **Estonia**, **Latvia**, **Lithuania**, **Poland**, **Hungary**, **Czech Republic**, **Slovakia**, **Slovenia**, Cyprus, Malta, **Romania**, **Bulgaria**, and **Croatia**). The first six countries on the list founded the EU in 1957. In 1973, the United Kingdom, Ireland, and Denmark joined; in 1980, Spain, Portugal, and Greece entered; and, in 1994, Finland, Sweden, and Austria gained membership. On 1 May 2004, the next 10 countries entered, coming mainly from Eastern Europe. On 1 January 2007, Romania and Bulgaria joined, and they were followed by Croatia on 1 July 2013. A few more countries are still expected to join in the coming years.

The EU originated from the idea of a customs union facilitating trade and using the various countries' comparative advantages when trading with one another. The EU was also seen by some as a way of reducing conflicts in Europe, especially the historical conflicts between France and Germany.

The development of EU **social policy** is a long and complex story. It started with the initial treaty in 1957, which increased labor mobility and **social security** for migrant workers. In 1971, a reform of the European Social Fund (ESF) included funding for vocational training, and the reform continued in 1974, with the Social Action Program (SAP), which, among other things, included the promotion of **employment** and a social dialogue in Europe, including the first EU **poverty** program. This was followed by a long period without any new initiatives, which ended in 1987 with adoption of the Single European Act (SEA). The SEA introduced recommendations about the **health** and safety of workers and stated the intention of economic and social cohesion. In 1989, a Community Charter of Fundamental Social Rights was adopted, including 47 initiatives, one of which was concerned with employment and remuneration.

In 1991, the Maastricht Treaty was concluded, which includes a "Protocol on Economic and Social Integration and a Social Dimension" (which does not include the United Kingdom). This was followed by recommendations on **convergence** and guaranteed minimum income in 1992 (recommendations are not binding on the member states, in contrast to directives).

Labor market policy was included in the Amsterdam Treaty in 1997, and the aim of the EU was described as working to include traditional economic aspects, as well as to ensure a high level of employment. In 1997, based on the Amsterdam Treaty, guidelines for National Action Plans for Employment were adopted in Luxembourg. These action plans, which would later be labeled the **open method of coordination (OMC)**, were an attempt to encourage a common understanding of the need for an **active labor market policy**. Additional areas of social policy (**pension**, **social exclusion**) went on to become part of the OMC.

Still, the EU does not have any real impact on **welfare-state** policies in the individual member states, because social and labor market policy, including **financing** of the welfare state, is decided by the nation-states. Only in relation to the free movement of workers, **health** and safety at the workplace, and equal treatment of men and women does the EU have a direct impact on the nation-states' policies. Nonetheless, the increased awareness on the supranational level of social and welfare policy, as well as the more economic aspects that the EU addresses, may influence the member states to pursue a more common policy, leading to some degree of **convergence**.

The EU's initiatives have already had a huge impact on the development of **social policy** regarding health and safety and equal treatment of men and women. The same is true for spending through the ESF and other regional and structural funds, where the economically weaker areas of the EU are supported. The EU's influence on welfare states in Europe is not only through directives and recommendations, but also due to court cases in relation to the free movement of workers and equal treatment, as well as the free movement of goods and **services**; therefore, the EU's impact on the development of the welfare state cannot be overemphasized and should not be neglected. The ongoing enlargement of the EU could indicate a trend toward more uniform welfare states in Europe, especially if it evolves into a more **integrated** economic and monetary union. Some have labeled this a **European social model**.

The EU has set goals for Europe in 2020. This is the organization's growth strategy, with the aim of high levels of employment, productivity, and social cohesion. Five goals have been established related to employment, innovation, **education**, **social inclusion**, and climate/energy.

EVALUATION. Evaluation is increasingly being used to find out how the **public sector** can get the most out of scarce resources. A growing number of **welfare states** are using **evidence** as part of their attempt to ensure the best possible outcome and guarantee that, given the economic options, individuals are getting the best support. Evaluation has been used for some time in **health care**, as in some cases the use of a given medicine might have a negative impact or adverse effect on an individual's **health**. Evaluation can be difficult given that the support can be related to contacts between different individuals. The gold standard is randomized control trials (RCT), where one group gets a treatment and the other (and in principle they should not know it) does not. By doing so, it is possible to measure whether the intervention has the expected outcome.

EVERYDAY LIFE. As a sociological term, this describes **family** life. It is a way of examining roles and relationships in day-to-day life. It is often used in sociological analysis to describe the home, neighborhood, and local **community** and the individual's lifestyles within them.

EVIDENCE. Ensuring that users, within the possible economic limits, get the best service, for example, in **health care** or social **care**, can best be carried out if there is evidence that one intervention works better than another. To do so, one needs to have a theory of why an intervention can help alleviate a problem. Furthermore, one needs to have solid empirical evidence gained by the **evaluation** of different kinds of intervention. There is a hierarchy of what ensures the best evidence, but also that even if it is not possible to get the strongest level of evidence, one can at least do one's best to find out what will ensure the best outcome. Evidence has been used in health care and **labor market policy** for some time; however, this is increasingly a central issue in all types of **welfare states'** policies and interventions, especially given that there are scarce resources, and the expectation is that this will also be the case in the years to come.

EXIT, VOICE, AND LOYALTY. This concept was developed by Albert Hirschman (1972) to describe the ways that individuals in society can respond to decisions and find solutions to different problems. They can exit (i.e., **migrate** or move to another area of the country), albeit this can often be so costly that, in practice, it is difficult to do so due to transaction costs. They can raise their voice, either in debate or by voting for a party that takes an opposing standpoint at the next election. Or, finally, they can be loyal and agree with the decisions made. In the **welfare-state** debate, this term has been used to argue in favor of a more **decentralized** way of organizing the welfare state. In a highly decentralized system, it may be possible to develop different combinations of **services**, transfers, and local **taxes** that the individual will have the opportunity to choose and combine as he or she prefers.

F

FABIANISM. This movement was formed by people in the **United Kingdom** who advocated a **collectivist** approach to **social policy** and argued that the capitalist system would inevitably crumble. They believed that a **universal** and collectively decided **welfare state** would be developed out of the old system. Fabians saw the **Beveridgian** approach as confirming their ideas about and visions of society's development.

FAMILY. An institution within which many different activities take place. It normally refers to parents and their children. In a larger framework, the family can include all those who are relatives, mainly in a biological sense. The term *nuclear family* refers to families consisting of parents and immature children. This is seen as the narrowest way of defining a family.

The concept of the family is related to different **welfare states** and their way of functioning. In many welfare states, especially those where the state only intervenes as the lender of last resort (i.e., **subsidiarity** exists), the family plays an important role in the delivery of **care** and different types of income transfers. In these systems, the family structure will have a strong impact on whether a person is covered (or supported) in the event that a specific **contingency** occurs.

The role of the family can be analyzed from various viewpoints, but the analytical unit generally tends to be the household instead of the family. The reasons for this are both practical and theoretical. The practical reason is that many statistics are based on the special unit, the household. The theoretical reason is that a household is the unit the individual is living in, and although this may consist of relatives, it may also consist of many other people, including friends, lovers, and companions. Family policy has been developed as part of the welfare states' support to those needing it, and also as part of how to reconcile **work and family life**. *See also* DEFAMILIZATION; FAMILY ALLOWANCE; FAMILY REGIMES; GENDER.

FAMILY ALLOWANCE. Support to **families** with children. This type of allowance is structured, and the criteria for receiving it vary among different **welfare states**. It is also known as **child benefit**.

FAMILY REGIMES. This term describes how various societies place different emphases on the role of the **family**. These range from full **defamilization** to reliance on the family as the main provider, as in the **Southern European welfare state** type. Regimes often describe the difference between the male **breadwinner** and dual breadwinner types of households.

FEMINISM. This is both a theory and a movement based on the belief that women are treated in a systematically different way (and mainly a disadvantaged way) compared to men in the **welfare state**. Feminist researchers have claimed that most research has not taken into consideration the specific sociological impact of differences in **gender** when analyzing the outcomes of the welfare state. Feminist researchers adopt different dividing lines in their research compared to other types of welfare-state research, for example, **liberal** and **Marxist**. In many countries, the issue of gender, among other things, has been used in relation to the analysis of **labor market** development, as in most countries women earn less, do more part-time work, and are often in more insecure jobs than men. Recent years have seen growing **equality** and also areas where young men are at disadvantaged position to women. *See also* CONVERGENCE.

FINANCIAL CRISIS. The financial crisis of the **welfare states** has been an ongoing issue for many decades due to the fact that such crises seem to be a repeating theme in the historical economic and political trends. The Wall Street Crash of 1929 is just one of several crises that, early on, had a profound effect on the overall level of **unemployment** and economic activity. These recurrent types of economic crisis, combined with pressure in the balance between voters' expectations for more welfare and states' lack of financial means, has also implied that fiscal pressure has been mounting on the welfare states for some decades now, except in times of rapid economic growth. This was further exaggerated in the wake of the collapse of banks and mortgage institutions in the **United States** in the autumn of 2008. The reduced value of real estate and huge losses in banks indicated that there was a need for financial injections in the banking sector in the United States, as well as in most welfare states in Europe.

In many countries, the implications of these financial injections were huge and resulted in rapidly growing deficits in the **public sector**. These deficits have been difficult to cope with given the overall increase in the public sector's debt. The huge losses, combined with an economic recession in many countries, implied an increase in unemployment and lower public-sector revenue, entailing even more pressure on the **financing** of the welfare states. Lower public-sector income implies a need for either an increase in **taxes** and duties or a reduction in public-sector spending. Most welfare states have used austerity measures by reducing spending on welfare expenditures, including **pension**, unemployment, and monitoring the number of public-sector employees, but, in Europe, increases in the value-added tax have also been seen. Countries in the Eastern and Southern parts of Europe have been especially hard hit, as well as such **liberal** welfare states as the **United Kingdom** and **Ireland**. Furthermore, the crisis has been an argument for reforms in the **labor market**, with a focus on additional **incentives** to take up a job by lowering the relative level of benefits.

The financial markets' mistrust of the abilities of several countries to pay back loans has further increased the burden on the welfare states because of an elevation in the interest rates on loans, requiring several countries, including **Greece**, **Ireland**, **Spain**, and **Portugal**, to receive international economic support to avoid defaulting. To reduce deficits, many countries adopted austerity packages, inferring strong cuts in public-sector spending and, albeit to a lesser extent, an increase in taxes and duties; therefore, the financial crisis has placed more pressure on the welfare state than in many other previous crises. It has also resulted in a high level of unemployment and, in many countries, an especially elevated level of youth unemployment. As a consequence of the relatively lengthy span of the economic crisis, there are also more people living at risk of falling into in **poverty**. The long-term implications for the welfare state cannot yet be evaluated given that the willingness to pay for welfare can change in times of economic growth. *See also* FISCAL CRISIS.

FINANCING. The means through which welfare support is funded. There are many different ways to finance the **welfare state**. It is important to understand these different approaches and their relation to welfare-state development and how the different ways of financing in different models can be interpreted.

In principle, it is not necessary to collect **taxes** and duties, but not doing so has economic consequences, including problems with the balance of payments, **public-sector** debt, **inflation**, and bottlenecks in the **labor market**. Taxes and duties collected will have an impact on allocation, stabilization, and **distribution** in the economy. Furthermore, they will cause some distortion, for example, the choice between work and leisure, saving and consumption, and the use of capital and labor in the production process. Taxes and duties may further change the consumption patterns of various goods and **services**. They could, for instance, switch the consumer's spending from tobacco to milk by putting a high duty on tobacco and none on milk. Taxes and duties can be imposed in all parts of the economy. They can be levied on households, firms, **markets** for goods (consumer or capital), or factor markets. In addition, they can be placed on wealth, inheritances, and so forth.

User charges and obligatory insurance membership can also be thought of as a way of financing the welfare state. **Social insurance** contributions may be another way of funding welfare programs rather than using income tax or duties.

The core elements of a good tax structure are that it will do the following:

1. provide adequate revenue
2. ensure an equitable distribution of the tax burden
3. minimize excess burden and be achieved with low administrative cost
4. achieve economic goals (stabilization, allocation)

Taxes and duties are often taken in the following forms:

1. income taxes
2. **social security** contributions
3. value-added taxes
4. duties
5. other (property, bequest, wealth)

The most frequently used methods to collect taxes are income taxes, social security contributions, and value-added taxes. The combination of these varies to a great extent between countries. One could argue that user payments and user charges are a way of financing part of public-sector expenditures. Obligatory insurance, privately organized and delivered, could also be an indirect way of financing the welfare state. Welfare states that have a more **universal** approach often rely on income taxes and value-added taxes, whereas welfare states with a more selective approach tend to use social security contributions. Welfare states taking a minimalist approach mainly rely on private **charity**.

The manner of financing the welfare state also depends on the historical traditions and development. The more mature welfare states seem to have a higher overall level of taxes and duties as a proportion of the **gross domestic product (GDP)** than the newer welfare states. Many Western European welfare states spend anywhere from 45 to 50 percent of their GDP on public-sector expenses. Not all of this is spent on **social policy** in its broad meaning, but it indicates the influence of the public sector on the economy and the need to finance it.

Different ways of financing public-sector expenditures have varying social policy implications with respect to who pays and who receives benefits from the public sector. Using contributions—and not making them obligatory—implies that only those who contribute will be covered. The criterion for coverage will often be having a job in the labor market, but it could be something else, for instance, voluntary payment to life insurance. A consequence of relying on contributions is a tendency toward a more polarized society, dividing those inside and those outside the labor market. In the field of **health care**, the difference between those paying into a contributory system and those not paying—as in the U.S. system—results in an unequal treatment of individuals, and, for some, no treatment at all.

Using income taxes and duties may indicate a more universal system in which the **right** to a benefit or service depends on being a citizen in the given country. In addition, taxes and duties may have the consequence of changing the distribution of resources as a result of their impact on individual choices. This can happen in two different ways. The first is between generations (intergenerational), and the second is within generations (intragenerational).

Intragenerational redistribution through the tax and duty system has the aim of ensuring that those with high incomes pay more in taxes than those with a small ones. This redistribution will be combined with public-sector spending mainly devoted to those with a small income, resulting in redistribution from rich to poor. The effectiveness of this redistribution depends not only on the level and composition of the tax and duty systems, but also on how the public sector spends its money.

During their lifetimes, some people may be among both those paying for and those receiving benefits. This is intergenerational redistribution. This is mainly in such areas as **care** and benefits for children and the elderly. Those who are elderly and perhaps receive a public **pension** or are being cared for have previously paid the taxes and duties. In this sense, one generation is paying for the next generation and expects that the coming generation will do the same for it. Taxes and duties are therefore of great importance to the welfare state and how it fulfills its goals. Furthermore, taxes and duties will have an impact on society's overall economic functioning and redistribution between and within generations.

Countries cannot simply impose whatever types of taxes and duties they see fit if they are open-**market** economies. **Globalization** has an impact on how an individual country can chose its tax packages. Taxes on companies, for example, will have an impact on the firm's location, and to attract foreign investment, countries are often willing to change to a lower level of these taxes compared to neighboring countries. Higher duties on goods that can be easily traded across borders are also more difficult to impose, as this might move the trade to neighboring countries. In addition, e-trade poses difficulties for national tax bases. Taxes on immobile factors have thus become increasingly important. Hence, although globalization has not created serious difficulties in financing the welfare state, it has imposed certain restrictions on choices about taxes and duties.

FINLAND. The **welfare state** in Finland started with a law on **industrial injury** in 1895. This was followed by an **unemployment** insurance law in 1917 (changed to unemployment assistance in 1960), a ruling on **pension** and **disability** in 1937, a law on **family allowances** in 1948, and a directive on **sickness** and **maternity** in 1963. Finland has gradually developed its system and has been a latecomer in many areas compared to the other Nordic countries. This may be partly explained by its history. From 1809–1917, the country was under **Russian** rule, and, thereafter, a two-year civil war **prevented** the real development of **social policy**.

Finland was hit hard by the changes in Eastern Europe in the late 1980s; therefore, it tightened the welfare system during the 1990s, although without making dramatic changes in its overall composition. Recent years have seen reforms of the **pension** systems, including guaranteed monthly pension and part-time sickness benefits. One goal of pension reform is to extend the retirement age. Today, in many respects, Finland's welfare state resembles the other **Scandinavian welfare state** types, but with a much more direct influence from the **Bismarckian** type and also membership in the **European Union**.

FISCAL CRISIS. This refers to the possible inability to pay for the **welfare state**, but, also in the writing in the 1970s, the built-in conflict between state and **market** provision and delivery of welfare. A fiscal crisis exists when the welfare state is having difficulties in **financing** the **welfare state's** expenditures and the **public-sector** deficit. In the aftermath of the **financial crisis**, countries in Southern Europe have had difficulties ensuring that they can borrow money to pay for the deficit until they are able to get a higher level of **taxes** and/or duties or a reduction in public-sector spending, if the need arises.

The fiscal crisis can also refer to the ability to fulfill voters' expectations for welfare benefits, thereby implying a **legitimacy** crisis in the welfare states. The fiscal crisis has had a visible impact on welfare spending in Southern and Eastern Europe, but also in such countries as the **United Kingdom, Ireland,** and **United States;** therefore, there has been a tendency to change welfare spending, as witnessed by numerous reforms in the **pension** systems in the last 10 to 15 years, with the aim of later retirement and the decreased use of taxes and duties to pay for pension, and instead the use of more funded pension systems.

FISCAL FEDERALISM. The understanding of which level of **government** has the **right** to **tax** and levy duties. It is often supplemented by a discussion of at which level taxes or duties are best imposed: supranational, national, regional, or local.

FISCAL POLICY. This refers to the **government's** intervention in the economy, either through **taxes** and duties or government expenditure. The intervention can have the purpose of expanding or contracting the economy. Fiscal policy was seen by **John Maynard Keynes** as one way of managing the economy to achieve stable economic growth. The use of fiscal policy could help achieve a more balanced economy, including balance of payments equilibrium and low **unemployment** rates. This approach was mainly inspired by a belief in macroeconomic policy. Questions were later raised about how the microeconomic level was affected by changes in fiscal policy, that is, the impact on **incentives** and the willingness to work and save.

As economies have gradually become more open, it has become harder to use fiscal policy in individual countries, especially the expansive version of fiscal policy, without creating balance of payment problems. Fiscal policy still plays a role in **preventing** huge swings in the economy, thus it can be used on a smaller scale, and it was also used by some countries in the wake of the **financial crisis** in 2008. A country facing a deterioration in the balance of payments or the level of unemployment may use fiscal policy in a limited measure to ensure better overall macroeconomic balance.

FISCAL WELFARE. Welfare distributed through the **tax** system. Fiscal welfare can, for example, be support to homeowners through a **right** to deduct interest payments. Fiscal welfare often has a negative impact on economic **distribution**. It can also be an alternative way to achieve certain welfare goals as opposed to **public welfare** or **occupational welfare**. *See also* SOCIAL DIVISION OF WELFARE; TAX EXPENDITURES; TITMUSS, RICHARD MORRIS.

FLAT-RATE BENEFITS. Benefits paid at the same rate to everyone who is eligible. This type of benefits is not **earnings related**. Even flat-rate benefits may be **means-tested** based on income and wealth, that is, only those with an income or wealth below a certain level will receive them. Flat-rate benefits were part of the **Beveridgian** description of a new **social policy** in the **United Kingdom** after World War II. The extent and size of this kind of benefits varies among different types of **welfare states**.

FLAT-RATE PENSION. A **pension** that does not depend on contributions or previous earnings. It can therefore also be labeled a **universal** benefit. Its level may depend on the number of individuals in the household, and it can also be **means-tested**.

FLEXICURITY. This term refers to a situation that combines a highly flexible **labor market,** as in the **post-Fordist** production system, with a high degree of **social security,** which is attained through **welfare-state** benefits and by ensuring a decent standard of living. It is a concept that describes the combination of flexibility and security in the labor market. The degree to which a labor market is flexible especially refers to how easy it is to hire and fire employees in a company, and thereby how companies can increase or decrease the number of people they have employed. Flexibility can also be related to internal changes at the individual workplace and how flexible the workforce is in moving from one type of job to another within the same company. Security, on the other hand, has as its focus the degree of security the individual workers has. This can be in relation to the dismissal time, but also employment security, for example even if fired, the individual can get a job again. Security also refers to the degree of income replacement in case of **unemployment.** Thus, there are many dimensions, and different countries may pursue different combinations of flexibility and security. There can therefore also be many different pathways to flexicurity. Instruments include rules about contracts and dismissal, **active labor market policy, lifelong learning,** and social security.

FRANCE. The history of **social policy** and **social security** in France has had a long-lasting impact on social security development in many other European countries. This is true even though we usually compare the development of **welfare states** with the situation in the **United Kingdom** and **Germany.**

The French Revolution drastically changed the picture of **charity** and the role of the **church** in France. Furthermore, in the 1791 constitution, it was declared that citizens had a **right** to assistance. In 1791, a right to **pensions** for seamen suffering **invalidity** was also established. In 1852 and 1856, France developed systems that provided **subsidies** to certain mutual funds covering **sickness** and invalidity for certain groups. Mutual assistance and insurance for a few groups were developed in the beginning and middle of the 19th century, but they did not provide sufficient support to those in need, and many groups were left out; therefore, in 1898, a **social insurance** system to cover **industrial injury** was introduced. It was a special system for a limited number of groups, but it was an all-encompassing system. These changes were followed in 1905 by an **unemployment** insurance law, a law concerning old age and **disability** in 1910, sickness and **maternity** laws in 1928, and a ruling on **family allowances** in 1932. During World War II, there were plans in France—as in Britain—to develop a more comprehensive system, but the approach was never implemented the same way it was in Britain. There seems to be no satisfactory explanation for this.

France has a mixed type of system, in which some aspects—family allowances, for example—are of the **universal** type, and when likened to other **European Union** countries, benefits are generous. Other features primarily build on the social insurance system. The French system has been developed within France's structure of central administration and is therefore highly centralized compared to other European countries.

However, it is mainly a **continental model**, and most of the **financing** comes from payments from those in the **labor market** and those who are insured. The **government** is not directly involved in the payment of social security in France, leaving this to the aforementioned partners, but this does not mean that the government is not actively involved in deciding the levels of benefits and structure of the system.

In recent years, debates have focused on the pension system and how to finance it given ongoing **demographic** changes. Lower pensions and additional years in the labor market were discussed as solutions, which were passed into law in 2011, including better **incentives** for elderly workers to stay in the labor market.

FREE RIDE. When someone enjoys the benefits of a good, service, or agreement but pays nothing for it. In **welfare-state** analysis, the concept has been used as an argument for state provision in areas where it is impossible to ask for payment—urban street lighting is an example—and therefore it is not possible to exclude someone from enjoying the good. A free ride is especially possible in relation to **public goods**. The possibility that some are getting a free ride makes it difficult to know the exact preferences and demand for many public **services**.

FREEDOM. The position where one is being independent and is free to make one's own decisions. In **welfare-state** analysis, this concept has been used when analyzing **capabilities**, but the conflict between state and **market** and its impact on the individual's ability to make his or her own decisions has also played a central role. The debate between advocates of **public choice** and promoters of a more central role for the state plays a part in this conflict.

FRIENDLY SOCIETY. Friendly societies were established in the 19th century in many countries to support and protect their members through mutual aid. They can be viewed as an early insurance-based solution.

FUNCTIONAL DISTRIBUTION. The distribution of income from production among the factors of production: land, labor, and capital. *See also* INCOME DISTRIBUTION.

FUNCTIONALISM. This theory describes the development and growth of the **welfare state** as a response to changing needs of either citizens or capital interests. In a historical context, this theory asserts that the development of the welfare state will mainly be explained by industrialization. Thus, capitalism needs to be revitalized and receive continued support from the state to develop and maintain high profit rates.

FUNDED SYSTEM. A specific way of **financing** and developing **pension** systems. Under this system, those who want to have a pension must pay a contribution. This can be either voluntary, part of a **collective agreement** made in the **labor market**, or compulsory by statutory law. In most countries, the system is based on voluntary or collective agreements. The voluntary systems will frequently be helped and given **incentives** to develop through state **tax subsidies**. Collective agreements can take many different forms, including agreements in individual firms, collective agreements for an entire sector or industry, or nationwide agreements for specific groups of skilled or unskilled workers.

Funded systems are based on the idea that the individual receives a pension in accordance with what he or she has paid in and the return on these savings. Funded systems may be built into a collective agreement covering certain risks, for example, **invalidity** or life insurance. The individual also will normally receive a pension in accordance with what he or she has paid into the system.

Various arguments exist in favor of and against the different types of pension systems. One advantage of a funded system is that it is possible to increase capital stock and thereby presumably also the future level of output, because this capital stock can be invested in productive capacity. The system is not typically seen as a tax by the individual and is therefore likely to cause fewer distortions between saving/consumption and work/leisure than taxes and duties are normally assumed to create. Another advantage is that the **government** will know the future size of **public-sector** expenditure in the area, and this will fluctuate little as a result of the proportion of elderly in society.

The problem with the funded system is that it takes a long time to implement. For instance, decisions about improving the level of benefits may take 30 to 40 years to be fully executed. The value of pensions can be easily reduced because higher taxes reduce the buying power of the pensioners. Another issue is that if savings are not used to increase production, there may be a balance of payments problem when the pensions have to be paid out. The pensions, as seen from society's point of view, can only be spent if the production capacity is in accordance therewith.

Some would argue that a funded system has the built-in disadvantage that when a government has reduced pressure on expenditure for the elderly, then the government will be able to spend more in other areas. If the saving is high, it may depress the overall rate of return due to the large amount of money used to buy stocks and bonds. Despite increasingly open capital **markets**, this only seems to be a problem for countries with more restricted access to international capital markets.

Unless strict restrictions are imposed on pension funds, there is a risk for the members of the funds if those administering them abuse them or do not invest the money in the best possible way. Members of well-run pension funds may then have higher pensions than those in poorly run ones. In the case of a company-based pension fund, where it is not possible to transfer pension **rights** when changing jobs, there may also be severe restrictions on the way the labor market functions.

Finally, it has been argued that big pension funds may apply political pressure—"pension fund socialism," as some have labeled it. Furthermore, large amounts of money collected in one place could have an impact on society, at least in terms of influence on the decision-making process. Each country should ultimately develop its own combination of these systems. Most countries use a pairing of the **pay-as-you-go system** and a funded system to pay for pensions.

G

GENDER. A person's sex may affect that person's position in society, and decisions can also be influenced by different perceptions of gender. A growing body of literature has tried to describe and explain how gender has had an impact on **welfare states** and their development. This type of research attempts to explain the different developments in society. It emphasizes the positions of men and women more than **class** or differences in status and income.

In many states, the position of women is often seen as weak, although there has been a movement toward more gender-equal societies in several countries. In welfare-state analysis, various concepts of a male-**breadwinner** (strong or weak) model of the welfare state have been introduced. Women have been seen as disadvantaged with regard to the average wage income in the **labor market**, and they also often do more of the house work than men. Women in most welfare states often hold only part-time jobs, and they have historically been weakly placed in the **democratic** system.

On the other hand, recent studies show that men, especially young men, achieve a lower level of educational attainment than women, as well as the fact that men have a shorter life expectancy. Both sexes thus have different disadvantages when compared to the other sex, although development toward a higher degree of gender **equality** has taken place. *See also* FEMINISM; GENDER MAINSTREAMING.

GENDER MAINSTREAMING. This refers to elements decided with the aim of ensuring that **gender** issues are included in the development, evaluation, and improvement of a gender perspective in policy processes. The intention has been to be aware of both direct and indirect gender issues arising from a given policy in a particular area. Furthermore, mainstreaming also implies trying to increase the level of gender **equality**. *See also* FEMINISM.

GERMANY. The current German welfare system is still inspired by Otto von Bismarck and the so-called **Bismarckian model**. Coverage for **sickness** was introduced in 1883, followed by support for **industrial injury** in 1884 and **invalidity pensions** in 1889. But even before the 1880s, certain groups had industrial injury and sickness insurance in parts of Germany. In 1838, for example, employers were made responsible for labor on railroads. In 1854, compulsory insurance for mineworkers was introduced, and, in 1871, employer responsibility for workers in specific parts of the industrial sector was enacted.

With the introduction of these laws in the united Germany in the 1880s, the state as an entity took over in areas of **social policy** that had previously been either ignored, only partly covered, or left to voluntary assistance. The reason for the successful development of the German system was that it was piecemeal and based on mutual aid, which for some already existed. Finally, it did not rely on state intervention alone; the system used a combination of state and private **financing** and organization.

The development of the welfare system was also a response to growing unrest among the working **class**, which arose due to the increasingly difficult and bad working and living conditions in the cities. Thus, the case of Germany exemplifies one of the explanations for the emergence of the **welfare state**—fear of social upheaval. In addition, economic insecurity after industrialization was taken into account when developing systems by giving better coverage to those **families** that could no longer rely on other types of income or their own food production.

The structure of the Bismarckian system has, to a large extent, stayed with the system since it was built; therefore, it still relies on **labor market** participation, coupled with some state financing and intervention. With the founding of the Weimar Republic in 1919, citizens were partially recognized as having some **rights**, but the main criterion was, and still is, that the individual was in the labor market. It was only in 1927 that a law on **unemployment** was passed, and **family allowances** were first introduced in 1954.

These late developments can be explained to a certain degree by Germany's defeat in both World War I and World War II, which naturally hindered the rapid and continued development of the social system. Furthermore, the role of the **church**—although weaker than before—still existed, and family responsibility was—and still is—a factor, as evidenced by the circumstance that children can be forced to pay for their parents.

After the changes in Eastern Europe in 1989, Germany was reunited in 1990. This brought about new difficulties for the German economy due to the fact that the welfare system had to be equal throughout the country. Today, the welfare systems are identical, and Germany has been able to cope with the reunification, despite the earlier differences.

The German welfare-state model follows a more traditional male-**breadwinner** approach than many other Western European welfare states; however, in recent years, there has been a focus on how to develop affordable and high-quality **child care** to make it possible for both men and women to be in the labor market.

Prior to the **financial crisis** in 2008, Germany implemented the Hartz Reform with the aim of ensuring an effective labor market by implementing a more successful employment policy. Development in Germany also includes more working hours and later retirement in some sectors, as well as lower wage income. In the wake of the crisis, Germany has used "Kurzarbeit" as an instrument to help bridge the gap for companies. Kurz-arbeit implies that workers work a few days and then receive **unemployment benefits** as a supplement. The implication has been that when the demand for labor has grown, it has been possible for companies to use their existing and qualified staff, and also that in this way, **unemployment** has been shared among the workers.

In most areas in Germany, the system is still building on the Bismarckian reforms, using contributory financing from employers and employees, although nowadays with broader support, especially for the vulnerable groups. **Social insurance** systems still remain the most central, including a specific system of Pflegeversicherung for long-term **care**. Germany is still a **corporatist** welfare regime type, albeit the focus on **social investment** perspective has increased, and it is increasingly affected by decisions made by the **European Union**.

GHETTO. A term for an area that mainly consists of one group in society and has certain common characteristics. A ghetto can, in principle, be both only for the poor or the rich; however, in public discourse, it usually has a negative connotation, implying an area with many social problems and risks of a high level of crime, a low level of **education**, and rundown **housing**. One widely known ghetto is the one in Harlem, New York, but there are also many in the Third World.

GINI COEFFICIENT. This measures the degree of **inequality** in a **distribution**, which can be income, wealth, or something else. It describes how far away or close a country is to a hypothetical situation of having an **income distribution** where each decile has an equal share (decile) of society's income. The Gini coefficient can be illustrated on a diagram with the proportion of the population measured along the horizontal axis and the proportion of income along the vertical axis. If the line in the diagram is straight from the left bottom corner to the upper right corner, then the income distribution is equal, and it has a Gini coefficient equal to zero. The Gini coefficient can vary between zero and one, and the closer it comes to one (which is a situation in which one person has the total income or wealth), the more unequal the situation is. Most Western countries experienced a gradual move toward a more equal distribution, measured in this manner, in the period after World War II. This stopped in the 1980s, when the degree of inequality remained almost the same, but some countries experienced a slight decline. Since the 1990s, there has been an increase in the Gini coefficient in many **welfare states**, implying more unequal economic distribution of resources. Inequality variations are still measured by the Gini coefficient in various welfare states. The coefficient is highest when measured before **taxes** and transfers in all welfare states. It is only one among various measurements of the degree of **equality**, although it is the most commonly used. *See also* LORENZ CURVE.

GLOBALIZATION. In economic terms, globalization refers to increased trade and travel, more open capital **markets**, capital's ability to move quickly from one point to another, and companies' willingness to relocate production to where labor is cheaper. It has been argued that globalization will undermine the nation-states' ability to form and develop their own **social policies**. There is also concern that global **market failures**, global monopolies, and global economic problems will persist.

The argument for globalization having an impact on **welfare-state** policies centers on the loss of autonomy of the individual nation state, as well as that global competition will weaken those forces in societies that have been the main advocates of welfare. It has been argued that competition, at a constantly lower level of **social security** by reducing contributions, will gradually undermine the welfare states.

The counterargument is that in a global world, there is an even greater **need** for social security as insecurity increases in many areas. The demand for welfare-state policies will grow and, at the same time, many countries have become richer as a result of increased global interaction, which has also increased the demand for welfare benefits.

Despite the fact that open-**market** economies have been under pressure from other countries' production, this has not led to a decrease in spending on **social welfare**. Furthermore, programs throughout the world have predominantly been increased, although some **retrenchment** can also be found. At the same time, globalization should also be expected to deliver different kinds of **services** and medicine at a cheaper price, thus reducing the economic burden on the welfare states.

GOVERNANCE. The coordination of interdependent social relations. Governance can be understood as existing in three different types: anarchy of exchange, hierarchy of command, and heterachy of self-organization. The first type is especially relevant with regard to the use of the **market**; the second in terms of state steering; and the last with regard to networks, including **civil society**. In this way, the distinction and interactions between the different modes of coordination and changes implies a balance between classical agents in the development of **welfare states: state, market, and civil society.** When governance changes, so does the relationship between the actors. Governance can therefore be seen as an overarching concept where the importance of the concept lies in the direct application of ways of steering in dissimilar areas, and how welfare policies are implemented. Furthermore, it has local, as well as national and supranational, aspects, where the interaction and combination of actors and institutions are important elements.

GOVERNMENT. This concept has no clear and unambiguous meaning. There are a variety of forms of government. In Western countries, it usually means that there is a body (the government) that, due to a constitution, has the **right** to make decisions about governing, and it should do so in agreement with an elected parliament. In some **democracies**—for example, the **United States** and **France**— an elected president has a great deal of influence on the decisions and the appointment of the government.

"Government" may also be given a broader interpretation, encompassing those making legislation, those responsible for implementing the laws, and the courts interpreting disputes concerning the laws. Used in this way, it describes a way of ruling a country where power is divided between different organs with different powers in the system.

The focus of **welfare-state** theory has shifted from concentrating on the functions and institutionalized structure of the government to analyzing the built-in consequences of governance on societal development and micro and macro decisions. Such analysis examines the impact of the **bureaucracy** and **pressure groups** on the growth of **public-sector** expenditures. Attempts are being made to analyze how the system itself contributes to growth in the public sector. *See also* GOVERNMENT FAILURE.

GOVERNMENT FAILURE. This is the opposite of **market failure** and refers to a situation in which **government** intervention in societies and expansion of the **public sector** becomes larger than is optimal. The **public choice** theorists especially argue the possibility of government failure. They refer to the Leviathan monster of the Bible, implying that the public sector may be crowding out the private sector. Other arguments for government failure revolve around the impact of **pressure groups** and the **bureaucracy**. It is impossible to measure the probable size of government failure, but it is obvious that as long as market failure exists, so may government failure.

GREECE. Greece was a relative latecomer in developing **social security** systems and a broad, all-encompassing **welfare state**. In the 6th century BC, there was some support for soldiers who had been disabled in battle, and, in the 5th century BC, it became possible for some individuals to receive a specific benefit if an assembly decided that they were eligible for it. This was an early variation of the **means-tested benefit**, and a stigma was attached to receiving it. With the decline of the old Athenian state system, these benefits apparently vanished. It was not until 1914 that a law on **industrial injury** was presented, followed by a law on **sickness** and **maternity** in 1922, old age and **disability** in 1934, **unemployment** assistance in 1945, and **family allowances** in 1958.

From 1967–1974, under a military junta, no real development of **social policy** occurred. Then, in the late 1980s and early 1990s, Greece experienced a rapid development of the welfare system in an attempt to match the developments of the rest of the **European Union (EU)**. Part of this was **financed** by regional support from the EU; however, since the **financial crisis** in 2008, there have been strong cuts made in the welfare system, and the youth unemployment rate has been particularly high. Greece has thus reduced its already limited welfare state even more.

Despite its historically close links to **Germany**, Greece belongs more to the **Southern European welfare state model**. Greece spends less on social security than do other EU countries, and it consequently has more rudimentary coverage than other EU welfare states. Greece has been one of the countries hit hardest by the financial crisis, a situation that has required loans from international lenders. Tough austerity measures have been enacted to get these loans and pay the interest, including cuts in **public-sector** spending, dismissal of public-sector employees, and an increase in the value-added tax and some duties. In addition, some public-sector companies have been sold off. There has also been a dramatic increase in the level of unemployment. Better **tax compliance** is seen as another way to reduce the deficit.

GROSS DOMESTIC PRODUCT (GDP). GDP measures the value of a society's production during one year, and, in principle, it is the amount of money that can be used for different purposes in one year in a society. It has to be split between public and private consumption and investment. Per capita GDP is often used as a measure of how rich a given country is. A critique of the measurement has been that it does not reflect the impact on the environment. For example, the increase in the use of resources is not reflected, and also, for instance, more traffic accidents would increase GDP, making the society a better place to live. This is also part of the reason why other measurements of the development of a good society, namely **happiness**, have emerged in recent years.

GROWTH OF THE PUBLIC SECTOR, THEORIES. There can be, and are, several explanations for the growth of the **public sector**—and in most countries they include the **welfare state**. They range from socioeconomic, ideological, and political institutional perspectives to consumer, financial, and producer perspectives. They include demand and supply arguments for development of public-sector expenditures. The need to correct **market failure** can be given as a reason for increasing public-sector spending. In the years to come, changes in **demography** may require an increase in spending for **health care** and **pensions**.

A useful typology could take its starting point in four dimensions with an impact on the growth of the public sector, all dealing with the direct or indirect impact. These four dimensions are voters, exogenous factors, costs, and change at the decisive level. The following is a demonstration of this typology and examples of the impact on the growth of the public sector:

voters	a) directly	Ex: demography
	b) indirectly	Ex: voting
exogenous factors	a) directly	Ex: business cycle
	b) indirectly	Ex: displacement
cost	a) directly	Ex: Baumol's disease
	b) indirectly	Ex: fiscal illusions
change at decisive level	a) directly	Ex: change in ideology
	b) indirectly	Ex: **bureaucracy** and **pressure groups**

In various countries and welfare-state types, there will be different reasons behind the growth of expenditures. It seems, however, that a mixture of reasons is needed to explain the development of the public sector. A specific reason for the growth of many more mature welfare states has been the change in the division of labor between **family** and society. Taking **care** of children and the elderly moved away from the family sphere as women gradually entered the **labor market**. In this respect, the growth of public-sector expenditure can be seen as a response to a change in demand for public-sector **services** and transfers.

It is impossible to provide a single explanation and **comparative analysis** of the growth of the public sector because frequent changes in the definition of what the public sector is in different countries has resulted in a lack of comparable data. Furthermore, **tax expenditures** are not included in all countries' statistics, and this creates major problems for comparisons between countries. The last 10 to 15 years have seen a standstill in the growth and, in some cases, even a reduction in the number of mature welfare states; therefore, the welfare states' relative share of societal income has been reduced in several countries. The implication is that the development and coverage of new areas are especially related to and possible when there is economic growth.

H

HANDICAP. *See* DISABILITY; DISABILITY BENEFIT.

HAPPINESS. The quest for happiness has been a built-in issue in societies for thousands of years. Greek philosophers already discussed and tried to define happiness. The focus was on having an independent life, a life in security, and with a maximum of pleasure. Nowadays, in modern terms, this relates to such issues as income, security, and being part of society. The concept embraces issues of how individuals perceive their lives in the past and the present, as well as their expectations for the future. It has been questioned whether an individual concept of happiness can be used in policy making given that it is individually measured. It seems that it can point to areas where, for example, the **welfare state** can support the individual by ensuring a **social safety net**, or make it possible to combine **work and family life** by establishing **child care**.

Happiness seems to grow with higher income, at least until a certain level, and some other general linkages also seem to prevail, for instance, married people and religious people, as the elderly and young are often happier than **divorced**, nonreligious, and middle-aged individuals. It is also so that healthy people often are happier than others, but we do not know whether this is due to their being healthy or because when they are happy they are also healthier. Happy people also tend to live longer than unhappy people, although again the causality is somewhat unclear.

Happiness has been seen as a central purpose in recent years, given that classical ways of measuring society's development, namely **gross domestic product**, do not reflect nonmonetary issues of **well-being** and everyday life. *See also* HEALTH.

HEALTH. Health and **health care** are central areas in the **welfare state**. In most countries, they are paid and delivered on a **universal** basis. In some countries, health care is financed by different kinds of insurance schemes, often in combination with user charges. The level of user charges varies from country to country, but these charges generally tend to have a negative impact on the **distribution**.

Health is of central importance for most people; therefore, public support for state intervention tends to be high in many welfare states. The problems within health care involve many ethical questions, and also questions with regard to **justice** and **equality**. They raise issues of how to set priorities among individuals with different types of illness and also stress the need for measures to **prevent** people from becoming sick. In the 20th and 21st centuries, health has, in general, been improving, as evidenced by the increase in the average **life expectancy**. This is a result of both curing sicknesses and reducing infant mortality.

Health care ranges from the direct delivery by general practitioners to specialized treatment at highly specialized hospitals. Thus, there are many different types of treatment involved and numerous different types of individuals with different educational backgrounds. This also makes the area of health care a difficult and complicated field to analyze.

Having good health is seen as an element in improving **well-being** and **happiness**. Voters' support of spending on health care is often high, lending support to the **Rawlsian** argument that no one knows whether they will one day be on the other side of the veil and **need** treatment. *See also* HEALTH INSURANCE.

HEALTH CARE AND HEALTH ECONOMICS. These are broad topics of importance in **welfare states** regarding their delivery of **services** to individual citizens. Health care refers to the individual's **health** independent of who is delivering the services. Health economics is a special discipline within economics that attempts to explain and analyze the development of health care expenditure; the individual's choice among different solutions; and the consequences of different combinations of public, private, and insurance-based solutions with regard to the problems of health care.

Most welfare states offer free access to hospitals, but some private provision also exists. The individual will often have to pay (partly or fully) for medicine and visits to the general practitioner. Some areas are provided for by both the public and the private sectors, and the distinctions are not always clear.

Health care often has the greatest amount of public support when measuring support for specific aspects of the welfare state in different societies, presumably because many people expect to use the system. It is organized quite differently in different countries, and the mix of public and private is diverse. At the same time, the demand for health care seems unlimited.

Analyzing the area involves ethical, economic, **justice**, and philosophical questions. For example, given scarce resources, who should be treated first, should we treat all diseases, and, if so, who should be treated by the **public**

sector and who should be treated by the private sector? Will the public sector, for example, supply abortions and pay for change and manipulation of genes? Should new technologies always be used, and how can one make sure that the costs are efficiently covered? Furthermore, how long should treatment continue for a person with no chance of a continuation of life? Is it acceptable to experiment with human beings to improve life chances for other individuals by testing different methods and different medicines?

As societies in more and more countries are graying, the economic pressure on health care has become more evident and led to a need for greater prioritization of the resources available, although many people are living longer and are healthier than previous generations. **Comparative analyses** of health care activities are often used to try to make the health care system as efficient as possible. This includes not only the administration and planning of the system, but also how users react to different ways of organizing and **financing** it. *See also* HEALTH; HEALTH INSURANCE; PRIMARY CARE.

HEALTH INSURANCE. A mechanism for individuals to cover risks of sickness and injury if they are not covered by state welfare. By paying a premium, the individual is covered for the cost of treatment. If the insurer knows about them, "bad lives" will have to pay a higher premium than "good lives." In this way, the use of an insurance system may create **inequality**. Naturally, by pooling the risk, which can be done by collective insurances or by the state, this inequality will not arise, as the individual is then covered, not depending on his or her own **health** and risk.

HEALTH MAINTENANCE ORGANIZATION (HMO). A system of controlling **health care** costs found primarily in the **United States**. Through its member medical providers, the HMO provides medical **services** to member patients, who pay a fee. HMOs assume different forms, and the services provided vary. A crucial element is that it is difficult to estimate how to balance the fee and the use of the system, combined with the fact that some are not covered at all. *See also* HEALTH INSURANCE.

HEGEMONY. In this system of **government**, the ruling **class** in a society dominates specific **norms** and values. Hegemony can be maintained either by political or ideological means. State hegemony means that the state's economic and military power and ideology are maintained during a period of time. *See also* DEMOCRACY.

HIDDEN ECONOMY. This refers to unrecorded economic activity, for example, when people evade paying **taxes** or avoid deductions in their **social**

security benefits by not reporting their income. There is no clear indication that the hidden economy should be larger in **welfare states** with a high overall tax burden, although economists sometimes claim this is so. It is argued that the **incentive** not to record economic activity is higher when taxes are high. Others claim that the combination of the risk of being caught and the fines attached have an impact on the size of the hidden economy. Yet, others emphasize that societal **norms** and values and whether it is generally considered acceptable to cheat the rest of society is more important in relation to the size. The distinction between the hidden and official economies is not always clear-cut. Helping friends and relatives, for instance, can be considered tax evasion if it takes the form of an exchange of work. The hidden economy is often referred to as the "black economy."

HOMELESSNESS. The condition of people who have no living accommodations or have only unsatisfactory and temporary accommodations. Homelessness is becoming an increasingly prevalent urban problem in many **welfare states**, with many people living on the streets, thereby often being **marginalized**.

HORIZONTAL EQUITY. A **distribution** in which equals are treated equally. In policy making, this means that individuals in the same situation should be treated in the same way, or the outcome of the distribution will not be equal. Horizontal equity and **vertical equity** are both concepts used in describing equity. For example, paying child **allowances** to **families** is using a horizontal equity approach; however, this also raises questions regarding vertical equity, as not all families with children have the same level of income; therefore, people with high income might get support. *See also* EQUALITY; GINI COEFFICIENT.

HOUSING. This term refers to provision of living accommodations. Housing and housing policy are a special area of the **welfare state** with the purpose of either delivering or supporting accommodations for people. The policy can be aimed at reducing the cost of living by different means. This can be through direct economic support to those who are building accommodations or through **housing benefits**. It can also be done indirectly through **tax expenditure** by allowing the deduction of interest payments on mortgages. In addition, it can include the use of physical planning to make areas available to build affordable new houses. Housing policy can also include the **right** of the **public sector** to rent out certain living quarters to, for example, single mothers and homeless people, at reduced or nominal rates. Housing policy also refers to whether such central amenities as sanitation, water, and heating are available. *See also* HOMELESSNESS.

HOUSING BENEFIT. Support provided to **families** to pay for all or part of the cost of their living accommodations. In most countries, this is **means-tested** (based on income and the cost of the accommodation) and directed toward low-income earners. In many countries, the ability to deduct interest payments on a house can be looked at as an indirect housing benefit. This, however, is not means-tested.

HUMAN CAPITAL. This term refers to the individual's personal **capabilities**, that is, skills, talent, and knowledge. These abilities can be acquired in different ways, including through **education**, training, or on-the-job experience, but for some they are also something that the individual is "born" with. Increasing the level of human capital is seen as central for **employment** and economic development.

Human capital will often be reflected in individual income, but some of it may not be transferred from one job to another. This is usually the case for the more specific forms of human capital. Furthermore, human capital cannot be transferred directly from one person to another, although individuals using their human capital when teaching others may be able to transfer their skills.

The theory of human capital, often connected with the works of Gary Becker, implies that an individual can invest in himself or herself via education, and that this type of investment will yield a return through higher income in the **labor market**. Requests for support for different types of education, for example, as part of **labor market policy**, implicitly use arguments from human capital theory, assuming that people obtaining more or better education will have a higher chance of getting a job and then be better able to take **care** of themselves. Human capital is different from **social capital**, especially because of its clear focus on the individual's personal competencies.

HUMAN DEVELOPMENT INDEX (HDI). A summary measurement of human development. It is calculated by measuring the average position on three basic dimensions of human development: a long and healthy life (**health**), access to knowledge (**education**), and a decent standard of living (income). It is calculated based upon international data to ensure consistency in the comparison. For more information, see http://hdr.undp.org/en/statistics/hdi/. The countries at the top of the HDI are mainly the richer countries in the Western world, with poor countries in Africa appearing at the bottom. *See also* HAPPINESS; WELL-BEING.

HUNGARY. Hungary's **social security** system followed two different paths and was markedly different before and after World War II. The country's history has undoubtedly had an impact on the development of these systems. From 1867–1918, it was part of the Austro-Hungarian double monarchy. From 1919–1949, it was a kingdom, and then, until 1989, it was an Eastern European **communist** country.

Until World War II, Hungary was strongly influenced by the **Bismarckian** system, and, as a result, its early **social welfare** measures were based on **social insurance**. This was the case for **sickness** and **maternity** in 1891, and **industrial injury** in 1907. Old age and **invalidity** support was also originally built on the basis of social insurance, but, from 1957 onward, **unemployment benefits** were the assistance system in these areas. **Family allowances** were introduced in 1938 as a **universal** system, and they remain a universal system today.

Following World War II, the social security system was based on the **right** to have a job, and thereby **social rights** in the communist system, which was closely connected with having a job. **Pension** rights were linked to having been in the **labor market** for a lengthy period of time. To a large extent, the system today is based on payments from the insured and employers. The state only takes responsibility for family allowances and guaranteeing against deficits in the insurance system.

Since the collapse of communism, Hungary has returned to the traditional **conservative model**, corresponding to a **Bismarckian** system, with a high reliance on the social insurance system and the necessity for the individual to gain social rights by being in the labor market. Recent years have seen reforms in the pension area and also the abolition of the **early retirement** measure (2012). Changes in **disability benefits** and other modifications indicate a leaner **welfare state** within the conservative welfare approach. Hungary has also been adopting changes as part of being a member of the **European Union**.

I

INCENTIVE. An encouragement for a person to perform a certain action. Analysis of incentives in the **welfare state** has concentrated on two areas: incentives to save and incentives to work. Incentives to save can take the form of **tax** relief or lower taxation of interest income. This has especially been used to get individuals to save for their own retirement. It has also been argued that saving for periods of **unemployment** is important. The debate about work has focused on the possible consequences of incentives due to **unemployment benefits.** Some see a low unemployment benefit as a better incentive for people to take up a job when one is offered to them than a high level of unemployment benefit would be. There is, however, no clear and firm **evidence** that this is the case, also given that having a job is important for most people. Incentives can also exist in relation to movement from one geographical area to another, for example, to pursue **education.** Incentives are mainly economic motivations, but they can include nonmonetary attractions, including good working and living conditions.

INCOME DISTRIBUTION. This describes the way money income is distributed in a society. There are two forms of monetary distribution, functional and personal. **Functional distribution** is how gross factor income is distributed among the different factors involved in production: wages (labor), profit (capital), and land. Personal distribution is how income is distributed among different individuals in society. It is often measured using the **Gini coefficient,** which describes how big a share different deciles (a tenth of the population) receive and how far this **distribution** is from a hypothetical distribution in which each decile has exactly a tenth of the personal income in a given year. Another way of measuring personal distribution is by comparing the income of the 20 percent of the general population with the highest income with the 20 percent with the lowest income. Other methods emphasizing different aspects of distribution are also used.

Many different problems are encountered in the measurement of income distribution in different countries—especially when discussing how the impact of this measurement on the degree of **inequality** can be interpreted. Some issues relate to the fact that not everything can be measured, that is, the statistical background for the data. The data will usually not include gifts and bequests. Furthermore, the **hidden economy** will not be included. Because such factors vary among different groups in a society, their impact on the distribution is obvious. If the income distribution is calculated by comparing income after **tax** deductions, then a further problem arises due to the differences between groups in the types of, and ability to obtain, tax deductions.

For comparisons between countries—and, in some cases, also within countries—differences in purchasing power parities must also be taken into consideration. Moreover, income has an impact on consumption. This is also the case for transfers and **services** from the **public sector**, which influence the individual household's ability to buy various goods and services, and thus its relative position in the income distribution.

Aside from measurement problems, difficulties in analysis arise as a result of behavioral differences among **families**. In some families, the savings may be high and thereby give rise to interest income, whereas others may spend the money during the year and not have any interest income. Differences in consumption may, therefore, not be a consequence of the income stemming from the **labor market**, but rather a result of different consumption patterns.

Individuals may also be at different stages of their life cycles. Income statistics typically include all individuals in society: those who are undergoing **education**, those who have just started in the labor market, those who have been in the labor market for a long time, and pensioners. Changing income during these periods may give rise to a misleading interpretation of the impact of the differences in the income distribution if these things are not taken into consideration.

Finally, differences in family size may have an impact on consumption per person, depending upon how many have to live on a specific income. Traditional statistics do not—and it would be difficult for them to—include differences among individual needs and how this may affect their economic position in society. For example, an individual who has a large income but needs to spend a high proportion of their earnings on medicine or **health care** due to permanent **disability** may not have the same consumption possibilities as a healthy person with the same income. The tax system can also have an impact on disposable income.

When looking at income distributions throughout time and making comparisons between countries, these aspects must be included in the analysis to obtain a coherent answer to questions about the degree of inequality in and description of income distribution in those countries. In addition to comparing income distribution, one can also compare the distribution of wealth and, increasingly, the degree of access to the **democratic** decision-making process as indicators of the degree of **equality** in different countries. *See also* COMPARATIVE ANALYSIS; HORIZONTAL EQUITY; VERTICAL EQUITY.

INCOME MAINTENANCE PROGRAM. This type of program is designed to alleviate **poverty** by providing **benefits in cash; social security; social services**; and/or **benefits in-kind**, for example, food stamps and school lunches. These programs attempt to repair the damage caused by **market** forces.

INDEXATION. This is the way in which the level of benefits changes. In some systems, indexation is linked to prices, and in others to wages. The way indexation is done thus influences the level of benefits and whether those receiving benefits have the same income development as others. Indexation linked to price ensures a constant buying power; however, in times of rising real income, it also implies that those on benefits do not have access to the same increase in living standards as others in a society.

INDIA. India is the second most populous country in the world, with more than 1.2 billion inhabitants. It became independent in 1947, and has since become one of the world's largest **democracies**. In 1948, a state insurance act required the provision of medical care, **sickness benefits** and **maternity benefits**, as well as benefits in case of **disability** or death in companies with more than 10 employees. A law covering **pensions** was passed the same year. Laws were adopted in 1923 and 1924 covering **industrial injury**, and an additional maternity benefits law dates from 1961. The statutory pension age is 55 for both men and women. The main part of the official welfare programs are the **social insurance** programs paid for by employees and employers. This also includes pensions that come from a mainly **funded system**.

A central welfare problem is the high number of people working in the **hidden economy**, as they are not covered by the social insurance laws and often have an income below the **poverty** line; however, recent years have seen a development in micro-insurance, making it possible for at least a partly limited type of insurance.

INDIVIDUALISM. The opposite of **collectivism**. Individualism is based on the individual's choice and connection to the state and society. It has been a major element in the development of various **liberal** versions of the **welfare state**. It is also part of the debate on **freedom**.

INDUSTRIAL ACHIEVEMENT MODEL. This model in many ways resembles the **Bismarckian** notion of the **welfare state**. It relies on the individual's participation in the **labor market,** to which **rights** are connected. Payments into the system may be compulsory, but they may also be voluntary or part of **collective agreements.** Systems may and will often be insurance-based. Benefits are related to income and previous contributions. In this type of model, **social welfare** institutions are only partly developed, and those outside the labor market are only covered to a small degree.

INDUSTRIAL INJURY. An injury that occurs at the workplace. Industrial injury was the first injury to be covered in most countries, because it was a requirement of industrialization, and many **families** were not covered against this type of risk when moving into the cities and taking up jobs at the new workplaces. In an effort to reduce these injuries, safety at work has been developed in many countries, improving living conditions because of fewer casualties.

INDUSTRIAL RELATIONS. The relations between employers and employees are termed the industrial relations system. The degree and use of the relation depends on how organized employers and employees are. Recent years have seen a weakening of the industrial relations system, particularly in Europe, especially due to weaker **trade unions,** implying a higher degree of wage bargaining taking place at a **decentralized** level, often in direct agreement between an individual worker and the company.

INEQUALITY. This concept concerns the way that resources are distributed in a society. Analysis of inequality should, in principle, include all resources available in a given society, but it often focuses on the economic **distribution** of resources in a society. There are various types of inequality: inequality in opportunity, inequality in economic income or wealth, unequal treatment, and so forth. Inequality is often measured by calculating the differences in income or wealth among various groups and individuals in a given society. Different measurements of inequality exist. The most commonly used indicator is the **Gini coefficient.** Some of the other indexes utilized are the Herfindahl, the Atkinson Index, Theil's entropy, and Dalton.

   Although adequate statistical information—even with its shortcomings—is available about differences in income and wealth, it is much more difficult to obtain information about other types of inequality. Studies will sometimes describe differences in access to **education,** the **labor market,** and so forth. These will often be based on case studies and therefore cannot be repeated as often as indicators of inequality based on income and wealth, for which statistics are available each year. *See also* EQUALITY; HORI-

ZONTAL EQUITY; MEASUREMENT OF INEQUALITY; POLARIZA-
TION; VERTICAL EQUITY.

INFLATION. The increase in prices from one period to another. For example, if a basket of goods costs 100 units in the first period and 105 units
in the next, the inflation rate is 5 percent. In many **social security** systems,
a correction for inflation is built in so that people receiving benefits will
have the same buying power from one period to another. During periods of
rapid inflation, systems that are not index-linked will experience fast deterioration for those living on benefits, and these individuals could eventually
end up living in **poverty**.

INSERTION. The French term for **integration**, mainly relating to the **labor
market**. Insertion policies are those that can reintegrate **marginalized** or
socially excluded groups. Having better social contacts can do this, but it is
often achieved through programs that try to get people back into the labor
market. *See also* FRANCE; SOCIAL EXCLUSION.

INSTITUTIONAL MODEL. This model originated from the **Beveridgian** way of thinking about **welfare states**. In this model, a more **universal**
approach is developed, and the individual's living standard is seen as part
of society's responsibility. **Citizenship** is recognized as the criteria when
receiving benefits, and a decent standard of living is part of the goal. Furthermore, the model is mainly financed through general **taxation**, and the **right**
to benefits is therefore not only for those participating in the **labor market**.
Redistribution is generally high in this type of model. It also has many characteristics in common with the **Scandinavian welfare state model**.

INSTITUTIONS. Institutions are places, organizations, and entities, for
example, hospitals, **child care** institutions, prisons, **families**, and **churches**,
and also concepts, relationships, and practices, for instance, the law, the state,
the family, and religion; therefore, the understanding in the social sciences of
what institutions are is not unambiguous. Capitalism, practices, rules, **norms**,
and **markets** can all be seen as specific types of institutions.

The following are some of the many definitions used in the social sciences
and the main area they are related to: 1) Institutions are a set of rules, compliance procedures, and moral and ethical behavioral norms designed to con-
strain the behavior of individuals in the interest of maximizing the wealth or
utility of principals (historical institutionalism). 2) An institution is a social
arrangement regulating the relationships of individuals and collective groups

to one another. This includes laws, customs, traditions, and "administrative guidances," while excluding biological fundamentals from sex to epidemiology (institutional theory). 3) An institution is collective action, control, liberation, and expansion of individual action (institutional economics).

These definitions have in common a description of how institutions can be seen as a set of organized structures that can have different goals and institutional structures. They further stress that institutions are not only formal organizations, but that they can also be structures of a whole or part of society. The way institutions work can, thus, have a profound influence on the **welfare states**.

INTEGRATION. The word *integration* comes from the Latin word "integer," meaning whole or complete, and in **welfare-state** analysis, this refers to how individuals or groups can be part of society's development. Integration can be done at both the micro and macro levels. On the macro level, it can involve the joining of different countries or groups in a society by making them have the same possibilities. It has mainly been used as a way to create common **markets** in which the free trade of goods and **services** can take place. It can also involve a higher and more common way of solving different problems within an area, for example, in the **European Union** or through the North American Free Trade Agreement. On the micro level, integration involves the individual's ability to be a part of the way society functions. An individual without a job may not be **integrated**. But lack of integration may also exist in relation to social contacts, culture, policy, and other areas. This type of integration is labeled **social integration**.

It is difficult to define and measure whether integration has taken place. Analysis can therefore focus on whether an individual is **socially excluded** instead of trying to measure the degree of integration. Furthermore, it can focus on either social or system integration, and also on how to move the society or individuals in such a way that they will be bound together (integrated) better than before.

In welfare-state analysis, integration has often focused on how different groups, for instance, women, migrants, people with disabilities, the elderly, and young people, are positioned in society. In recent years, greater emphasis has been placed on integration in the **labor market** due to the higher impact on people's welfare of being in the labor market in relation to both income and social contacts. In addition, with the **migration** of refugees and illegal immigrants from outside the **European Union** and the **United States** into these areas, new elements of integration have been raised. Integrating those coming from another cultural background has proven difficult in several welfare states, but it appears to be necessary to ensure integration, cope with the change in **demography**, and reduce the conflicts and tensions in various societies between those who are integrated and those who are socially excluded. *See also* INSERTION.

INTEREST GROUPS. Groups of individuals who wish to promote or argue for a certain decision and join together to apply pressure on decision makers. They are manifold and exist in many countries. In **welfare-state** analysis, interest groups have been seen as part of the explanation for the expansion of the **public sector**, which has responded to various interest groups' desire for influence in specific areas.

It is difficult to know how big the interest groups' impact really is, as they form a part of the societal decision-making process, and different groups have different interests. Some apply pressure for increases in specific areas, while others may argue for a lowering of **taxes** and duties. An asymmetrical decision-making process has been used as an argument to suggest that interest groups have an impact on the growth of public spending in relation to welfare areas, because those gaining a positive value from expansion in a specific area are few, whereas those paying for it are many.

Interest and **pressure groups** have undoubtedly had an impact, but it is impossible to make a quantitative assessment of their influence. Furthermore, there are interest groups who have the opposite interest, for example, lobbying for lower taxation, thereby lowering public-sector spending. *See also* TRADE UNION.

INTERGENERATIONAL ISSUES. Different generations may have varying views, expectations, and ideas about how the future looks. In **welfare-state** analysis, this often refers to the fact that there is an at least tacit agreement among the generations that one generation pays **taxes** to finance **social services** and benefits for the previous generation with the expectation that the next generation will pay for their specific **needs** for welfare **services**. This also relates to the idea that the need for support from a welfare state varies throughout the life cycle.

INTERNATIONAL COUNCIL ON SOCIAL WELFARE (ICSW). This body was founded in Paris, in 1928. It is a nongovernmental independent organization that represents national and local organizations in more than 70 countries throughout the world. They work in such core welfare areas as how to combat **poverty** and help people living in distress. In their own countries, the ICSW's organizations provide help for a wide range of people who are poor, ill, disabled, unemployed, frail, or oppressed. They help young people, older people, **families**, indigenous peoples, migrants, refugees, and others who are experiencing special hardship or vulnerability. The organization collects information and works as a network for the member organizations.

INTERNATIONAL LABOUR ORGANIZATION (ILO). The ILO was established in 1919, as part of the Treaty of Versailles, as an international organization with the purpose of working for social **justice**, which it believed could help in ensuring peace. It is a **tripartite** body in which employers and employees as groups each have 25 percent of the vote, and the **governments** have 50 percent. Since 1946, the ILO has been part of the **United Nations**. Today, 182 countries are members of the ILO.

Among the important functions of the ILO is the adoption of conventions, which are used as guidelines for structuring and organizing social and **labor market policy** in many countries. An important example is Convention No. 138 on the working environment. Conventions have also been issued on **social security** and **discrimination**. Countries that have ratified the conventions are bound to follow them. The fundamental conventions revolve around issues of labor, protection of **rights**, equal remuneration, discrimination, and child labor. They are therefore important signposts to understanding issues in relation to welfare, especially what is part cf the **labor market**, although the concrete enactment and interpretation is done at the national level. Thus, the conventions are sometimes rather broad in their descriptions. *See also* TRADE UNION.

INTERPERSONAL COMPARISONS. Comparisons of different **utility** levels among numerous individuals that raise the question of whether it is possible to find a societal welfare function on the basis of which normative advice can be found to make the best choice among possible options. As individuals, we are able to reflect on and know the utility we receive from a specific good or bundle of goods. It would be much more difficult to know on an aggregate level—that is, for all individuals—what utility each individual derives from different goods. One person's pleasure in a good bottle of French wine cannot be compared with another person's dislike of French wine because of, for example, political reasons or taste.

To compare utilities, one can compare levels of utility and changes therein. When comparing levels, the present situation for different individuals are evaluated. When comparing change, what happens to different individuals when moving from one set of solutions to another is examined. Ordinalist comparisons only compare the different levels of utility, whereas a cardinal approach compares both levels and changes therein.

The problems involved in comparing utility may be fewer when referring to more traditional goods, for example, the basket of goods necessary to survive, but it is difficult—or perhaps impossible—to compare people's tastes or pleasure in many cultural events. Some like to watch football, whereas others hate it. It is impossible to find an overall societal welfare function because individuals' preferences will have a great impact and are difficult to combine. For instance, when comparing apples and pears, some would call both fruit, but that is not enough if one wants to find an overall societal welfare function. Recent years have seen a development of studies on **happiness**, as this reflects the individual's subjective evaluation of life and can therefore be used in comparison among individuals. *See also* COMPARATIVE ANALYSIS.

INTERSECTIONALITY. A term referring to the fact that different degrees and types of issues may overlap, for example, a person might be disadvantaged due to **disability**, but this disadvantage could also be related to **gender**, age, or **ethnic** aspects. Different positions can thus intersect and strengthen or weaken, for instance, the degree of **social exclusion** or **social inclusion** in a society. Hence, the concept points out that analyzing just one specific element and/or approach might have the risk of overlooking that being disadvantaged or advantaged in one aspect can also imply a better or worse position when combined with other elements.

INVALIDITY. A person's inability to take **care** of himself or herself. In most **welfare states**, it is possible to receive an invalidity (**disability**) **pension**. The size of the pension may depend on the degree of invalidity and the ability to work in the **labor market**.

IRELAND. Ireland has been highly influenced by Catholicism, but its historical links with the **United Kingdom** have also had an impact on the development of the welfare system. In 1921, Ireland received the status of a dominion within the British Commonwealth, and, in 1922, it declared itself an independent state but remained within the Commonwealth. In 1949, it became a fully independent state outside the Commonwealth.

In Ireland's welfare system, benefit laws were established early on, including one covering **industrial injury** in 1897, old age in 1908, and **disability** in 1911. **Sickness benefit** and **maternity benefit** systems, as well as **unemployment benefits**, were also introduced in 1911. **Family allowances** came along in 1944. To a large extent, the system is based on the criterion that the individual must be in the **labor market**, but, at the same time, there is state involvement and coverage of vulnerable groups.

The Catholic influence in Ireland has not only brought about a rudimentary development of the **welfare state**, as in other Catholic countries, it has also been a factor arguing for the social responsibility of the state, albeit this has been reduced in recent years. The Irish system has state involvement, a high degree of responsibility within the **family**, and many voluntary organizations involved in supplying social help for the various groups in **need**.

The system is a mixture of the **Beveridgian** model and the **Southern European welfare state model**. **Financing** is mainly a combination of state financing and contributions from employers, employees, and the self-employed. Ireland experienced rapid growth in its economy during the 1990s, which has continued in the first years of the 21st century. This has reduced **unemployment** but also increased **inequality**. Within the **European Union (EU)**, Ireland spends the least proportionately on **social security**. The country was hit hard by the **financial crisis** in 1998 and needed a loan from the EU to cope with the resulting challenges. A high level of **public-sector** deficit and debt has forced the island nation to reduce welfare-state spending, including reforms of the **pension** system. *See also* CHURCH.

ITALY. Italy followed many other Catholic countries in its development, but its **social policy** was also influenced by its close connection to **Germany** and its fascist government. At the same time, Italy has had a strong working **class** and, for a long time, one of the strongest **communist** parties in Western Europe. These factors, in combination with the influence of the Catholic Church, have profoundly affected the development of the Italian welfare system.

Italy became a unified kingdom in 1860. It participated on the losing side in both World War I and World War II. The fascist period from 1922–1943 was doubtless a reason for the presence of **corporatist** elements in the system. Political instability in Italy can be seen as an explanation of the limited and sporadic development of social policy during the postwar period.

In 1861, an **invalidity pension** for mineworkers was introduced. Laws on **industrial injury** were introduced in 1898, followed by a ruling on **maternity benefits** in 1912, and decisions on **unemployment benefits** and old-age pensions in 1919. Legislation on **family allowances** was enacted in 1937, and on **sickness benefits** in 1943. The Italian system is mainly built on participation in the **labor market**, but, at the same time, it has such **universal** components as **health care** and family allowances. Still, in all areas, the main financial principle is contributions from either the inhabitants, employers, or employees.

Different parts of Italy apply different welfare models. The northern part of Italy has been increasingly developing toward a more **continental** and **conservative model**, whereas the southern part still has many features and structures that resemble the **Southern European welfare state model** of limited state intervention. **Care** for those in real **need** is first and foremost the responsibility of the **family**; the state rarely steps in to help the individual.

Italy has undergone rapid economic development in the past 20 to 25 years; however, since the **financial crisis** started in 2008, problems with state deficit and debt, as well as high levels of **unemployment**, especially for young people, have imposed dramatic changes. During the long period of economic development, the welfare system has been expanding, and it is thus in a period of transition; however, despite the increasing level of coverage and universal health care system, its main characteristics can still be described as a Southern European welfare state type. Reforms in recent years point even more in that direction, although contribution and participating in the labor market, as in the more continental model, seem to be more important for the individual's coverage. A new series of austerity measures, which include an increase in the retirement age, **privatization** of state-owned enterprises and properties, and steps to improve labour market efficiency, have been enacted in the wake of the financial crisis.

J

JAPAN. Historically, Japan was isolated for long periods of time until 1867, and since then it has been involved in several wars, which means that it has been difficult to develop a welfare system. On the other hand, the growth in the economy since the beginning of the 1950s has made Japan a rich country.

Japan belongs to what has been labeled the **Confucian welfare-state** type. Its welfare state has been developed quite recently. **Industrial injury** was the first **social security** system to be introduced, in 1911. It was followed by **sickness benefits** and **maternity benefits** in 1922; old age and **disability benefits** in 1941; **unemployment benefits** in 1947; and, most recently, child **allowances** in 1971.

In Japan's constitution of 1947, it is stated that the individual has a **right** to a decent minimum standard of life and access to **health care**. Japanese **social policy** is based on a highly centralized model, with part of it being managed by the employers in the **labor market**. The **family** also plays an important role in the Japanese system in taking **care** of those unable to help themselves. This is partly the reason why it took so long for **pensions**, for example, to be introduced. It was also only in 1973 that the Japanese **government** declared Japan a welfare state.

With families, companies, and societies structured hierarchically, the system relies on a top-down approach to social policy. The Japanese work ethic and strong commitment by companies to lifetime **employment** have also reduced the need for a public welfare system. If, as recent developments indicate may happen, more people are left without lifetime employment, and families assume less responsibility, new **needs** will arise. At the same time, Japan has a population structure with an increasing number of elderly due to a comparatively high **life expectancy** and low number of births, implying a pressure on the pension system, which has also been changed. Japan has a large **public-sector** deficit, although it is **financed** internally. A large part of the system is **market**-based; therefore, it is difficult to say that the system resembles anything seen in other parts of the world. Rather, it is a specific kind of Southeast Asian model with a strong emphasis on family values, but also one that is reliant on the market in a more **liberal** sense.

In 2011, a large earthquake hit northeast Japan, with a tsunami that caused devastating damage to property and changes to the landscape. The **government** enacted several social policy initiatives to help those affected by the disaster, and it has had to do more since many people could not return to their homes.

JUSTICE. One of the core concepts of many social-science disciplines. It is also often used in political debates to argue for a specific solution, which will be more "just" than other solutions. The problem is that it is difficult to define what justice is—and it is even harder to measure it. The term is, therefore, often used interchangeably with **equality** and the negation thereof, **inequality**.

Two major types of justice are distributive justice (how to distribute goods and **services** among citizens) and commutative justice (referring to the treatment of individuals who do not follow certain rules). **Welfare-state** analysis focuses on distributive justice. This concept can be found in the old Athenian society and Aristotle.

Distributive justice can also be defined as absolute or relative. Absolute distributive justice means that everyone gets the same goods given the same situation. Relative distributive justice refers to different criteria for deciding how to distribute goods in a society, including the following:

1. To each according to what he or she deserves.
2. To each according to what he or she has done.
3. To each according to what he or she needs.
4. To each according to his or her abilities.
5. To each according to his or her position in society.

It is clear that these criteria will give rise to quite different recommendations for the **distribution** of goods in a society—and even if a society agrees on one of the criteria, it may still be difficult to interpret and decide what, for example, the individual deserves. Nevertheless, the concept of justice is often used in many fields of social science. For example, the argument for progressive **taxation** rests on it, that is, those who are most able to pay should pay higher taxes than those without the same ability.

Another way to achieve distributive justice is to make a distribution according to the following:

1. property **rights**
2. whether one is **deserving** or **undeserving**
3. **needs**

It is obvious that a distribution according to property rights could be very unequal, because it will have its conservative roots in the historical distribution of goods in a society. The other two principles would also be tough to apply, as it is quite challenging to decide what the individual deserves and what needs the individual has. Moreover, it could be argued that not all needs should be satisfied. An individual who has a need to fly to the moon, for example, cannot expect the rest of society to pay for this. Using property rights as the starting point in relation to justice could also be said to rely on a libertarian notion in which the individual's **freedom** is the central element in a just society.

John Rawls, in his famous book *A Theory of Justice* (1972), suggests that the concept of justice should be viewed in terms of some basic principles and before the individual knows his or her position, that is, behind the veil of ignorance. His argument is that if the individual does not know his or her future place in society, then he or she will be more prepared to take into consideration the position of weaker individuals.

Rawls applies two basic principles in his analysis. The first principle is that each person is to have an equal right to the most extensive total system of equal basic liberties compatible with a similar system of liberty for all. The second is that social and economic inequalities are to be arranged so that they are both a) to the greatest benefit of the least advantaged, consistent with the just savings principle, and b) attached to offices and positions open to all under conditions of fair equality of opportunity (*A Theory of Justice*, 1972). These principles include both equality and liberty, but also that certain minimum conditions should be taken into consideration when distributing resources in society.

More libertarian theorists argue that justice is the outcome of the way **market** forces work. Furthermore, they hold that differences in economic or other conditions due to the market's behavior is not a reason for intervention. A more **Marxist** approach would be to argue not only for just possibilities, but also to distribute to each individual according to need. The concept of justice is also used when trying to create a **social welfare function** in which equal distribution is one goal—or at least maximizing **utility** in society.

Obviously, no simple and one-dimensional definition of justice exists; therefore, it is impossible to apply the principle as more than a concept in arguments for or against different types of state intervention and the development of the **welfare state**.

K

KEYNES, JOHN MAYNARD (1883–1946). Keynes was born and lived in the **United Kingdom** and educated at Cambridge. He became widely known with the publication of *The Economic Consequences of the Peace* in 1919. During the 1920s and 1930s, he dealt primarily with monetary policy and how to use it so that full **employment** would also be possible. His thoughts on this were published in *Treatise on Money*, published in 1930.

From that point onward, on he worked his major contribution to economics: *The General Theory of Employment, Interest, and Money* (1933). This book has become one of the most influential of the 20th century and has had a profound effect on the role of the **welfare state** by stressing the possibility of a macroeconomic approach and the use of **fiscal policy** as a way to counterbalance the cyclical movement in economies with the use of public investment; however, Keynes did not dismiss the use of monetary policy. Furthermore, he questioned the functioning of the **labor market**, money, and the way investment decisions were made.

Keynes's theoretical work opened up new ways of thinking, which had an impact on economic and **social policy** after World War II. In 1940, Keynes published *How to Pay for the War*, suggesting new methods as opposed to just using the **classical economic** approach.

KOREA, REPUBLIC OF. Also known as South Korea, this is a relatively rich East Asian country, with close to 50 million inhabitants. The Republic of Korea was a latecomer in the development of welfare policies. It was in 1953 that a law on **industrial injury** was first passed as a **social insurance** system. **Sickness benefits** and **maternity benefits** were enacted in 1963, although first as an obligatory system from 1976. The National Welfare Pension Act was enacted in 1973, and it was not until 1993 that the **unemployment** insurance act came into being. The system looks like a **Confucian welfare model**, with high reliance on the role of the **family**, albeit in recent years it has gradually been more heavily influenced by the state through legislation. This was, for example, the case with a new old-age **pension** system (2007), **financed** out of general **taxation** and focusing on the most vulnerable individuals in the country. The statutory pension age is 60 for both men and women, although the pension reform from 2007 provides coverage beginning at the age of 65.

L

LABOR FORCE. Those employed and unemployed in the **labor market**. It is often described as those individuals in the labor market between the ages of 15 and 66, but, in principle, it should include all who want to find work and are actively searching for **employment**. The reason for the age range is mainly that (in most Western countries, at least) most people under the age of 15 are still living at home and undergoing **education**, and most of those people who are 66 or older are retired. Nonetheless, changes in time spent in the educational system and **early retirement** policies in many countries make the validity of this age range debatable.

Changes in the labor force have an impact on the number of people employed and unemployed. Growth of the labor force means that even if there has been an increase in the number of jobs, the number of unemployed individuals has also increased. An increase in the labor force can impose a pressure on the wage level if there is **unemployment**. *See also* LABOR MARKET POLICY.

LABOR MARKET. Although it is labeled a **market**, in principle, the labor market consists of many and varied markets where labor is bought and sold. Labor markets can be different in different geographical areas, but they can also vary depending on qualifications, age, and sector (e.g., jobs are often different in the **public sector** and private sector). Labor markets are, for many people, an important place to ensure a job, and thereby income, and at the same time a place for social contacts. Theoretically, the labor market will, in a classical understanding, be cleared (be in equilibrium) given that those who are willing to accept the ongoing wage rate will then be employed; however, it is often the case that there are different kinds of **unemployment**. *See also* DUAL LABOR MARKET; LABOR MARKET POLICY; SEGMENTED LABOR MARKET.

LABOR MARKET POLICY. This policy involves measures designed to improve the functioning of the **labor market** in the **welfare state** and reduce **unemployment**. Labor market policy can be either passive or active. Passive labor market policy has two different aspects—compensation and matching. Compensation takes the form of **unemployment benefits, early retirement** benefits, and early social **pensions**. The amount and duration of unemployment benefits have been widely discussed in relation to the impact on people's willingness to take a job. They have also been discussed as a core issue in securing and avoiding large-scale **inequality** and with regard to the **stigmatizing** effects of being unemployed. Passive labor market policy has as its overall aim economic compensation for any damage the individual incurs by being unemployed.

Active labor market policy (ALMP) will ideally ensure that the **labor force** has the necessary qualifications to fulfill the requirements of the employers when demand is shifting from one area to another. The necessary qualifications will exist if productivity is equal to the wages paid. ALMP will, thus, only increase **employment** in the long run if there is a **market** for the goods produced and a marginal profit from increasing the number of people employed.

ALMP can influence both demand and supply in the labor market. Influencing the supply of labor can be achieved through various leave schemes; vocational training and mobility grants can also accomplish this. Demand can be influenced by qualification programs in companies, on-the-job training, subsidized employment, quotas, and **finance** policy. Matching labor market policy involves employment **services**, which have the purpose of trying to make demand and supply in the labor market meet.

The effects of different types of ALMP depend on the economic environment in general, the possible deadweight losses of a new activity, and the long-term **demographic** situation in the labor market. It is generally assumed that ALMPs will have a positive effect if they raise the **human capital** and the economic environment is positive for changes in the level of unemployment, including changes in the international economic conditions. Activation in private companies also has a positive outcome. Activation can further have a focus on work first or an increase in human capital. Recent years have seen an increased focus on work first in many welfare states.

Finally, in relation to the welfare state, an ALMP may reduce **marginalization** and also the **dual labor market**. Labor market policies also often have a regional dimension to ensure the balanced development of a society.

The use of active and passive labor market policies varies widely among welfare states. They are most developed in the **Scandinavian welfare state model**. *See also* KEYNES, JOHN MAYNARD.

LAISSEZ-FAIRE. A policy of nonintervention by the state. It is therefore often a **conservative** policy in which the existing **inequalities** in a society will prevail. Moreover, the consequences of **market** forces on, for example, **unemployment** and **inflation** will not be counterbalanced by public intervention.

LATIN RIM. *See* SOUTHERN EUROPEAN WELFARE STATE MODEL.

LATVIA. This small Baltic country first gained its independence from the **Union of Soviet Socialist Republics** in 1991, and, in May 2004, it became a member of the **European Union (EU)**. Changes in the economy and the movement toward a **market**-based economy have resulted in **unemployment** and **poverty** for many Latvians. The first laws concerning **social security** were passed in the 1920s, but the legislation was rewritten after independence, and laws on **family allowances** and **unemployment benefits** only went into effect in 1991. The system is built mainly on **social insurance**, with the exception of **health care** and family allowances, which are paid by the state. It is, thus, primarily a **conservative model**, but with some elements drawn from the **Scandinavian welfare state model**. Latvia's **social policy** is also influenced by the development in the EU.

LEAVE SCHEMES. Leave schemes are intended to give people **incentives** to temporarily exit from the **labor market**. They exist in various countries, with different benefits and criteria attached to them. The schemes can be designed to give incentives to undertake **education** or training. The idea is that the individual with a state grant can leave the labor market for a given period of time, living off the leave-scheme benefit, and ultimately increasing **human capital**. There are also parental leave schemes whereby individuals can take **care** of children or other relatives needing assistance. Finally, leave schemes also exist where the main purpose is a sabbatical leave, that is, an individual can leave the labor market for a previously agreed span of time without specifying the cause. Faced with expected shortages in the **labor force** due to **demographic** changes, these schemes have been reduced in many countries during the past few years.

LEGITIMACY. Having broad societal support. Questions often arise about whether decisions and developments in the **welfare state** have broad societal support, that is, whether something is done in the right way and whether those making the decisions have the **right** to do so. The problem with this concept—as with others—is that it involves **normative** value judgments about whether decisions have popular support. In welfare-state analysis, the concept has been used to discuss whether the state has sufficient support for the continuation of the welfare-state project, or if support has decreased throughout time, opening the question of its continuation.

The crisis of legitimacy, due to an inability to fulfill the expectations of the welfare state, has been widely debated. It has been put forth as an explanation of the emergence of the **New Right** and the fact that it has been possible in some countries to make major cutbacks in welfare-state benefits. The expectations of the welfare state were, among other things, that **unemployment** would be permanently low, and that growth in the economies could improve living standards for most people, and at the same time reduce **inequality**. Given the high level of unemployment in many countries from the mid-1970s onward, and the increase in unstable economies, confidence in the welfare state has been diminished.

On the other hand, the expenditures on **social policy** in most countries have either continued to rise or been stabilized at a high level. Seen in this light, there may have been a legitimacy crisis, but it must be over or at least be of reduced importance compared to what it was. Support for the various welfare states' activities varies. The highest support in most countries is for **health care** and **pensions**; there is less support for **social assistance**. Austerity measures adopted in many welfare states in recent years do not seem to have reduced the electoral support for the welfare state.

LIBERAL. This is a believer in **liberalism**, a particular approach to societal development. Liberals were originally in opposition to the conservatives, but today the difference is less clear-cut. Liberals argue for slow but gradual change, believing that the individual is the best person to know his or her own interests. Given such an **individualistic** approach, there is less scope for state intervention. Still, liberals accept intervention to promote stable economic development and guarantee internal and external security. *See also* LIBERAL MODEL.

LIBERAL MODEL. This model places a large degree of emphasis on the **market** as the main provider of welfare and is therefore based on **means-tested benefits**, for which the level of compensation is low. It is based on limited state intervention, for those "really" in need. The **public sector** is mainly responsible for **financing** in these limited areas, as well as for **health care**, at least to a certain extent.

This model puts **freedom** and individual property **rights** high on the agenda and before intervention. It is not committed to intervention to create full **employment**, relying on the market to accomplish this task. It has its historical roots in the Protestant work ethic and therefore, as a rule, finds that the individual should be able to take **care** of himself or herself. As a result, countries in the liberal model group often spend less public money on welfare than other countries, and a higher degree of **social insurance** can be found. The **United States** and the **United Kingdom** are two such countries. *See also* LIBERAL; LIBERALISM.

LIBERALISM. A political ideology inspired by French philosopher Jean-Jacques Rousseau, Scottish economist **Adam Smith**, and English philosopher John Stuart Mill that argues that people can and should be free to act in their self-interests, and only in a few and very well-defined cases should state intervention take place. It favors **democratic** rule, but with a view that the state should not be expanded too much.

In relation to **social policy**, **liberals** argue that too much welfare provision could reduce people's **incentives** to become employed and thus create distortions in the **labor market**. Intervention to create jobs is seen as a hindrance to long-term, stable development, and the **market** should have a chance to clear by making changes in real wage levels instead of intervention, which may build on more rigid structures and less flexibility in the labor market. **Social welfare** should be minimal, and the public supply of welfare should be limited as much as possible. On the other hand, liberals acknowledge that those in **need** should be helped, but they make a distinction between the **deserving** and the **undeserving** poor.

LIFE CYCLE. The individual's changing position throughout his or her lifetime, starting with being dependent on others and often ending with being so again. In between, the individual will usually be able to take **care** of himself or herself. In certain cultures and societies, different phases of life are endowed with certain duties and tasks. For example, in certain cultures, the elderly are seen as being wise.

In relation to **social policy**, this life cycle gives rise to different problems. The first is whether everyone should be supported if they have been able to save money to use when they become pensioners. Furthermore, it opens up the question of who the poor are. Is an elderly person who has had the ability to save for retirement poor if he or she has not done so? Should those who only for a short period of their lives are unable to finance their livelihood (e.g., young people) be considered poor and in **need** of support?

The second problem is that part of the **welfare state** consists of agreements between generations; for example, it is possible to receive **services** and benefits during different periods of the life cycle that are paid for by another generation, but it is then expected that the new generation will pay for the next. As long as these intergenerational agreements hold, they do not cause specific problems, but they will if they break down. *See also* AGING OF SOCIETIES; LIFETIME INCOME.

LIFE EXPECTANCY. The number of years a person is expected to live. Figures can be the number of years of life expected from birth onward, but they can also be the number of years of life expected after, for example, having reached the age of retirement. Life expectancy has been increasing due to especially lower levels of child death and better **health**, and this has given rise to the debate on the **aging of societies**.

LIFE PERSPECTIVE. This refers to the fact that people have different **needs** and perceptions during their lifetimes. People's need for **services** and/ or other types of support from the **welfare state** thus change during a lifetime. *See also* LIFE CYCLE.

LIFELONG LEARNING. This refers to the fact that, in modern societies, the required level of qualifications is constantly rising; therefore, individuals will continuously need to get an **education** and further their education to have the necessary qualifications to get jobs or keep them in their jobs in the **labor market**. As a result, many **welfare states** now pursue lifelong learning initiatives as a way of also supporting **flexicurity**.

LIFETIME INCOME. The income earned and accrued during a lifetime. The argument for using lifetime income when comparing different groups in a society is that this makes it possible to take different parts of an individual's life into consideration. That is, periods when income is earned are considered, but also periods as a pensioner or when one is undergoing **education**.

Lifetime income can be measured in two ways. The first, although not often used, is to follow a generation during its lifetime and gather information about its total income. This makes it possible to compare the total lifetime income of different groups. It should, in principle, include earned income, interest income, and transfers from the **public sector**. It should be calculated at the same price level. Furthermore, one could argue that income tax and **social security** contributions should be deducted. The problem with this type of calculation is that, being *ex-post*, it is difficult to make a change in welfare policy that can counterbalance the situation if, for example, the level is then too low.

The second way is to calculate a stylized income path for different groups in the **labor market**. It may or may not include their **pension** income, periods of **unemployment**, taxes paid, and expectation of future real income increases. Based on these calculations, it can be shown which groups, during a lifetime, are better off and which are worse off. This can then be used to make recommendations for **social policy**, that is, which individuals are the neediest in relation to lifetime income. The concept's weakness is that it is a stylized calculation, and society changes throughout time. Groups that have been low-income earners may change position, and groups with high income may see their relative position decline. *See also* LIFE CYCLE.

LITHUANIA. This small Baltic country gained its independence from the **Union of Soviet Socialist Republics** in 1990, and became a member of the **European Union (EU)** in 2004. The years since independence have been characterized by dramatic economic changes, and **unemployment** and **poverty** are the main social problems. Although some laws relating to **social security** originated earlier, the current laws stem from the 1990s onward. Unemployment was the first area to be covered, in 1919, and old age, **disability, sickness**, and **maternity** were covered beginning in 1925. Systems covering **family allowances** (1990) and **industrial injury** (1991) were first introduced after independence.

The welfare system is based on **social insurance** to a high degree, but for family allowances and medical care, it is a **universal** system. In this sense, the structure combines elements from the **Scandinavian welfare state model** with those of the **conservative model**. Being member of the EU also influences the options and possibilities of the development of welfare.

LOCAL SOCIETY. A short way of referring to, on the one hand, a specific local entity, but also indicating traditions, roots, and social cohesion. The local society can also be the level at which welfare benefits and **services** are organized and/or **financed**. Furthermore, local activities can be important in everyday life.

LONG-TERM CARE. Care that is given during an extended period of time, especially for the elderly or those with long-term illnesses. Long-term care is often expensive; therefore, if more elderly are in **need** of care, expenditures will rise. The high expenditures for one person is also the reason why this is done collectively in **welfare states**, as it is impossible for the individual to foresee whether he or she is one of those who will be in need of care later in life. *See also* AGING OF SOCIETIES.

LORENZ CURVE. This tool illustrates the **distribution** in a given society by having the individuals in a society on the x axis in an accumulated form, for example, the total number of people in the society on one axis, and the total number with wealth or income on the y axis—also in accumulated form—having either income or wealth. The resulting curve describes the degree of **equality** or **inequality**. If a straight line results, the situation is described as totally equal. If the line deviates, then the size of the area of the curve inward toward the straight line indicates the degree of inequality. It is possible to use the Lorenz curve to compare the degree of inequality between different years in a single country and also between countries, as long as the lines drawn from the different years or countries do not intersect. Those closer to the straight line will have a more equal distribution compared to those father away. *See also* GINI COEFFICIENT.

LUXEMBOURG INCOME STUDY (LIS). An international organization that collects data, thereby enabling research on income and wealth. It has two important databases: the Luxembourg Income Study Database (LIS) and the Luxembourg Wealth Study Database (LWS). They can be used for international **comparative analysis**, especially on differences in income and wealth.

M

MALTHUS, THOMAS R. (1766–1834). Malthus was a British economist whose main contribution was his *Essay on the Principle of Population as It Affects the Future Improvement of Society*. His thesis was that it would be impossible to produce enough food for an ever-growing population mainly restrained by war and **poverty**. He therefore suggested that wages should only be at a subsistence level to reduce the **demographic** pressure, assuming that with a low level of income, the working **classes** would be less prepared to have more children. His ideas have had a strong impact on many **conservative** approaches to **welfare-state** ideology, which extend his theory to stating that the level of benefits should not be very high.

MARGINALIZATION. The state of not participating in mainstream society. Those who are not participating in certain mainstream activities are considered to be marginalized. They can be so in various ways, for example, not participating in voting, cultural events, local activities in schools, and **child care** institutions. Marginalization can be permanent or temporary. It is temporary when, for a while, some individuals (for example, those in prison or hospitalized) are unable to participate actively, but when they leave these institutions, they may be able to partake and may even be easily reintegrated into society. For others, a temporary marginalization may lead to permanent marginalization by reducing contact and the ability to function with other people.

Marginalization in the **labor market** for those of working age has been seen as a core problem in many countries because welfare systems are highly dependent on people having jobs, and their **social security** coverage is low if they do not have them. Furthermore, the lack of a job apparently makes contacts with others unstable for many individuals and also reduces their economic ability to participate in various activities. Working individuals seem to be more **integrated** into society, which implies a need for **labor market policy** as a way of reducing marginalization. *See also* SOCIAL EXCLUSION.

MARKET. The arena for the exchange of goods and **services**. It is characterized by the supply and demand of goods and services. The exchange of goods and services is based on the price, given full information and knowledge of the quality thereof. The **labor market** is a specific type of market in which the demand and supply of labor have consequences for the levels of both wages and **unemployment**. This is a varied market, which, in most countries, varies in terms of geography, qualifications, age of workers, and types of jobs available.

The delivery of goods and services to specific groups in the population will either be provided by the market, and if **market failure** occurs, it will perhaps be provided by the state. If both fail to produce, **civil society** is left with the responsibility.

Markets have strong and weak elements. Markets with goods produced by a large number of suppliers and with many demanding the goods seem to be the most efficient at delivering at a reasonable price. Monopolies, on the other hand, result in higher prices and perhaps also lower quality. This is why in most market economies, the state has enacted rules to ensure competition. The principle of supply and demand has increasingly been used in **welfare states**, and also within the **public-sector** provision as a means to try to make provision more effective. Weighting the level of responsibility to provide services among the market, the state, and civil society often results in a dichotomy between effectiveness and equity in the welfare state.

MARKET FAILURE. A common term for the situation when the **market**, left to itself, does not generate an efficient output of goods and **services**. A common example is pollution, where the cost of pollution is not reflected in market prices. Different types of market failures can occur. These include the lack of production of certain goods; monopolies, including natural monopolies; disequilibria (**unemployment**, **inflation**, balance of payment deficits); and information problems.

Market failure has been a core argument for **public-sector** intervention in the economy. Most accept some types of public intervention, for example, defense, police, foreign policy, and administration of common rules for society's functioning; however, there is greater disagreement about the **need** for social programs and real **welfare-state** intervention.

Different types of market failure are often related to imperfect competition. In welfare-state analysis, it is especially in connection with a lack of supply of certain goods and disequilibria in the economy that the question of market failure arises. There may be a lack of supply of certain goods needed by handicapped groups because their demand is too low for production to generate a profit; in this situation, if the goods were produced, few people with disabilities would be able to buy them.

Disequilibria have several consequences in relation to **distribution** and the structure of society. One is that unforeseen price inflation redistributes wealth between those with and those without fixed assets. Another is unemployment. High unemployment in a market economy generates income and other problems for many **families** and a need for public intervention to reduce unemployment. Market failure has, therefore, directly and indirectly been a central reason for the development of the welfare state in many countries, to counterbalance the consequences of market forces that, if left to themselves, could create serious problems for individuals and families.

Some argue that even if one accepts the idea of market failures, they have a less harmful effect on society's overall level of welfare than **government failure**. This cannot be decided at a theoretical level but needs to be resolved by empirical analysis of the specific area in question.

MARKETIZATION. A process in several—mainly European—countries, in which elements from the **market's** way of functioning are used in the production of welfare **services**. This can be done by **privatizing** public production and/or delivery of a **social service** or by letting private companies play a role in the production of social services. The private impact can assume various forms, and the producers can have different degrees of **freedom**. At one end of the scale, this can be a fully free **right** to provide services under market conditions, with full competition, including prices determined by the market. At the other end, it can be giving the right to produce the service based on a fixed set of prices from the **public sector** and with a specified set of conditions to fulfill relating to quantity and quality. Sometimes marketization refers to the use of market-type mechanisms within the public sector itself when providing services, for example, competition between various providers.

MARSHALL, T. H. (1893–1982). Marshall was a sociologist who taught at the London School of Economics from 1925–1956, and was professor there beginning in 1944. His contribution to **welfare-state** analysis was to distinguish between different types of **rights** and how they were connected. His notion of **citizenship** has been a cornerstone of many analyses of why and how one could and can distinguish between welfare states. Marshall introduced the distinction between civil, political, and **social rights**. He stressed that in early society, only civil rights were developed; in the 19th century, many countries established political rights for their citizens, but it was only in the 20th century that the right to income or transfers was established. Many welfare-state models do not use citizenship as the basic criterion for being eligible for benefits, but rather participation in the **labor market**. Marshall also worked on an analysis of welfare-state policies in the **United Kingdom** from 1890–1945, to describe how **social rights** had been expanded. His vision of the welfare state was built on the conflicts among **democracy**, welfare, and **classes** in society.

MARX, KARL (1818–1883). Marx was born in Trier and studied at Bonn and Berlin. He wrote *The Communist Manifesto* in 1848, with Friedrich Engels. In 1849, he fled to London, where he spent the rest of his life. His main contribution is his historical analysis of society at that time, which included the inevitability of the **class** struggle that arises from the built-in conflict between workers and capital. This thesis was especially developed in *Das Kapital*, written in 1867. Marx's analysis of social structures and conflicts in capitalist societies and their consequences has been used in many **welfare-state** analyses to describe and explain the social conflicts within the welfare state. The development of the welfare state has also been interpreted in **Marxist** terms as a consequence of the ongoing struggle among different classes in society. Marx's expectation that capitalist society would inevitably break down and be transformed into a **communist** society is not supported by historical developments thus far. Nevertheless, his analysis of the different classes' living standards and the consequences of capitalist production yields much useful information about the functioning of capitalist societies.

MARXISM. This ideology was built on **Karl Marx's** ideas and his analysis of society. The main thesis is that internal **class** conflicts will occur continuously in society until there is a revolution in which the ruling class disappears. Marxism has been a driving force behind many revolutions in Eastern Europe and Third World countries. It was the official ideology of the **Union of Soviet Socialist Republics**, the People's Republic of **China**, and many other countries, especially in Eastern Europe.

Presently, support for Marxism seems to be rather weak, although class analysis is still used in many types of analysis of the development of the **welfare state** and the degree of **inequality** in different countries. In addition to its use in welfare-state analysis, the concept of class is still deeply rooted in interpretations of historical developments in numerous countries. *See also* COMMUNISM.

MATERNITY BENEFITS. Benefits given in relation to the birth of a child. In most countries, these benefits are only given to the mother during a certain period, when she can take **care** of the newborn child while receiving a public benefit. The duration and amount of the benefit vary between countries. In some countries, maternity benefits also exist for men to allow fathers to have closer contact with their children.

MEANS-TESTED BENEFIT. A benefit for which the individual is only eligible upon fulfilling certain income and wealth tests. As a result of being means-tested, certain groups are disqualified from the **right** to a benefit because they have too high a level of income or wealth. The specific criteria, a combination of income and wealth, differ in different countries. Means tests can be so strict that few people can receive the benefit, or they can help to ensure **legitimacy** in the welfare state by only giving benefits to those most in **need**. These tests can also carry a degree of stigma, especially if the means test includes more than looking at such objective criteria as income or wealth. Means-tested benefits are especially used in countries that utilize the **liberal welfare model** and **conservative welfare model**.

MEASUREMENT OF INEQUALITY. A measurement that is part of the analysis of the degree of **equality** in a given society. The first problem that arises when measuring **inequality** is deciding which type of inequality is being investigated. Is it inequality of access to different types of goods and **services**, or is it inequality in relation to nonmonetary goods? Research has focused on inequality in income and wealth, as this is possible to measure, whereas other types of inequalities require more qualitative data, which makes it difficult to get a comprehensive picture of the degree of inequality.

There are numerous tools for measuring inequality, including the Atkinson Index, Theil's entropy, the **Lorenz curve**, and the **Gini coefficient**. Pen's parade is a simple way of presenting inequality by showing the income of members of a society from top to bottom. The measurements try to answer the same question: What is the level of inequality in a specific country? They can have different ways of interpreting inequality, and this is the main reason for so many different forms of measurement.

The central question when using these indexes is how one should interpret the figures calculated and their relation to the numbers at the bottom of the income **distribution**. Should more weight be allotted to those at the bottom of the income distribution, and should there be a specific reduction in an index of inequality if those at the bottom are especially well taken **care** of? Another problem is how other changes within the income distribution should be calculated, and how they should be shown within the statistics. If the changes in income distribution, for example, are only within the top 20 percent, but with a tendency toward a more even spread of resources, the question arises of whether this should then be reflected in the calculated index, or should only those with an income below the average income be taken into consideration? Answers to these questions involve making various **normative** decisions.

Most research measuring inequalities uses the Gini coefficient, which describes how far the distribution is from a hypothetical distribution in which each decile of the population has one-tenth of the income or wealth. Some of the problems in relation to measurement and interpretation of this are that the statistics do not necessarily tell the full story since there is a **hidden economy**, which includes gifts and bequests, public services, and so forth, and since individuals may be at different points in their **life cycles**, which at least has consequences for an interpretation of whether they are in **need**. The impact of the size of the household, and, in relation to this, which units are used when making the measurement, also raise questions about how to measure the degree of inequality.

An analysis of whether some individuals are poor throughout their entire lives or for shorter periods of time is also used as a way of trying to analyze **poverty**. These types of analysis are more difficult because they require collecting data during a long span of time. Nonetheless, analyzing a country or comparing countries throughout time by using the same statistics and information does produce valuable information about the development of inequality. Even if the data are not precise, they may provide hints about how to use the information in **welfare-state** policies and the possible need for redistribution.

MEASUREMENT OF WELFARE. This measurement is one of the fundamental problems in **welfare economics**. Its starting point is the individual's **utility** of different bundles of goods. The ability to describe total welfare in a society depends on being able to add together the individual person's welfare functions. In theory, this is simple: Add the individuals' utility curves together to get the society's total welfare.

Problems arise when trying to interpret the consequences of, or trying to find the exact value of, the individual's welfare. Although in principle we can just add these together, they are based on different bundles of goods and **services**, determined by the individual's income constraints. An individual might have chosen another bundle if his or her income constraint had been different and had presented him or her with other options; therefore, by adding utility curves, one indirectly assumes that the present **income distribution** is the acceptable income distribution in a given society.

Furthermore, when adding the utilities, it is necessary to compare different goods, which may have different functions for individuals. Some goods are **basic needs**, while others are luxury goods. Thus, a reduction may be harsher for some (those with only basic needs covered) than for others if changes in distribution are made that require these groups to give up some of their resources. Consequently, value judgments are involved when making comparisons and adding together the information. The measurement of welfare is therefore highly **normative**, and information will be based on valuation in a specific time and specific historical context.

Using the information on individuals' utilities could also give rise to many different problems of interpretation. For example, should resources be taken away from a handicapped person if a healthy person can achieve higher welfare levels with these extra resources? Society's total welfare, measured as total utility, may be increased, but it will perhaps be at the expense of particularly vulnerable groups.

Finally, it is difficult to determine a specific figure when trying to measure value—should it be in monetary terms, level of satisfaction, or some other scale? Scale problems and decisions about which scale to use when measuring welfare are therefore also major issues. *See also* HAPPINESS.

MEDIAN VOTER. Someone who is able to shift the majority from one group to another. In mathematics, the median is found exactly in the middle of the **distribution**. In the analysis of the **welfare state** and **growth of the public-sector** expenditures, the concept of the median voter has been important in trying to explain why, and how, it is possible to gain a majority; therefore, it may be important to support voters in the middle of the political spectrum, as they will be able to help form a majority. Changes in attitudes of the median voter can have a profound effect on overall decision making. It is also argued that there may be an expansion of public expenditures in areas where the median voter has preferences.

MERIT GOODS. Goods that, when left to the **market**, will be produced in insufficient amounts compared to what society would wish if it were to maximize its welfare function. The term was first defined by Richard Musgrave in 1959, in *The Theory of Public Finance*. Musgrave used the example of luncheon tickets, which should ensure that children have meals with a high nutritional value. The market would do this by pricing the goods, and this would leave children from low-income families unable to buy the food. By having the state provide luncheon tickets, it should be possible to make sure that all children will get the food.

Today, a more common example is **education**. The market could provide education for payment, but fewer individuals might enter education, which could therefore result in an overall reduction in the level of education. This could be because the individual's expectation of income after education, and thus the improvement in **human capital**, is less than society's expectation.

Aside from the economic arguments, it could be said that **democracy** needs a well-educated population to make sure that everyone can participate in society's decision-making processes.

The debate about merit goods involves many **normative** judgments because of the difficulties in knowing and determining a society's welfare function. It is a political decision whether the **welfare state** should provide a specific good, to be decided by weighting whether a good has such a high value for society that it should be supplied, even if, in principle, it could be provided by the market.

METHODOLOGICAL INDIVIDUALISM. The belief that the individual's evaluation should come first when making decisions. An individual's choice should thus have priority compared to societal wishes to intervene. This philosophy has consequences for many areas of the **welfare state**, as it implies less state intervention and therefore a higher reliance on **market** provision and market-based solutions. Some limits exist where the reference to the common good may imply a restriction of the individual's behavior.

MEXICO. The development of **social security** programs in Mexico was slow compared to its big neighbor to the north, the **United States**. The explanation may be its relatively weak economic performance, slow economic growth, and a long period of political instability at the beginning of the 20th century, which came to an end with the introduction of a new constitution in 1917, after which several reforms were made. The first law covered **industrial injury** (1931) and was followed during World War II by laws concerning **pensions, sickness benefits**, and **maternity benefits. Unemployment benefits** and **family allowances** are only weakly developed, but there is a requirement that employers must pay dismissed workers an amount of money for a certain period. Mexico's system is, in general, a **social insurance** system, so primarily those in the **labor market** are covered. Otherwise, only specific individuals are covered—and mainly on a voluntary basis. A relatively low level of benefits also limits the system.

MIDDLE EAST WELFARE. A short term for welfare approaches in such oil countries as Saudi Arabia, Kuwait, Qatar, Bahrain, Oman, and the United Arab Emirates. Israel can also be considered a Middle East country where **civil society** has a strong role related to the provision of welfare. In addition, Turkey can be regarded as belonging to the Middle East. These countries are, to a certain extent, influenced by the **Southern European welfare state model**. They have a focus on the role of the **family** and are peculiar by being **welfare states** exclusively for their citizens. Foreign nationals, including legal residents and legal long-term employees, are ineligible to receive the benefits of the welfare state.

Due to high levels of income from natural resources, on average, citizens have a relatively large income and therefore have been able to develop a different kind of welfare system. How long they will be able to uphold the present situation regarding welfare depends upon the price of oil and how they save their present income for future use. They also differ by not having a specific, labeled type of welfare state. Furthermore, the role of the **market** is weaker than in other welfare states. At the same time, religion plays a role in the formulation and understanding of the role of a welfare state.

MIGRATION. The movement and change of residence of an individual. Migration can be immigration (moving into a country) or emigration (moving out of a country). It can also be movement within a country, but it is mainly thought of as movements of citizens between different countries. Migration can be permanent or temporary. Temporary migration may occur because someone wishes to take up a job for a short period of time in another country, working two or three years abroad and then going back, but sometimes what is expected to be temporary migration turns out to be permanent.

Migration can be either voluntary or forced. Voluntary migration occurs when a person or **family** moves from one country to another of his or her own free will. Forced migration occurs when a person or groups of individuals are forced to move from one country to another. Voluntary migration may be induced by various causes. The major reason is large differences in the level of welfare (and differences in wage levels); movement is expected to improve the living conditions of those migrating from one country to another. Differences in **unemployment** rates, or lack of manpower in some countries compared to others, may be another reason for this type of movement. Increasing **inequality** between the richer and poorer parts of the world may also be a reason for increased migration in the future. This likelihood has been part of the debate regarding how to best help poor countries achieve economic development, since economic development may reduce the migration from poor countries to rich countries.

The large movement of workers from Southern Europe and Turkey to Northern Europe in the late 1960s was due to a lack of manpower. Those who moved therefore had a chance to get a job and achieve a higher standard of living than in their home countries. Within the **European Union (EU)**, there is now a **right** to free movement mainly on the condition that the individual can find a job. Otherwise, and for third-country nationals, it is difficult to enter an EU country—except as a tourist. The same situation exists in the **United States** and many other countries. This makes it difficult to migrate to a country unless it is to study or take up a job that has been arranged beforehand.

Involuntary migration is often connected with wars (both between countries and civil), making it necessary for many people to flee as refugees. International conventions state that the first safe country that a fugitive enters should take **care** of that individual. It may be difficult for countries that are neighbors to big conflicts to cope with increased migration. Thus, within the **United Nations** systems, most countries have agreed to accept a limited number of refugees each year.

A large influx of migrant workers or refugees may make it challenging to keep a society fully **integrated** and may also create greater domestic tensions, especially when the nation's economic circumstances are not good. Racism and xenophobia can result from large influxes of individuals with a different cultural background. This seems to be one of the reasons for many countries imposing more stringent criteria concerning entry rights. The degree of tension naturally also depends upon which measures are used when trying to integrate people into society.

Migration has been discussed in relation to its impact on **welfare-state financing** and delivery. If a large proportion of migrants require social transfers, this may create problems for the welfare systems, depending to a large extent upon the degree to which the migrants are able to enter the **labor market**. Although this has varied in different states, the first generation of migrants usually has more difficulty in entering the labor market; therefore, they have a higher chance of being **socially excluded**. At the same time, the second generation of migrant workers and people who are being naturalized have a higher degree of affiliation with the labor market and are more integrated into societies. Integration may, thus, take several generations. Hence, integration of migrants into the labor market is a formidable challenge facing the welfare states in the years to come.

On the other hand, migration can also have a positive influence on a country by generating a more multifaceted view and a greater understanding of other individuals. The migrants' inspiration can become the source of new ideas and new production methods. Further migration can have a positive impact by reducing the **dependency ratio**, if the migrants are, on average, younger than the population.

Those countries from which the migrant workers come may also benefit in the form of remittances from those working abroad, which positively contribute to the inflow of foreign capital. This has been the case for many of those countries that, in the 1960s and 1970s, had a net migration to Europe, and it still is for many sending countries. Furthermore, if those migrating make it possible for others to take over their jobs, that may reduce the overall unemployment in the home country. It is generally impossible to know the precise effects of migration, and the impact at the micro and macro levels may be different—even if the economic and social consequences are substantial.

MINIMUM INCOME. The level of income necessary to avoid living in **poverty**, or the income needed to achieve a decent living standard. The level of the minimum income is, to a large extent, dependent on the levels of welfare in the country in question. **Welfare states** generally do not have a guaranteed minimum **basic income** for their citizens, although many welfare states have a basic **pension** for those not having other sources of income.

MORAL HAZARD. This risk arises when people's actions are influenced by a given structure of **incentives**. The term is often used in relation to insurance. Moral hazard exists, for example, when a person, after being insured against fire or theft, takes fewer precautions than before becoming insured. The individual will have less incentive—due to the insurance—to do something, and will, in this respect, have a **free ride** in relation to the insurance company. Moral hazard can also exist when an individual is working less than expected at a workplace or can more easily accept the loss of his or her job because he or she will receive **unemployment benefits**.

In **welfare-state** analysis, it has been argued that too high a **public-sector** provision of, for example, **health care** makes people less careful about their own **health**. Furthermore, systems with benefits that are too generous have been used, especially in **public choice** theories, as examples of why people are less willing to take up jobs, relying on **sickness benefits** and so forth. There does not seem to be firm **evidence** on a societal level that this is the case, but a thorough analysis would be difficult to make.

NATURAL RATE OF UNEMPLOYMENT. The rate of **unemployment** that a society would eventually move toward given the structure of the economy, the **labor market**, and related regulations. It is questionable what the level of the natural rate of unemployment actually is. One definition has been the rate of unemployment when the **inflation** rate is stable—sometimes referred to as the nonaccelerating inflation rate of unemployment (NAIRU). By relating unemployment to a stable inflation rate, it can vary greatly in different countries and will also change throughout time.

NEED. Something an individual is lacking, physical or psychological. It can be food and **housing** to survive, but also be social contacts with other people. **Basic needs** should normally be fulfilled before the individual expresses the need for loving and caring. Needs are individually bound, and the size is **normative**, which makes it difficult to decide which needs should be covered and which should not, because needs are seen as unlimited. The **welfare state** primarily supplies such basic needs as food (or income to buy food) and housing; to a lesser degree, it supplies loving and caring. In some welfare states, homes for the elderly, self-help groups, and support **services** for voluntary groups are established to reduce loneliness among specific vulnerable groups.

NEGATIVE INCOME TAX. A tax paid to those having an income below a certain defined level. It has been used to define a minimum income level that all members of society should have, and, in this way, it resembles a **means-tested** general benefit given to those with the lowest income in a society. It can be said to reduce the number of people living in **poverty** if the minimum is defined as the poverty line.

NETHERLANDS, THE. One of the mature European **welfare states**, which can basically be characterized as a mixture of the **continental model** and the **Scandinavian welfare state model**, as it has certain elements of and similarities to the **Bismarckian** model due to its combination of the **universal** system, with insurance-based systems. The Netherlands experienced slow and late industrial development. It was only in 1901 that a law on **industrial**

injury was established, and, in 1912, a change in the **Poor Law** was passed. During World War I, an **unemployment** system was developed, and only after the war (although the country was neutral during the war) were new elements in the **social security** system developed, that is, coverage in case of old age and **disability** in 1919, and laws supporting **sickness benefits** and **maternity benefits** in 1931.

Although inspired by the Bismarckian model, the Netherlands turned to the **Beveridgian model** after World War II, and a more universal welfare state type gradually emerged, which, among other things, included general **pensions**. During the 1960s, the country, like many other welfare states in Europe, experienced rapid development and the expansion of its welfare system.

With respect to old age, the Netherlands has a universal system in which an individual may pay into a supplementary pension system above the state-supported level. The sickness and maternity benefits are also mainly based on a universal approach, whereas industrial injury, **unemployment benefits**, and some of the medical benefits are mainly for those in the **labor market**. The Netherlands is one of the countries in the world where spending on social protection as a proportion of the **gross domestic product** is highest, although some **retrenchments** were made in the last 15 to 20 years. The **European Union** has been central for the Netherlands since it became one of the original members in 1957. Thus, the free movement of workers has also been part of the country's development. As a result, **social policy** is another influence on welfare development.

NEW FAMILY. A term that describes the situation when a **divorced** person meets and starts living with another person. This can, but does not necessarily, also imply living together with new children belonging to one or both of the new members of the couple. *See also* FAMILY.

NEW LEFT. The term for those who tried to redefine the aims and goals of the **welfare state**. It argued in favor of a more just society, but at the same time strove for a higher degree of individual responsibility. *See also* NEW RIGHT; THIRD WAY.

NEW PUBLIC MANAGEMENT (NPM). A specific way of understanding how to manage and steer **public-sector** administration, especially that focused on the use of **marketization** as part of management. **Integrating** competition within the public sector's delivery of **social services** has also been part of this approach. NPM can be seen as one of the strategies criticizing the public sector for being inefficient, and the **bureaucracy** for mainly expressing self-interest in the development of the public sector. It is also largely inspired by **public choice** theorists and emphasizes how to make the public sector more efficient and responsive to user **needs**.

NEW RIGHT. A term commonly used to describe a specific way of thinking that evolved in the 1980s about the state's intervention in the economy. Many New Right thinkers have seen the state, and especially social programs, as economic problems that should be reduced to create a better overall economic situation. The result would be a situation in which those living in poor conditions could get a job.

The New Right emerged in many countries as a response to growing budget deficits, which the group claimed crowded out private investments. They believed that the way to reduce budget deficits and continued increases in state debt is to reduce **social welfare** benefits, not raise **tax** levels. New Right theorists wanted a more flexible **labor market** that would enable wages to go up and down in line with demand and supply. Furthermore, they argued for a reduction in **labor force** protection because, for example, protection against dismissal could make the labor market too rigid.

New Right recommendations included placing greater emphasis on using monetary policy as a measure to cure **inflation** and stimulate economic development, and less, if any, emphasis on **fiscal policy**, which would, in this context, mainly consist of reductions in **public-sector** expenditure. This way of thinking has been highly influential in many Western countries—especially the **United States** and **United Kingdom**. New Right theorists traditionally argue in favor of a **conservative** type of **welfare state**. *See also* NEW LEFT.

NEW ZEALAND. The **social security** system and **social policy** in New Zealand are a mixture of models and ideas about the **welfare state**. Inspired by participation in the British Commonwealth, it has some similarities to the **Beveridgian** notion of a welfare state, but also a high reliance on the **labor market** as a provider of welfare, as well as strong **means-tested** programs.

The old-age **pension** was the first **social security** law to be introduced (1898), and a ruling on **industrial injury** followed in 1908. Then came a long period of time during which no real initiatives seem to have been taken, but, in the 1920s and 1930s, a series of new laws rapidly followed, starting with **family** benefits in 1926, **unemployment benefits** in 1930, **disability** pensions in 1936, and **sickness benefits** and **maternity benefits** in 1938.

The system is based on a general way of **financing** the different contingencies, and, in this respect, it resembles the **Scandinavian welfare state model**. Only for industrial injury is there payment by employers. In many areas, an income test is used to find out if the individual is eligible for a certain type of benefit.

In the late 1990s, New Zealand adopted a more **liberal** approach to welfare-state delivery, with a high degree of **retrenchment** of the state's intervention in welfare-state issues. The model began moving toward a much more liberal form of welfare state. At the beginning of the 21st century, more emphasis on welfare-state intervention has returned.

In 2007, a KiwiSaver subsidized retirement savings plan was introduced to supplement the **flat-rate universal pension**. New entrants into the **labor force** and new employees who do not have a KiwiSaver account are automatically enrolled in a KiwiSaver plan but may opt out. There have also been changes in the **early retirement** benefit system and improved support to assist unemployed individuals in getting back into the labor market.

NONCONTRIBUTORY BENEFIT. A benefit that requires fulfilling certain criteria to receive it. It is often based upon a citizen's **right**. The criterion for receiving benefits can include a **means test**, but the benefit can also be based on fulfilling certain other criteria (age or having children). **Child benefits** are an example of a noncontributory benefit in many countries.

NONGOVERNMENTAL ORGANIZATION (NGO). An institution or body that is not directly managed or steered by the **public sector**. NGOs include various voluntary organizations and the **voluntary sector**, including the **church**. They may receive economic support from the state to carry out their activities. The main criterion is that they are independent of the state apparatus. In cases where they receive economic support, full independence may be difficult to achieve. For voluntary organizations, the possibility of having public support may therefore be looked upon with mixed feelings. The positive aspect of state support is the enhanced possibility of carrying out activities; the negative aspect is **dependency** on the state apparatus.

The NGOs' influence has been increasing in most **welfare states** since the 1980s, after a long period during which they played only a minor role. They can be effective because they are independent of the public sector and thereby have a better possibility of gaining access to vulnerable groups that do not like contact with the public sector. The increasing role of the nongovernmental sector is one of the reasons for the debate about the connection among **state, market, and civil society**.

In several **welfare states**, the NGOs' role has also included the ability to do **voluntary work**, which can include more personal contacts with, for example, lone elderly individuals. It is difficult for the state to both **finance** and find labor for this kind of work. At the same time, NGOs also fulfill a need of many of those people participating in the voluntary work, as it gives them some self-satisfaction. There is a constant debate regarding a variety of understandings as to how to also include **civil society** in the welfare states' activities and avoid voluntary failure. *See also* BIG SOCIETY.

NONPROFIT ORGANIZATIONS. These organizations deliver welfare that is often based on state **financing**, but without the purpose of creating a surplus for the organization. They are especially important in continental Europe. They resemble **nongovernmental organizations** in some ways.

NONTAKE-UP. When a person eligible for a benefit does not claim it. Reasons for nontake-up can be that the individual either does not know about the **right** to a benefit, or he or she feels **stigmatized** and is therefore not willing to ask for a benefit. Administrative rejections or administrative lack of precise knowledge of the individual's right can also explain nontake-up. In several **welfare states**, appeal systems exist to help people who do not feel that they have been given proper treatment in the administrative system. *See also* TAKE-UP RATE.

NORDIC MODEL. Welfare states often have different names by different authors depending on the author's focus. The Nordic model refers to welfare states in **Denmark, Sweden, Norway**, and **Finland**. *See also* SCANDINA-VIAN WELFARE STATE MODEL.

NORMATIVE ANALYSIS. An analysis based on value judgments about whether an outcome or policy is desirable or undesirable, and how to change things to achieve the best possible outcome. Normative analyses, in contrast to **positive analyses**, ask such questions as, What ought to be done? Normative analysis is especially prevalent in areas concerning **justice** and **equality**, as these involve many normative issues. But discussions about what constitutes a good society can also involve a normative analysis. Research on **welfare states** will normally try to avoid a normative stance and approach. *See also* NORMATIVITY.

NORMATIVITY. A **normative analysis** that is value-based, that is, an analysis based on such questions as, What ought to be done? Normativity can be both conscious and unconscious. Within politics, normativity can, for example, take the form of more or less explicit references to party ideology and aims. Normative approaches can sometimes be difficult to avoid due to the individual's historical background. *See also* NORMS.

NORMS. Rules or sets of rules that serve as common guidelines for individual or collective behavior, and by means of which deviation can be punished.

Formal norms can be sanctioned by legal actions, whereas informal norms involve other types of sanctions, for instance, being cast out from the group. A social norm describes how individuals are expected to behave. Some norms can be broken without punishment, for example, bad behavior at a party. Friends, relatives, and employers may sanction other types of norms, and the law sanctions certain norms. The type of sanction can vary depending on the degree of deviation from the norm. Norms can also vary among countries and welfare systems. Cheating the public system may be morally more acceptable in one system than in another. Norms can also influence the understanding of who is **deserving and** who is **undeserving**. *See also* NORMATIVITY.

NORWAY. Norway belongs to the **Scandinavian welfare state** type and has a very **universal welfare state**, which has been supported by the country's oil income. Norway has also accumulated an oil fund that is expected to help **finance** the welfare state in the future, and for this reason the **aging** of the population seems to be a minor problem compared to other European countries.

In many respects, the development of **social security** in Norway followed the pattern in other parts of Northern Europe, although the coverage of old age and **disability** was relatively late (1936). The first law on **industrial injury** was passed in 1895, inspired by the German example, followed by a law on **unemployment benefits** in 1906, and laws on **sickness benefits** and **maternity benefits** in 1909. After World War II, a law on **family allowances** was adopted, and other laws emphasizing the state's considerable involvement in societal development and coverage were extended and new groups taken into consideration.

The Norwegian system is a universal one, with a high degree of public support and general financing, although employers and employees pay a specific contribution to the state; however, these contributions resemble general income **tax** in many respects. The considerable level of public involvement and general financing, combined with the universal access to welfare-state support, indicate that Norway's system is a Scandinavian welfare state type. In recent years, **pension** reforms have tried to ensure a sufficient level of pension, as well as a balance between decisions on retirement and the level of pension to be received, by making pensions more dependent on the age of retirement. Norway is not a member of the **European Union**, but, in many ways, it still follows the rules and traditions of the organization.

NOTIONAL DEFINED PENSION. A way of combining a **pay-as-you-go pension** system with **rights** dependent on the number of years spent in the **labor market**, and, in principle, also the expected number of years a person will receive a pension. The implication is that if you work longer and retire at a time where projections are that there will be fewer years left to collect the pension, the pension will be higher. **Sweden** and **Italy** have introduced this type of pension system.

NOZICK, ROBERT (1938–2002). Nozick was mainly known for his book *Anarchy, State, and Utopia* (1974), in which he argues for a minimal state. His is mainly an ultraliberal approach to societal development. He inspired the **New Right** and many **liberals** in their thinking about the **welfare state** and its development, for example, the need to reduce the welfare state where possible. His views included the belief that our entitlements should only be based on our own efforts and abilities. This requires individual responsibility and, therefore, less **need** for state intervention. It is thus a highly **individualistic** approach, expecting that when individuals do what they deem to be best, society as a whole will also benefit.

NUDGE. This conveys the idea that it is possible to push people in a positive direction without violating their **right** to make their own choices. This can be in the direction of having a healthier lifestyle, by, for instance, arranging food so that the healthy foods are seen first and using smaller plates so that the portions will be smaller. Another example is having fewer parking places so that people must walk longer distances to reach their destinations. It is sometimes labeled libertarian paternalism, as it combines individual **freedom** to make decisions with a paternalistic approach by trying to push people in a specific direction.

O

OBAMACARE. The popular name of the 2010 **health care** reform in the **United States** known as the Patient Protection and Affordable Care Act. The aim of the reform is to buy insurance for the 44 million uninsured U.S. citizens. It has been heavily opposed by the Republicans, indicating a clear disagreement on the role of the **market** versus the state. Another goal has been to make medication cheaper for elderly citizens, while at the same time curbing the growth in spending. The United States is among the countries in the world spending most on health care. *See also* FINANCING.

OCCUPATIONAL WELFARE. Welfare obtained through one's occupation, that is, from one's employer. It is sometimes labeled "fringe benefits" to distinguish it from traditional wage income, but occupational welfare is broader and can consist of different elements, including **pensions, sickness benefits, health care** coverage, **child care, education,** and training. Part of occupational welfare is supported through the **tax** system (*see also* FISCAL WELFARE).

Occupational welfare can be in addition to the state's welfare; this is the case, for example, when the **welfare state** has a ceiling on economic support in case of sickness or **unemployment** and the employer pays something above this ceiling. Sometimes occupational welfare can be part of a **collective bargaining** agreement. In some countries' welfare-state systems, occupational welfare **financed** through **social security** contributions is the most important element of the welfare state (*see also* BISMARCKIAN MODEL).

Occupational welfare was one of the three elements in the social division of welfare identified by **Richard Titmuss** (1968). The **distribution** of occupational welfare tends to create **inequality** against women and individuals with a low income in the **labor market**.

OLD-AGE PENSION. *See* PENSION.

OPEN METHOD OF COORDINATION (OMC). A method developed in the **European Union (EU)** that attempts to develop a common understanding of a specific policy area, and at the same time accept local and national decisions on how to reach a specific goal. The EU has used the OMC method in such diverse areas as macroeconomic policy, **employment** policy, **social inclusion, pension** reform, the information society, and research and innovation. The process varies, using either soft or hard measures to develop the area. In most areas, a soft method is used, with naming and shaming being the hardest sanction for countries not following the agreed overall goals.

The OMC uses the following four stages:

1. Fixing guidelines
2. Establishing indicators
3. Translating guidelines into national practice and regional practices
4. Monitoring, evaluating, and comparing as a mutual learning process

The aim of the OMC method is to achieve agreement on common aims and goals in the various areas, especially where the competencies of the EU are weak, which is the case in most areas of social and **labor market policy**. The expectation is that agreeing on the goals would and could help in attaining **convergence** among the EU countries, and also be the first step on the path toward a **European social model**.

P

PARETO EQUILIBRIUM. A term used in economics that conveys the idea that when the economy has reached a Pareto equilibrium, no further change can be made without making at least one person less well off. It takes its name from **Vilfredo Pareto**. It is mainly a hypothetical concept, however, indicating that if to improve the situation of one person it is necessary to take something away from another, there may be **normative** issues involved in making the decision of whether to do so. In this way it also supports the idea that existing structures should not be changed when having to reduce the economic situation for some citizens.

PARETO, VILFREDO (1848–1923). Born in Paris, Pareto made numerous contributions to economics, sociology, and political science, although he was trained as an engineer. Within political science, he was especially famous for his work on elites and his acceptance of authoritarian regimes. In economic science, Pareto's main contribution was what has become known as the Pareto principle. In accordance with this concept, redistribution should be continued as long as one person's situation can be made better without making other individuals' situations worse. This is called a Pareto improvement. This criterion can, on the one hand, be seen as a way of using overall resources in such a way that societal welfare is maximized and can thus serve as an argument for optimizing scarce resources. On the other hand, it is a **conservative** criterion in the sense that the existing **distribution** cannot be changed by using this criterion, and, as a result, a very uneven distribution would be continued if this were the starting point. *See also* PARETO EQUILIBRIUM.

PAY-AS-YOU-GO (PAYG) SYSTEM. This term is mainly used to describe a specific type and way of **financing pension** systems. In this system, the expenditure on pensions is financed as a direct **public-sector** expenditure; therefore, it is not part of the current public- or private-sector saving in a country. In a PAYG system, the present generation pays the pension to the pensioner, with the expectation that the next generation will do the same for it.

There are advantages and disadvantages to this type of system. The advantages are that it is possible to make immediate payment of pensions to the pensioners, and the decisions about changes in the level of pensions can be implemented directly. Seen from the pensioner's point of view, a PAYG system can eliminate the risk of **inflation** if the system has an indexation of benefits built in. Such a system can be a way of guaranteeing all pensioners in a society a minimum standard of living, thereby fulfilling one of the goals of a **welfare state**.

The primary disadvantage is that it does not in itself increase resources. The system must be financed from current **taxes**, duties, or contributions. If financed out of taxes and duties, it may have a negative impact on the **labor market** because it creates **disincentives** to work. If financed out of **social security** contributions, it may have a negative effect on competitiveness due to its impact on costs. Finally, it may create a negative **incentive**, keeping people from saving for pension purposes if they are guaranteed a decent living standard as pensioners.

The balance between minimum standards and decent living standards, and redistribution in society and the possible negative impact on savings and work due to different ways of financing pensions, is the central issue for political systems when deciding whether such a system should be used and how to implement it. Many welfare states have moved toward a combined system, attempting to have sufficient financing for the pensions while guaranteeing a minimum income for those who have not been able to save for pension purposes.

PENSION. A periodic payment of income from the state or another source to people who are above a certain age or fulfill specific criteria. Pensions and pension systems differ among the **welfare states**. The pension system can include both an old-age pension (the individual is entitled to a pension upon reaching a certain age) and an **invalidity** pension (an individual is entitled to a pension when certain contingencies occur and the possibility of supporting oneself is not possible). Some countries also provide pensions for those who, for various reasons, for example, psychological causes or social events (a deserted or **divorced** wife without prior work experience), are no longer able to take **care** of themselves. The **right** to a pension can be based on various criteria, including **citizenship, employment (collective agreement** or statutory), or private insurance. A citizen can have the right to a **universal** state pension, or the right can be based on fulfilling certain criteria.

Pensions are often presented as a tier system. The first tier consists of the public pension, the second tier the occupational pension, and the third tier the purely private pension. The mix depends upon the structure of the particular welfare state. Most countries use all of these elements to cope with varied expectations about the living standard after retirement; various positions in the **labor market**, including specific options for the self-employed and coverage for those with only a weak affiliation with the labor market; and variations in society's willingness to support the elderly.

The benefit varies in different situations. In a citizenship model, it is either a flat rate or **means-tested**. Employment-related and private-insurance pensions will typically depend on the individual's previous contributions to the system. The citizenship model will typically involve a **pay-as-you-go (PAYG) system** (either paid by general **taxes** and duties or earmarked contributions), whereas employment and private-related systems will be **funded systems**. The public, through certain tax benefits, may support the private system indirectly. The positive side of a PAYG system is that it is easier to change the real level faster, but it can also have a negative impact if reduced. The main problem relates to how to pay if there is a lack of financial resources in the welfare state. The risk with the funded system is the possibility of the fund not being properly invested or going bankrupt, as was the case with the Maxwell fund in the **United Kingdom**; therefore, in most countries, funded systems are regulated in such a way that those putting in money have strict rules to follow regarding where and how to invest the money. Another problem with a funded system is that if people do not save sufficiently, they will still be in risk of **poverty** when reaching the age of retirement.

Pension systems were developed to cope with the increasing number of elderly who had no income after leaving the labor market, and who were thus unable to take care of themselves. In many welfare states, the elderly have traditionally been looked after by their children and other relatives.

The first pension systems were designed for specific groups in the labor market to give them **incentives** to continue to work, with the clear awareness that their specific working conditions involved high risks of suffering **industrial injury**, followed by the consequence that they would no longer be able to support their **family**. This was especially important at a time when the system depended on the male **breadwinner** model.

In **France**, a right to pensions in cases of invalidity was created for seamen in 1791. This was in response to the growing number of seamen without any income due to invalidity resulting from their work. In 1844, **Belgium** followed with an obligatory invalidity and old-age pension for seamen. In 1854, an invalidity pension for mineworkers was introduced in **Austria**. In 1861, **Italy** established such a system. More generally, old-age pensions were introduced in the late 19th century. In **Denmark**, this was done in 1891, followed by Italy in 1898, and **Germany** in 1899. Most countries established general pension insurance between 1900–1940.

In the past 10 to 15 years, a combination of state universal pension and a funded system have been developed in many countries. To some extent, this has been a response to the growing problem of a higher proportion of elderly individuals. This has sparked a discussion about **dependency ratios**, that is, how many people will have to be paid for by those working in the labor market.

With the average **life expectancy** increasing during the past 30 to 40 years, and a falling birthrate, the proportion of elderly in the population compared to those of working age has been growing. It remains to be seen if this is a large economic problem, and that will depend upon, among other things, general economic growth. In several countries, the age of retirement has been increased as a way of coping with the number of years for which pensions will have to be paid. Recent years have seen dramatic changes in pension systems in most welfare states, particularly large increases in the age when one can receive a pension, making this dependent on life expectancy and, to a larger degree, upon earned income while in the labor market. This also indicates that incremental change can lead to a stronger deviation from the original path, and in the case of the pension system, this has led to a higher reliance on **occupational welfare** and less dependence on state-financed and subsidized welfare. Changes also seem to imply international learning effects as many of the changes seem to move—with national variations—in the same direction (*see also* CONVERGENCE).

The generosity of public pensions varies among the welfare states, and they are generally most generous in the universal welfare states. Aside from pensions, many elderly receive other forms of support, which means that comparing only the level of pensions would result in an incorrect impression of the living standard for pensioners in various welfare states.

In most countries, pensions are among those benefits that are most strongly supported by the electorate. There are two reasons for this: 1) The elderly are seen as **deserving**, and 2) most people expect to need a pension themselves when they reach the age of retirement. *See also* DEFINED BENEFIT PLAN; DEFINED CONTRIBUTION PLAN; EARNINGS-RELATED BENEFITS; FLAT-RATE PENSION; GENDER; SUPPLEMENTARY PENSIONS.

PERMANENT EMERGENT WELFARE STATE MODEL. A description of welfare regimes in the Sub-Saharan area that, due to historical traditions, colonialism, lack of **democracy**, and slow economic development, are constantly updating and developing their **welfare-state** model. This does not imply that all countries have the same type. Rather, it suggests that continuous changes in different elements in welfare states are enacted and changed.

PERSONAL SOCIAL SERVICES. Services individuals receive from the **welfare state** outside the scope of **health, housing, education,** and **social security.** They can take the form of home help for the elderly, homes for the elderly, housing for the **homeless,** or **child care.** They can also include **social work** for an individual person. These services are directed at both groups and individuals. Personal social services are **benefits in-kind** instead of **benefits in cash.**

The importance of personal social services varies among the different welfare-state models. The more **universal** models have more of this built into the system than those models that rely more on the **market** or **families.** Recent experiences have shown that even in state-**financed** systems, delivery through the market has been more profound, including the use of various types of **vouchers.** Measuring quality in personal social services is difficult due to the extent of individual **needs** to be covered.

PLURALISM. A political philosophy emphasizing the need for different groups in society to be actively engaged in and have the ability to participate in society's development. It is felt that different groups being actively involved will keep **democracy** alive by not leaving the decision making solely to a limited power elite. In pluralist thinking, power will not only be in the hands of the state, but also held by different groups in society, which can be **churches, nongovernmental organizations,** and so forth. This can also be a value position arguing for diversity and inclusion of many different actors in the decision-making process.

Critics of pluralist thinking argue that, in reality, there is **inequality** in access to the decision-making process, due to social **segregation** and differences in economic and political **capabilities.** This is further accentuated by the fact that access to the media plays an increasing role in decision making. Thus, those who have access to or own the media will be better able to participate in the democracy. Recent years have seen development in **social services** in **health care,** and **care** for children is also seen as part of the social investment state, as well as a way of supporting possibilities of combining work and **family** life.

POLAND. Despite its close connection with **Germany** and **Austria,** Poland was a latecomer to the development of **social security** programs. In 1889, an **industrial injury** insurance system was introduced in the part of Poland occupied by Austria. The slower rate of industrial development in Poland seems to explain why this was so, combined with the fact that Poland has been occupied by other countries several times. It was only after World War I that it again became an independent country. After independence, laws were adopted covering **sickness** and **maternity** in 1920, **unemployment** in 1924, and old age and **disability** in 1927. After World War II, the system was strongly influenced by the **Union of Soviet Socialist Republics**. Thus, there was considerable state responsibility for the support, including, among other things, a commitment to **employment** for everyone. At that time, the system resembled the **communist welfare-state** system. The system in Poland relies heavily on wage-related benefits, without a clear connection between what has been paid in and the benefits to be received.

After the changes in Eastern Europe in the 1980s, the system has also been altered, and one of the main problems has been how to **finance** these changes. This includes how to ensure the purchasing power of those receiving benefits from the state, as well as how to administer the system. It is still highly centralized and influenced by the **labor market** partners, primarily **trade unions**. This seems to be a consequence of the fact that the changes in the 1980s began with an uprising of workers, who then started a new movement (Solidarity).

Family allowances, which are **means-tested**, and **health care** are now a **universal** system, but the bulk of the support is a **social insurance**-based system, although in most areas with some state guarantee. In 1999, a two-tier **pension** system was enacted, in which the first tier's obligatory payment to a pension fund is coupled in the second tier with individual accounts. The system today thus greatly resembles a **continental** and **conservative model**. Like most Eastern European countries, Poland is a member of the **European Union (EU)**. Recent years have seen reform in the pension system and the abolition of the **early retirement** system.

POLARIZATION. The widening of social and economic differences between groups of people in society, for example, between social **classes** and between men and women. With increasing **inequality** in some countries, it is argued that there is also increased polarization, which can then cause an increase in crime. Polarization due to **ethnic** differences has also been witnessed in several **welfare states**.

POOR LAWS. A common term for policies that aim to relieve individuals from **poverty** and destitution. The first law was the Poor Law of 1388, enacted in the **United Kingdom**. It established that the local area was responsible for providing assistance to individuals. This law was changed in 1834 to make it more general and establish a more common level of support throughout the country. At the same time, workhouses were established, in which those needing benefits had to work, but conditions in these facilities were such that only a few individuals applied for benefits.

In many countries, Poor Laws distinguished between the **deserving and undeserving** poor. They made it relatively easy to receive assistance, albeit with a few, hard conditions when one was deserving (although the benefits were low), but the undeserving in the United Kingdom were often forced to work hard in workhouses. The expectation was that this would reduce the number of individuals applying for assistance.

Poor Laws were later developed into **social assistance** schemes, because after the Industrial Revolution, Poor Laws were no longer able to cover the new risks, and it was seen as too harsh to require that those in **need** should do hard physical labor in workhouses. Yet, the legacy of the Poor Laws system can still be witnessed in many countries. *See also* ACTIVE LABOR MARKET POLICY (ALMP).

PORTUGAL. Portugal's system belongs to what has been labeled the **Southern European welfare state model.** It is based on the **family** and family structure, although participation in the **labor market** and coverage thereafter was in its historical development and is still important. In 1913, a law covering **industrial injury** was passed, followed in 1935 by laws on **pensions, sickness benefits**, and **maternity benefits**. In 1942, a law on **family allowances** was enacted. Only after the so-called Flower Revolution in 1974 was a law on **unemployment benefits** passed. The long period of dictatorship and fascist rule from 1932–1974 and the poor economic situation are major reasons for the late development of **social policy**.

Following the transition from dictatorship to **democracy** after the revolution, a rapid development of the social system took place in the 1980s and 1990s. During this period, Portugal was the country in the **European Union (EU)** with the fastest growth in **public-sector** expenditures for social policy. The main element of the policy is still participation in the labor market. Pensions are the exception; those not covered by the labor market are covered by a state subsidy for a minimum pension. The pensions are low and **means-tested**. Thus, the system is still relatively ungenerous, although Portugal is required to fulfill a EU recommendation for a guaranteed minimum income for all citizens. Since the **financial crisis** in 2008, the Portuguese **welfare state** has been witnessing strong cuts in public-sector spending, including the abolition of the **early retirement** benefit and changes in the pension system.

POSITIVE ANALYSIS. This describes a situation in completely objective terms, without any **normative** judgments. Positive analysis answers such questions as the following: What is the scale of **unemployment**? What will happen if x, y, or z happens? These are central questions for the analysis. This is in contrast to **normative analysis**. Positive analysis can thus help decision makers find the most effective **social policy** interventions, for example, in **active labor market policy (ALMP)**; however, recent years have seen a tendency in the area of **health care** and ALMP to use scarce resources as best as possible by use of **evidence**-based policy.

POSITIVE DISCRIMINATION. Discrimination not against, but in favor of, certain disadvantaged groups. It may consider, for example, how to help women and excluded minorities. Positive discrimination can thus help ensure that weaker groups get a better position in society than would otherwise be the case. *See also* AFFIRMATIVE ACTION.

POST-FORDISM. This refers to the production system that followed the mass production system first introduced by Henry Ford. The post-Fordist production types are characterized by flexibility in the **labor market**, production, and regulation. It can also be argued that post-Fordist systems are characterized by less protection of the workers due to the higher degree of flexibility in the labor market; therefore, jobs are less secure. This has raised the issue of **flexicurity**.

POVERTY. An old concept in **social policy** and **welfare-state** analysis. Many of the original social policy measures were aimed at helping the poor. At that time, and as is still the case today, the concept seems to encompass both **deserving and undeserving** people living in poverty. The deserving were the decent poor who had been residing in an area and tried as best as they could to take **care** of themselves. They were incapable of doing so because of, for example, mental or physical **disabilities**. On the other hand, the undeserving were those supposedly living in poverty because they were shiftless and lazy.

The first attempt to measure poverty was the research done by **B. Seebohm Rowntree**. He only tried to analyze the absolute level of poverty by focusing on food; therefore, he did not include problems that—at least in contemporary societies—should also be considered, for instance, access to **services** and **integration** into society.

The European Commission has, in line with those original thoughts, presented poverty as being when individuals or **families** have such limited resources that they are excluded from the minimum acceptable way of life of the member state in which they live. According to this definition, poverty is not only an economic aspect, although it is central, it also refers to the entire debate about **social inclusion** or **social exclusion**.

However, poverty is a concept with many different definitions, some of which have led to a focus on **equality** instead. The two main types of poverty are absolute and relative. **Absolute poverty** refers to the situation in which the individual (or family) does not have access to a certain level of goods and services. An absolute poverty line is therefore defined by a certain basket of goods multiplied by the prices of those goods. It could be supplemented by a certain percentage to cover items not included in the basket (e.g., nonfood items) or for inefficiency when buying goods.

Relative poverty takes into account the relative wealth of society. Hence, it refers to what is deemed a decent standard of living. A relative poverty line could therefore be a certain percentage of the average or median income in a society. The European Union Commission, for example, uses 60 percent of the median income per person after **tax** as its relative poverty line. In this example, the size of the family is taken into consideration. The use of relative poverty lines indicates that a person who is poor in a given society may not be so when compared to the living standards of other countries.

The advantage of using a relative line is that it is a stable measurement throughout time, and it provides a better possibility of comparing poverty levels among countries, although the level will vary depending on the level of income in a society. Still, many problems arise when attempting to compare the level of poverty in a given year, including the choice of poverty line, family size, the difference between savers and spenders, purchasing power parities between countries, and the impact of the **public sector**. Some people, for example, may be living in poverty when only taking their income as a point of reference, but due to **benefits in-kind** from the public sector, they have a decent standard of living. A possible relatively high living standard can also be due to wealth accrued earlier in life. These problems with measurement show that data should be interpreted with caution.

Two explanations of poverty that are frequently referred to are the structural and the industrial. The structural explanation takes the personal situation as a starting point, for example, the fact that some people are born poor or born to become poor. This type of explanation also points to **unemployment** and **segmentation of the labor market** as having an impact on poverty and its level. In addition, **inflation** is included as a factor, and those analyzing poverty from a structural point of view recommend as policy action creating jobs and income guarantees for those who are not covered; however, in countries with low level of wages, for some groups, it can be argued that some are living in poverty.

The industrial explanation looks at the supply side of the **labor market** and changes in industrial structures. Furthermore, it examines **human capital** and how this can have an impact on the individual's chances of living in poverty. The industrial explanation suggests that **education** and industrial policy, combined with labor market flexibility, are the main measures that should be used to combat poverty.

Many different suggestions have been made to reduce poverty, but the choice is a **normative** one. In recent years, a movement has arisen that reduces emphasis on poverty and reinforces emphasis on social exclusion. This is because social exclusion and looking at the more vulnerable in society provide a broader focus, and it seems to be less **stigmatizing** to talk about the "socially excluded" than about those living in "poverty." Still, policies to avoid and/or reduce poverty are central in many countries, including how to **prevent** people from living in poverty. *See also* POOR LAWS; POVERTY TRAP.

POVERTY TRAP. This term refers to the situation in which people living in **poverty** have no or only a limited chance of improving their economic position. This will be the case if an increase in income fully reduces the benefits received from the state. In most cases, the poverty trap is not only the result of a reduction in social benefits, but of a combination of changes in benefits, **taxes**, and contributions to be paid out of increased income. The poor will therefore have difficulty in improving their situation without having a big increase in their wage income so that they can both enjoy a higher disposable net income and cope with the reduction in social benefits.

PRECARIAT. This is related to factors that may or actually do reduce individuals' resources in such a way that they become **marginalized** or **socially excluded** in a society despite having a job and earning an income in the **labor market**. Being in a precarious situation is, for example, when a person having a job only earns an income below the **poverty** line and can thus be described as being in the precariat. This is also associated with what is known as the **working poor**.

PRESSURE GROUPS. Organized groups of people with the purpose of achieving certain goals. In **welfare-state** analysis, they are mainly seen as groups that put pressure on political decision makers to expand certain areas of the **public sector**. Some pressure groups want better conditions for the unemployed, some for the disabled, and so forth. It has been argued that the existence of these groups has had an impact on the **growth of the public sector**.

Even if in theory it seems natural that pressure groups have an impact on the growth of the public sector, this is not really supported by empirical **evidence**, at least not when looking at developments on the macro level. Yet, it would be naive to ignore the possible impact of pressure groups, because even though they only promote one or a few issues, which, in relation to total expenditures may seem small, if many small changes in an upward direction are made, there will be an overall higher level of public-sector spending.

At the same time, these groups may be driven by a specific knowledge of **need** in certain areas because, for example, one of their **family** members needs specific treatment. Pressure groups can, thus, be a way of providing inputs into political decision making. Many individuals who are active in pressure groups are also active in **nongovernmental organizations** and **voluntary work**. *See also* INTEREST GROUPS; TRADE UNION.

PREVENTION. The process or act of preventing something from happening or reducing the risk of some social event becoming worse. In **social policy**, prevention is discussed to determine whether something can be avoided. If a preventive measure is taken, then curative measures do not have to be taken. Finally, prevention can involve less damage and less pressure on **public-sector** expenditure if the risk of a social **contingency** occurring is reduced by the intervention.

Prevention can include favorable working conditions, which will reduce the number of **industrial injuries**, as well as good **education** and programs, which will decrease the possibility of **social exclusion** and **poverty**. Prevention can include early **health** checks that make it possible to find out if people are at risk of becoming sick at an early stage, instead of waiting until they fall ill. Prevention can also be used to avoid negative **social inheritance** by being aware of the impact of different types of continuous **need** for public support and helping children, especially, lead better lives.

Prevention can be justified on the grounds that it is better to prevent than repair, and that it may be cheaper to prevent damage at an early stage than at a later stage. On the other hand, prevention may also be costly, because it involves use of money to make the necessary search for those who may, if certain conditions persist, be the victims of a social event. *See also* PRIMARY CARE.

PRIMARY CARE. A form of **health care** that does not require that individuals go to a hospital to be treated for sickness. Primary care includes general practitioners, as well as district nurses and small clinics outside the hospital system. The distinction may sometimes be unclear, but the main distinguishing factor is how health care is provided. Primary care is often cheaper than care at a later stage because the problem is treated earlier. In many countries, general practitioners also do the first screening for the **need** for treatment at a hospital. *See also* PREVENTION.

PRINCIPAL-AGENT THEORY. A theory used to describe the relationship between two individuals, institutions, or actors. One issue is that the principal wants a certain amount of work or services provided and wants the agent to deliver this. The problem for the principal is that it is not always possible to know exactly what the agent can deliver, or the right price or size of support that can be delivered. The agent might withhold information, or, for example, due to a professional viewpoint, might want to deliver a kind of **service** other than what the principal is willing to pay for. When having a purchaser/provider split in the delivery of welfare, this is an important aspect to include to ensure that society gets the best value for its money.

PRIVATIZATION. The takeover of a publicly provided and delivered good or **service** by the **market**. The **New Right** has been one of the most outspoken proponents of privatization of the **public sector**. The argument has been that without clear profit goals in the public sector, public production leads to inefficient delivery, whereas private provision would optimize resource allocation. It has been further argued that privatization is a major prerequisite for lowering **taxes** and duties. Arguments against privatization include the fact that it can result in **market failure**, and that there may be a hindrance to some people getting the good if it is in the hands of a profit-maximizing private company.

Despite the prevalent rhetoric in many countries, privatization has mainly been carried out on a large scale in such **liberal welfare states** as the **United Kingdom**. Most other welfare states have changed parts of the delivery system but maintained a considerable public-sector involvement, directly or indirectly. **Marketization** has also been interpreted as a kind of privatization, but marketization uses elements from market systems, among which is competition between providers, to increase the pressure on producers to deliver more efficiently. This is sometimes combined with the use of **vouchers**. The use of private and public delivery, combined with variations in **financing**, indicates that the distinction between public and private delivery in relation to welfare-state services may become less useful.

PROGRESSIVE TAXATION. A method whereby the level of **taxes** paid results in a more equal **distribution**, because those with higher incomes pay more. Progressive taxation is most often connected to the income tax system, but it can also be applied to value-added taxes and other duties if they are imposed in such a way that those with higher incomes pay both absolutely and relatively more than those with lower incomes. *See also* PROPORTIONAL TAXATION.

PROPORTIONAL TAXATION. A method whereby the **taxes** paid as a fraction of income remain constant as income rises. Thus, if the level is 30 percent, then everyone will pay that proportion in taxes regardless of the size of income; however, proportional taxation may involve at least some degree of progression if it is combined with a threshold before paying tax. *See also* PROGRESSIVE TAXATION.

PUBLIC CHOICE. This term can be defined as was done by Dennis C. Mueller (*Public Choice III*, 2003) as the "economic study of nonmarket decision making, or simply the application of economics to political science." The assumption of this concept is that the individual is a rational **utility** maximizer. James Buchanan (*The Political Economy of the Welfare State*, 1988) writes that it "essentially takes the tools and methods approach that have been developed to quite sophisticated analytical levels in economic theory and applies these tools and methods to the political or **governmental** sectors, to politics, to the public economy."

Public choice theory is concerned with the **growth of the public sector** and the **welfare state**. This growth has often been seen as a consequence of the impact of the **bureaucracy** and **pressure groups** on the decision-making process. The public choice theorist's argument is that although each individual decision may be rational, the overall result is irrational and leads to an overexpansion of the **public sector** because there is an asymmetry between those paying for the expenditures and those receiving the benefits. Those receiving will be few and those paying many; therefore, pressure from the few will lead to higher expenditures than would otherwise exist. Furthermore, according to public choice theory, the possibility of forming coalitions and gaining a majority leads to a higher level of expenditure than would otherwise be expected.

Public choice theorists have especially criticized the lack of a **market** mechanism within the public sector and analyzed preference aggregation, party competition, **interest groups,** and bureaucracy. They also question the concept of **market failure**, pointing out that nonmarket failure (**government failure**) will also occur. Their criticisms include that it is difficult to define and measure the output of the public sector, including the lack of a profit goal. The public sector often resembles a monopoly, with its consequences for prices and production. In addition, there is no clear connection between costs and revenues. Public choice theory has compared the public sector with the Leviathan monster from the Bible, arguing that the public sector would swallow up the private sector.

During the last 20 to 30 years, the development of the welfare state in many countries has been influenced by the public choice theory argument about the consequences for the private sector of a growing public sector. The argument has been used to exert pressure on decision makers to reduce the growth of the public sector and, in some instances, even to reduce the level of spending. *See also* RATIONAL CHOICE THEORY.

PUBLIC GOODS. Those goods that one person's use of does not diminish another person's use of. They can be consumed collectively (e.g., fire brigade, military, foreign policy) or individually (e.g., air, beaches, parks, roads). In **welfare-state** analysis, public goods have been used as an argument for state intervention because, in many areas, there is not a **market** to deal with the delivery of public goods. Among the characteristics of public goods is that it is not possible to establish a price because one person's use of the good does not reduce another person's use of the good; therefore, a public good cannot be sold on the market. **Health care** can be sold on the market, but a public system is necessary, because otherwise not everyone would have access to necessary treatment. When everyone has access to a **service**, it is a public good, since one person's use of it does not reduce others' possibility of using it—except in such rare circumstances as transplantation, where a lack of donors may reduce others' possibility of using that specific good.

Historically, many systems developed as a response to the fact that the market, left to itself, did not provide sufficient **care**. Thus, state systems in the areas of **industrial injuries**, **social assistance**, and **unemployment benefits**, among others, were developed even if they were not, in a strict sense, public goods.

Most writers on these issues, including **Adam Smith**, agree that the **public sector** should provide public goods, but they disagree about what exactly can be defined as public goods. Borderline cases have been discussed, for example, where the market may provide goods, but consumers do not have the possibility of paying for them. This is often the case for people with handicaps. Another instance is where the goods supplied by the public sector make it possible for many individuals to have access to certain remedies. Because different individuals can use these throughout time, they resemble a public good, without being so in the definition's purest sense. A related concept is **merit goods**.

Public goods may change throughout time, as is the case, for example, with lighthouses. Even when they change throughout time, analysis shows that some goods will not be provided by the market, and therefore can only be provided by state intervention. This has been the reason for public-sector intervention in specific areas. Some instances include help remedies for people with disabilities and welfare technology for the elderly.

In the wake of the debate on the impact of **globalization**, it has been argued that global public goods also exist in relation to environmental issues, security, and financial-market stability. Understood in this way, public goods can be seen at the local, regional, national, supranational, and global levels.

PUBLIC SECTOR. The short term for activities delivered and/or **financed** by the **welfare state**. If an activity is financed to at least 50 percent of the cost, it should be included in the public sector in the national accounts even if delivered by a private company. Thus, the boundary between the public and private sectors is less clear than often portrayed, a main reason being that to provide the necessary **service**, the welfare state often uses private firms. *See also* PUBLIC WELFARE.

PUBLIC WELFARE. Welfare delivered by the **public sector**. Public welfare was one of the three ways in which, according to **Richard Titmuss**, welfare could be delivered. It includes most of the elements often studied in the analysis of **welfare states**, among them **care** of dependent individuals and other **services** and **benefits in-kind** and **benefits in cash**. Public welfare is often most dominant in countries following the **Scandinavian welfare states model**; it is less prevalent in, for example, the **Southern European welfare state model**. Public welfare is relatively well-described in international statistics, and less so in **occupational welfare** and **fiscal welfare**. *See also* SOCIAL DIVISION OF WELFARE.

Q

QALY. The quality-adjusted life year (QALY) is a measurement of the quality and quantity of life. It is used when assessing which intervention gives the greatest increase in QALY for the least cost. QALY is based on the number of years of life that would be added by a **health** activity. Each year in perfect health is given the value of one. The value is zero for being dead. A year with, for example, some kind of **disability** will have a value above zero but below one. It is criticized from an ethical point of view because its use, when deciding interventions, will **discriminate** against the elderly and/or people with disabilities. On the other hand, when comparing two types of intervention, it can be used to decide which produces the greatest gain.

QUALITATIVE ANALYSIS. A method of analysis that is not based on precise quantitative measurement. Methods used include interviews, which try to get information on a specific subject from the informant. The interviews can be conducted in a variety of ways. Observation of behavior and case-based analysis can also be utilized.

QUALITY OF LIFE. A concept that refers to the **well-being** of individuals and societies. Quality of life is typically measured by such indicators as income, wealth, and **employment**; however, monetary and nonmonetary aspects are often included, as is also the case with **social indicators**. The Organization for Economic Cooperation and Development measures the quality of life in their study called "How's Life" (www.oecd.org/statistics/howslife .htm). The measurements also include issues on environment, civic engagement, and so forth.

QUASI-MARKETS. A **market** that is neither fully private nor fully public in its provision of goods. It is a system of delivering goods and **services** that takes elements from a "normal" market and combines them with **public-sector** intervention. These markets also differ in that providers do not necessarily have a profit motive, and consumers do not necessarily have money power, but rather power in the form of **vouchers** or **rights** to treatment or choice between various providers.

The development of quasi-markets has been seen as a way of breaking the state monopoly without fully reducing the possibility of state intervention. They can combine more effective provision of goods and services with equal access; however, whether this is the case depends on the concrete example and structure of the quasi-markets. Equal access and **equality** seem possible to achieve in the area of hospitals, whereas they seem less likely to occur in primary **education**.

R

RACISM. Discrimination against another racial group in a society, which can occur on the grounds of race, religion, or **ethnicity**. Direct discrimination is outright exclusion of certain racial groups from participation in, among other things, the **labor market** or the **educational** system. Indirect discrimination is nonlegislative exclusion from participation in certain social activities, for example, an employer avoiding employing people of a specific race. Racism can be difficult to measure and evaluate, except in the clearest cases; for example, employers may argue that they have simply employed the most qualified individuals. With the increase in **migration** between countries, different types of racism and/or discrimination against individuals who come from other countries have increased in many countries. *See also* MARGINALIZATION; SOCIAL EXCLUSION.

RATIONAL CHOICE THEORY. A theory that recognizes the individual's behavior when taking part in collective activity to obtain a certain goal. Rational choice theory is based on an economic understanding of **rationality**. Thus, rational choice is usually understood as a conscious and consistent choice that maximizes the decision maker's **utility**. In contradiction to traditional economic theory, however, it focuses not on the individual alone, but on individuals acting collectively. Rational choice theory is used in economic, social, and political analyses, for instance, those focusing on **family** consumption patterns or voting behavior. *See also* PUBLIC CHOICE.

RATIONALITY. In its basic form, rationality is an argument based on reason or logic, that is, conclusions, positions, or beliefs reached on the basis of conscious and consistent reasoning or logic. The understanding of rationality differs greatly within the social sciences. In traditional economic theory, an individual behaving rationally does so on the basis of a conscious and consistent logic to maximize his or her benefit. This understanding of rationality can be termed *goal-oriented rationality*. In sociology, the German **Max Weber** distinguished between four types of rationality, each characterized by a specific form of action (behavior):

1. Goal-oriented action, which, as mentioned, is identical to the common economic understanding of rationality and rational behavior. Furthermore, Weber added, it is perhaps the most dominant form of rationality in modern Western societies. It is part and parcel of capitalistic **markets** and **bureaucratic** organizations.
2. Value-oriented action, where the individual acts on the basis of a belief in a certain way of judging the action's inherent value, that is, evaluating actions on grounds of ethics. Like goal-oriented action, value-oriented action is an individual form of rationality. The judgments are made by individuals, but on grounds of socialization and interaction with other human beings.
3. Affectual action, that is, action based on feelings.
4. Traditional action, that is, action based on identification with customs and traditions. It is a counterpoise to types 2 and 3. This is traditional (i.e., premodern) rationality threatened with erosion by types 2 and 3. Despite this tendency to erode, traditional action is vital in theory, as well as in practice. It is a tool to explain, among other things, the social actions of human beings, **solidarity**, and **community**.

Some economic theorists argue that rational behavior can include such nonegoistic traits as sympathy, making possible an individual or collective **distribution** of wealth from the rich to the poor. It has also been argued that individuals cannot choose on a one-dimensional scale, making a ranking of choices impossible—and possibly implying the existence of what has been labeled "rational fools." Even if this is so, rationality is still a core concept in many economic **welfare-state** analyses; however, it is challenged by other approaches, namely behavioral economics and positive psychology.

Finally, it must be noted that individual rational choice does not necessarily imply an optimal societal outcome. This is due to the existence of **market failure**, where an individual's decision may be rational for the individual person, but may at the same time create disadvantages for other individuals, for example, pollution.

RAWLS, JOHN (1921–2002). Rawls was an American philosopher whose main contribution was his widely used and discussed book *A Theory of Justice*, published in 1972, in which he outlines and discusses many of the central concepts relevant to the analysis of **distribution**, including **equality** and **justice**—and, significantly, which principles should be used when defining and interpreting these concepts. Rawls's starting point is that, in all societies, it is possible to agree on some basic principles. These will be agreed upon before one knows his or her situation in the given society, which is decided behind the "veil of ignorance." This leads to the maximin principle, according to which the individual will describe at least what is a minimum acceptable living standard and acceptable distribution in a society. In the modern **welfare state**, one could argue that this principle lies indirectly behind decisions about benefits for handicapped or disabled individuals, because no one knows whether he or she will become disabled.

Rawls defines two basic principles. The first is that each person is to have an equal **right** to the most extensive total system of equal basic liberties compatible with a similar system of liberty for all. The second is that social and economic **inequalities** are to be arranged so that they are both, a) to the greatest benefit of the least advantaged, consistent with the just savings principle, and b) attached to offices and positions open to all under conditions of fair equality of opportunity (*A Theory of Justice*, 1972). These principles indirectly imply that liberty comes before equality, and, in this sense, Rawls's way of thinking seems to be in line with the **liberal** position on welfare-state analysis.

Criticism of Rawls's theory has focused on the conflict between liberty and equality, but also on the theory's indirect acceptance of an unjust distribution. One reason the distribution of income in Rawls's theory may end as being very unequal is that most individuals behind the veil of ignorance may expect to be those with the highest income. In this case, they will not redistribute a lot to those unfortunate ones who end up being poor. Differences in risk aversion will make it difficult to get the preferences for the individuals to **converge**, making it impossible to come to any conclusion about a just distribution.

Despite these criticisms, Rawls's book has made an outstanding contribution to the debate about justice, which is a central part of the analysis of the welfare state and the development of welfare societies. Rawls's understanding of justice may also be regarded as a reason why, in most welfare states, the support for **health care**, including hospitals, is often higher than for other welfare measures, as most people do not know whether they are going to **need** treatment, so they will prefer to have a good system in place.

REFLEXIVITY. This describes a situation in which each individual is confronted with a variety of risks in the postmodern society. Each individual will then have to constantly reflect on the impact of these risks and make choices based thereon, not only in relation to daily life, but also concerning long-term decisions, for example, living standards in retirement.

REPLACEMENT RATES. Rates that result from the calculation of benefits for a receiver of different kinds of benefits as a percentage of wages. They are often calculated in relation to the **average production worker** or other de-fined income levels. The level of replacement rates can be compared between countries and is often used as an indicator of the generosity of the various **welfare states**. They can be calculated before and after **tax**. Replacement rates are generally higher in countries that follow the **Scandinavian welfare state model**. In most countries, in the wake of the **financial crisis** in 2008, there has been a decline in replacement rates.

REPUBLIC OF KOREA. *See* KOREA, REPUBLIC OF.

RESIDENTIAL CARE. Care of individuals that takes place in some kind of residential area. It can be homes for the elderly, certain handicapped groups, or certain groups not well-**integrated** into society. **Universal welfare states** seem to have more public residential care, whereas in other welfare-state types, residential care is less developed, and more emphasis is placed on the role of the **family**. Whether residential care or care in the individual's own home is the best is contested.

RESIDUAL WELFARE STATE. A state characterized by the individual only receiving benefits if all other possible support has been exhausted. It is, in this sense, connected with the concept of **subsidiarity**. In a residual welfare state, support will only be provided as a safety net for those who otherwise would not be able to take **care** of themselves, and where the **family** is also not able to do so. In this model, private and **market**-based solutions are preferred to state solutions. The majority of countries that employ it are in Southern Europe; however, even here, it must be borne in mind that no country follows the typical pattern to the letter. Many countries developing **welfare states** will, for economic reasons, often have to start with a more re-sidual approach and then gradually move toward a more **universal** one with a higher level of coverage. Thus, a country with a residual welfare system does not have to maintain it in the long run.

RETIREMENT AGE. *See* STATUTORY RETIREMENT AGE.

RETRENCHMENT. This concept tries to describe the possible cutbacks and changes in **welfare states**, mainly due to financial pressure, as in the wake of the **financial crisis, demographic** changes, and, in the late 1980s and early 1990s, and again following 2008, persistently high levels of **un-employment**. In most countries, the relatively high level of support for welfare-state programs has made it difficult to change popular welfare-state initiatives. Historical developments in spending do not indicate that retrenchment on the overall level has taken place. This does not imply that certain areas have not been changed. Still, many systems retain the same structure as when they were started.

RIGHTS. What the individual/**family** has in certain situations, as defined in each **welfare state**. The rights may be based on **citizenship**; however, they may also be based upon previous contributions. They may depend upon whether a certain **contingency** arises, for example, **unemployment**, sickness, maternity, or retirement, but may also depend upon income and wealth, that is, being **means-tested**. How rights give rise to benefits varies from one welfare state to another and largely depends on the historical structure and development of the welfare state. In insurance-based systems, rights are often defined in the **social insurance** system, but they can have the same effects and implications as those defined in more state-organized systems. *See also* ENTITLEMENTS.

RISK SOCIETY. This concept stems especially from Ulrich Beck's book of the same name, published in 1986. It argues that in modern societies, new types of risk arise that the individual will have to try to cope with. This also implies a **need** for many to try to find ways of ensuring a higher degree of safety in relation to economic and other issues.

ROMANIA. Romania is a relative newcomer to the **European Union (EU)**, only joining in 2007. It has more than 20 million inhabitants. The country is a former Eastern European command economy, with only limited development of the welfare system under **communism**. Still, the first system relating to old-age **pension** was brought into being in 1912, and, in the same year, an **industrial-injury** scheme was implemented. This was followed by **sickness benefits** in 1930, **family** benefits in 1950, and **unemployment benefits** in 1991. With the exception of family benefits, which are **universal**, the system is a **social insurance**-based system.

Like other countries in Eastern Europe, there have been dramatic changes since 1990. Furthermore, there has been a **need** for a reduction in spending after the **financial crisis** in 2008. In Romania, this has, among other things, implied a change in the generosity of the pension system to reduce the **public-sector** deficit. Many people from Romania are using the free movement of workers in the EU to gain jobs due to the high level of **unemployment**.

ROWNTREE, B. SEEBOHM (1871–1954). Rowntree was a social scientist from the **United Kingdom**. He was the first to attempt to measure **poverty** by trying to determine the necessary goods for a **family** so that its **basic needs**

were covered. In his study on poverty (1901), conducted in York, England, in 1899, he based his views of the level of expenditure on the "necessary nutrients at the lowest cost possible." At that time, this chiefly meant bread and items used to make porridge and so forth. He added an allowance for clothes, **housing**, and heating. This could be described as the necessary basket of goods to survive. The method is problematic in many ways, as it is difficult to assess what is necessary for a family, but it represented an effort to measure poverty based on **needs** instead of what (especially later on) have been seen as the main methods—percentages of average income.

RUSSIA. Russia is the largest part of the former **Union of Soviet Socialist Republics (USSR)**. It can therefore be difficult to establish when the first laws were enacted, as some of them come from the period of the USSR, and some from pre-Soviet times, when the country was also called Russia. Most of the laws have been amended since the dissolution of the USSR.

The first law in relation to old-age **pensions** was established in 1922, but, in Russia, **industrial injury** was established as the first area to be covered in 1903, followed by sickness and maternity in 1912, with **family allowances** being addressed last, in 1944. After that, the system was, thus, a **communist** type, where obligatory work and low **housing** prices were the main ingredients.

The present-day system is largely a **social insurance** system, although with a high degree of mandatory elements, with a combination of **financing** from employers and the state. As in most countries, family allowance is a **universal** system financed out of general **taxation**. The level of benefits is relatively low due to the economic problems the country is facing.

S

SAFETY NET. This refers to the last level of various types of support that ensure a decent standard of living, and also for integrating people into society. The safety net may consist of various levels of economic and other types of support, and the holes in the net may be of differing sizes, implying that, in some countries, the risk of falling through the net is greater than in others. **Social assistance** is often the last element in the welfare systems.

SAVINGS. The portion of a person's earned income that is not spent during a year. Savings can, in principle, be both negative and positive. Negative savings mean that the individual has spent more than he or she has earned and therefore needs to take out a loan. Positive savings mean that not all the income has been spent. Most people have negative savings when they are young (during their **education**, when they are establishing a **family**), and then positive savings until retirement, when the savings again turn negative (using up the money one cannot take along).

In relation to **welfare-state** analysis, savings have been important in connection with **pensions**, because many people put money aside during their years in the **labor market** so they can have a good pension. These kinds of savings are often supported by **tax** expenditures. The relationship between welfare spending and **incentives** to save is often debated. One argument is that if the welfare state provides benefits that are too high, then people will not have incentives to save. It is also argued that the same result will occur as the consequence of a high level of income tax, including taxes on interest income. On the other hand, it is maintained that the individual's preferences are very diverse, and that for this reason, the impact on savings of various types of welfare benefits and taxes is apparently not very high.

The ability to save is related to the overall income, implying that chiefly high income earners will be able to save. Saving for pension purposes is, in several welfare systems, either obligatory through state-decided social contributions, or as part of **collective agreements**. This saving for pensions is, thus, something that everyone in the **labor market** will be doing. The negative impact of this is that those outside the labor market, in more unstable jobs and with high levels of **unemployment**, will often have fewer options and a decreased ability to save money, and these individuals might even be forced to use the savings already accrued; however, savings for pension purposes is often done in pension schemes or funds where the individual will only be able to use the money after having reached the age of retirement.

SCANDINAVIAN WELFARE STATE MODEL. This model is characterized by an all-encompassing nature and high reliance on state intervention in society, referring to **Denmark, Norway,** and **Sweden.** It is sometimes described as the Nordic welfare model, thus including such countries as **Finland** and Iceland. It also involves less reliance on the **market** as the main provider of **social security.** Access to, and **rights** to, social security benefits are mainly a consequence of being a citizen of the country one is living in. The model also involves a higher and more frequent use of general **taxes** and duties as a way of **financing** the **welfare state.** Its greater reliance on state intervention indirectly implies less scope for involvement from voluntary organizations, **churches,** and **labor-market** partners. The levels of benefit in this model have generally been seen as quite generous compared to systems in place in other countries.

The Scandinavian welfare state model was built as a compromise between the different **classes** in society and was seen as a possible way of combining capitalist and socialist development by maintaining a reasonably high degree of **equality,** stability in the labor market, and a free-market economy. In the late 1980s and early 1990s, the Scandinavian welfare state model came under pressure due to the more open economies in the world, increasing international competition, and changes in the economic and political systems of Eastern Europe. Some movement toward a more **continental model,** with more emphasis on **social insurance,** has thus occurred, although only to a limited degree.

The model still has the characteristics of **universality** and good coverage, although increasing emphasis is being placed on voluntary organizations and self-help groups, along with pressure for a reduction in **public-sector** expenditure. The focus on full **employment** and a high degree of equality can also still be seen in the Scandinavian welfare states. Comparing the welfare states in Scandinavia with other countries shows that they still are a more distinct welfare-state type, despite the fact that, in some areas, there has been some **convergence** with other European countries. *See also* SOCIAL DEMOCRATIC WELFARE MODEL.

SCHUMPETARIAN WORKFARE STATE. This model is named after the **Austrian**-born U.S. economist Joseph Schumpeter (1883–1950). It marks the transition in the **welfare state** from being general and all-encompassing to focusing primarily on the **labor market** and **rights** in accordance with **employment**. A Schumpetarian workfare state focuses on ways to strengthen the competitiveness of the economy, including a higher degree of flexibility in the labor market. Consequently, welfare-state policies in a Schumpetarian welfare state support flexibility and improved competitiveness more so than creating jobs and **equality**, as in the **Beveridgian** and Keynesian interpretations of the welfare state.

The reason this type of welfare state has arisen is growing international competition and specialization and the need for increased innovation. The focus is on **labor market policy**, which increases flexibility and indirectly reduces pressure on **public-sector** expenditures because of a constantly elevated level of employment. It includes a shift from a Fordist to a **post-Fordist** production mode. The Schumpetarian workfare state has many similarities to **liberal**, neoliberal, and neocorporatist ways of thinking about the relationship between state and **market**, including public-sector involvement in **social policy**.

It can be argued that an emphasis on work as a condition for receiving benefits is not new, as in most cases since the time of the **Poor Laws** it has been a requirement for receiving benefits. In most **unemployment benefit** systems, it has also always been a precondition for receiving **unemployment** benefits that the individual is actively seeking a job.

SCROUNGERPHOBIA. This fear is part of the occasionally hysterical debate about "scroungers," or people who are cheating the **social security** system. In the **United States**, scroungers are known as "chiselers." This term also indirectly includes the distinction between the **deserving and undeserving**, but the debate is primarily about whether individuals who do not have a **right** to receive a benefit nevertheless do so, for example, individuals who have a job but receive **social assistance**. In some countries, the debate about scroungers in the welfare system has been used as an argument for reducing the level of benefits.

SEGMENTED LABOR MARKET. This term describes a systematization and concept of the **labor market** as consisting of not just one **market**, but several. In the theory of segmentation, this means that at least two separate markets exist. One market is the core labor market, where the jobs are secure, with high wages and possibilities for promotion. These jobs require a certain level of skill (either through **education** or job training). Individuals working in the core labor market run little risk of being **unemployed**.

The second market—the periphery—is characterized by jobs with low wage levels, which are often unstable and insecure, and workers have a small possibility of promotion. Those in the second market therefore have a higher risk of being unemployed for shorter or longer periods of time. Hence, they implicitly have a greater **need** for public support. Those in the periphery tend to be the young, women, migrant workers, the unskilled, and, more recently, elderly workers.

Segmentation of the labor market suggests that if individuals are to be more permanently **integrated** into society, they should have the possibility of access to the core labor market. It is here that **social security** also seems to be higher. Furthermore, those in the core of the labor market can have other interests in relation to wage and other working conditions than those in the periphery.

SEGREGATION. The division in society of different groups or individuals. Segregation may be in different **housing** areas, among different groups in the **labor market**, and so on. Segregation also implies **marginalization**. The processes and causes of segregation may derive from different types of policies or be a result of market forces. Segregation may have an impact on **social inheritance**, and it may also be influential in **stigmatization**. Furthermore, more segregated societies seem to have a higher incidence of crime. Segregation may also occur due to increased free choice about, for example, **education**. *See also* GHETTO; SOCIAL EXCLUSION.

SELECTIVISM. A type of **social policy** emphasizing and making a selective **targeting** of benefits—either **benefits in-kind** or **benefits in cash**—to those most in **need**. A selective approach implies a **normative** choice between different groups in society and deciding who will be supported. As part of the economic pressure on **public-sector** spending, the focus in several **welfare states** has been on more targeted **social security** benefits.

SELF-EMPLOYMENT. The self-employed are individuals who, at their own risk and investment, run a company or deliver certain services. They have a different status in **social security** systems, as keeping control of their previous work records, income, and so forth, is more difficult. Still, being self-employed is a way of having a job in the **labor market**, and the trend has been to try to build systems that can cope with the specific problems of the self-employed by, for example, also making **unemployment benefit** systems for the self-employed, at least in some countries. Self-employed individuals also have to find ways to ensure that they have money saved for their **pensions**. This is true to a higher degree in the nonuniversal **welfare states**. The self-employed can either have a higher or a lower income than employed people. When using **European Union** rules on free movement of **services**, they are not obliged to follow rules on minimum wages.

SEN, AMARTYA (1933–). Amartya Sen, professor of economics and philosophy at Harvard University until 1998, and since then professor at Cambridge University in the **United Kingdom**, has contributed widely to the debate and discussion on **equality** and **inequality** and social choice. He has been awarded several honors, most notably the Nobel Prize in Economics in 1998. Sen has written several books that focus on trying to examine equality from traditional economic viewpoints and include **normative** elements and the political decision-making process. His writings have been influenced by his Indian origin, including important contributions on **poverty** and famine. He has analyzed questions of rational behavior and how **rationality** and social choice can interact. Sen can thus be labeled a social choice theorist. His concept of **capability** is widely acknowledged as being central to the understanding of equality in opportunities.

SERVICES. This refers to the provision of an activity, and thereby not a specific good, namely food, clothing, or **housing**. In relation to welfare, it refers more to **care**, which can be for children, the elderly, or other groups in **need**. **Health care** is another example of care often provided by the **public sector** in different **welfare states**.

SHARED CARE. This describes the situation when a child is living for approximately the same amount of time with both parents in the case of a **divorce**; therefore, the **care** of the child is in the **family**. *See also* CHILD CARE.

SICKNESS BENEFIT. This benefit is provided when the specific **contingency** of sickness occurs. It is organized and structured differently in different countries. In some it comes within the **public-sector social security**; in others it is related to being a member of, and having paid into, a private sickness-insurance fund. Some systems have waiting periods before individuals are able to receive the benefit (one or more days). The benefits are typically a percentage of previous income, with a ceiling. In some countries, **collective agreements** have built into a higher benefit beginning on the first day of sickness. In some systems, the principles of the sickness-benefit system are also used in calculating the level of maternity and paternity leave.

SICKNESS INSURANCE. This is a way of guaranteeing people income during a period of illness. In many countries, this is done not by the **public sector**, but by private insurance companies. The agreements may be generated by the individual insurance, but it is frequently part of the collective system, or the state makes it obligatory that the individual (employer/employee) must pay into an insurance company.

Individual sickness insurance can be provided for all citizens except the chronically ill. Insurance companies estimate and calculate the risk and thereby decide the level of a premium with no risk of **moral hazard** or **adverse selection**, because they have the chance of asking for the previous health records before granting an insurance policy. If this is done, however, it will cause problems for individuals with poor health, as they may have difficulty getting insured. This is less of a problem if sickness insurance is made obligatory by the state or if the individual belongs to an employer's group plan. Sickness insurance for larger groups of people who pool their risk is often cheaper than buying an individual insurance, this thereby also being an argument for a **welfare state** or obligatory **social insurance** approaches. *See also* HEALTH INSURANCE.

SLOVAKIA. Slovakia is a country in Central Europe that was established on 1 January 1993, following a referendum. It has approximately 5.5 million inhabitants. Slovakia was previously part of what is now the **Czech Republic**. The country's welfare system was, thus, to a high degree, developed as part of the old **communist** type of system. **Industrial injury** was the first area to be covered, in 1887, followed by **sickness benefits** and **maternity benefits** in 1888. In 1906, **pensions** for salaried employees were established, followed by pensions for wage earners in general in 1924. **Family allowances** were adopted in 1945.

The present system is largely an obligatory **social insurance** system, except for family allowance, which is a **universal** system. In the pension system, the insured pay part of the costs, the employers approximately one-fifth, and the state about one-third. The level of benefits is generally rather low. Membership in the **European Union** has also had an impact on the development of the **welfare state**.

SLOVENIA. Slovenia is a small country in Central Europe with a population of approximately 2 million. The country became independent in 1991, after breaking away from the former republic of Yugoslavia. Today it is a member of the **European Union**. Most of the first laws date to when it was part of Yugoslavia. **Pension, sickness, maternity,** and **industrial injury** benefits were all established in 1922, followed by **unemployment benefits** in 1927 and **family allowances** in 1949.

Before independence, the system was based on work for everyone. Slovenia presently has a stable economy and benefits that try to ensure a guaranteed minimum income for all citizens. The pension system is a **social insurance** system, with the contributions mainly coming from the insurers, but also from employers, and with the state providing a guarantee in case of deficit. The principles are the same in the other parts of the **social security** system, with the exception of the family allowance, which is state-**financed**.

Slovenia has been hit hard by the **financial crisis** that began in 2008. Reforms in social security, including the pension system, have therefore been introduced. Beginning in 2013, a new pension reform law went into effect that increases the retirement age for both men and women and changes how old-age benefits are calculated, with the aim of reducing the **public-sector** deficit.

SMITH, ADAM (1723–1790). Smith was a Scottish philosopher and economist during the Scottish Enlightenment. He studied at Glasgow University and later went to Edinburgh to teach. From 1751–1763, he held a chair in moral philosophy at Glasgow University. Smith's contribution to economic theory has been a foundation for many **liberal** thinkers and advocates of a free-**market** economy. It is mainly found in *Inquiry into the Nature and Causes of the Wealth of Nations*, published in 1776. His reputation as a philosopher was mainly established by *The Theory of Moral Sentiments*, published in 1759.

Smith's main contribution was that he believed that decision making by many individuals would be complementary and that most would act in their own self-interest. This has led numerous other authors to research and conduct further analysis on the conflict between state and society.

Even though Smith was a firm believer in the market, in *The Wealth of Nations*, he advocates that certain duties be preserved by the state. He charges that, among other things, the state should attend to defense, **justice**, and foreign policy, but he also says that, "The third and last duty of the sovereign or commonwealth is that of erecting and maintaining those public institutions and those public works, which never can be for the interest of any individual, or small number of individuals, to erect and maintain because the profit could never repay the expenses" (1970). This is, in fact, still at the core of present-day discussions and problems in relation to **welfare-state** analysis, and part of the argument concerning **market failure**, as well as an argument for state intervention.

SOCIAL ASSISTANCE. This is the main way of **distributing** state benefits that are not based on previous contributions; therefore, it is paid out of general **taxes** and duties. Eligibility criteria differ from country to country, but they are frequently based on the principle that other types of help are no longer available, as well as on a **means test**. In most countries, social assistance is received by those who are ineligible for **unemployment**, **sickness benefits**, or different types of **pensions**. It is thus the last part of the social **safety net**. Various criteria for receiving assistance can be attached, including work and/

or **education**. Some developing countries have attached as criteria that the children should follow primary education.

Social assistance varies in size and is often higher in the **welfare states** following the **Nordic model** than in the **liberal** ones. The size of the assistance is often measured by looking into the **replacement rate**, the expectation being that it is higher in the Nordic countries than in Central European and Southern European countries. Hence, the level of benefits also indicates how developed a welfare state is.

SOCIAL CAPITAL. This refers to forces in society that can be used for active involvement in societal activities. Social capital is thus often measured by looking at the membership of and active participation in various organizations, including voluntary organizations. Social capital can be seen as elements that are also important for the **third way** politics in welfare development, for they are a manner of integrating forces in the **civil society** in societal development. Consequently, to some degree, social capital also expresses the **solidarity** in a society and, at least in a broad interpretation, the society's cohesive forces. Social capital was made famous by Robert Putnam's book *Bowling Alone* (1995), where the expression "bowling alone" indicates a change in American society from a time when people used to engage in activities together, whereas now an increasing number do such activities alone. *See also* NONGOVERNMENTAL ORGANIZATION (NGO).

SOCIAL CHANGE. This refers to the changes taking place in the abilities and possibilities of individuals in different societies throughout time. Social change and the different ways it has developed in various countries have had an impact on the way **welfare states** have been built. Knowledge of social change may be used to explain differences in political outcomes under different social and cultural conditions. In **Germany**, social change in the 19th century resulted in new **social security** systems with a considerable reliance on the **labor market**. The way social change occurs is based on political, administrative, and economic conditions in different countries. The way changes are transmitted will have a different impact on and consequences for the way the welfare state is structured and changed.

SOCIAL CHOICE THEORY. This theory examines how different individuals' value judgments will have an impact on societal development; it focuses on the maximizing of welfare in a given society. This has mainly been done by using strict formal axioms to describe what the outcome of different choices would be in a given society. Included in this theory is how individual **rationality** has an impact on society's many decisions and, in turn, how social considerations can have an impact on the rationality of the individual. Social choice theory is closely connected to **welfare economics**. It also gave rise to **public choice** theory. Social choice theory research includes many of the questions about **justice, equality**, and **distribution** involved in finding a **social welfare function**.

SOCIAL COHESION. A term for the degree of **social inclusion** in different countries and their ability to ensure political and social stability. Social cohesion in a more sociological sense relates to the ability to develop connections and relations between members of a given society. It can also be used in relation to the debate on **social capital**.

SOCIAL CONTROL. The process by which some people and their behaviors are controlled by others or by **norms**. Social control can be used to get people to act in ways that society or specific groups want them to. In relation to **social policy**, social control may mandate that an individual can receive only **social security** benefits if the person does what he or she is told by the authorities. This can consist of engaging in **community work**, getting an **education**, or just going to a specific place each morning. Social control then involves a reduction of the individual person's **freedom**, but it is the price the individual will have to pay to receive public support. Social control through norms may vary throughout time, and for the individual it may have the consequence that it is difficult to know how to act. In welfare models that emphasize **family** help, the norms may implicitly apply pressure on fulfilling the norms of the family structure.

SOCIAL DEMOCRATIC WELFARE MODEL. This model has a **universal** character and is primarily state-**financed**. **Citizenship** is the key factor when deciding who is eligible for a given benefit. In many ways, it resembles the **Scandinavian welfare state model**. It is labeled so because in the Scandinavian countries, the development of welfare policies was especially due to social democratic-led **governments**.

SOCIAL DEVIANCE. A theory of how to understand deviations from social **norms** in a society, and that these deviations may give rise to **stigmatization** and **marginalization** of people in a society. Historically speaking, this can be people having a sexuality that differs from the norm. It can also be people who are not prepared to work.

SOCIAL DIMENSION. This concept refers to social aspects of societal development. It especially relates to a debate within the **European Union (EU)**

in which this was the other side of the coin to the free movement of capital and labor. The higher mobility of capital and labor was expected to increase the use of **market** forces, which could therefore create greater **inequalities** within and between the EU countries. The social dimension can thus indirectly be seen as the price capital in Europe, paid to have a freer and more open market; however, it can also be seen as a wish to keep competition in working conditions and **social policy** from dominating European economic and social development.

There are two positions in Europe in the debate on social dimension. One is that a social dimension would go against the notion of an internal market. The other is that the social dimension was the best way of avoiding social dumping on a European scale. The Social Charter, negotiated in 1989, was therefore only agreed to by 11 out of the 12 member states, with the **United Kingdom** deciding to opt out. The Social Charter covers **freedom** of movement; **employment** and remuneration; improvement of living and working conditions; social protection; freedom of association and **collective bargaining**; vocational training; equal treatment for men and women; information; consultation and participation for workers; **health** protection and safety at the workplace; and protection of children, adolescents, the elderly, and the handicapped.

The charter's prescriptions are general and nonbinding, but it was followed up and included in the Maastricht Treaty, with the United Kingdom still rejecting it, but the new member states (**Sweden, Finland**, and **Austria**) accepted it. In May 1997, the United Kingdom accepted the social dimension after the Labour Party, under Tony Blair, won the general election. It was later included in the EU Amsterdam Treaty, and the 10 new member states since 2004 have also accepted a social dimension, as it was also part of the Nice Treaty. This will involve some change in social policy, mainly to improve the lowest possible level of social protection within the EU.

The social dimension is, thus, not very precise and does not involve binding elements for the individual countries, but, on the other hand, it does show that a more uniform **social security** system may develop in the future on a European level. The social dimension of European development is also sometimes referred to as the ability to create a social Europe. *See also* CONVERGENCE.

SOCIAL DIVISION OF WELFARE. This term describes a concept proposed by **Richard Titmuss** in *Essays on the Welfare State* in 1958. He distinguishes among the following three levels of welfare: **public welfare, fiscal welfare**, and **occupational welfare**. These three levels refer to different ways of delivering and financing welfare. Public welfare refers to the welfare supplied and financed by direct state intervention. It is this type of welfare that most statistics on social expenditure show, and cross-national comparisons often have this as the starting point for the way in which the different countries' systems are connected. Fiscal welfare refers to what is directly or indirectly provided for by the **tax** system. This may take the form of tax allowances and tax relief. Fiscal welfare has an impact on **public-sector** income by reducing it when giving these specific allowances. Occupational welfare is the benefits and **services** provided by employers in the private **market**. These range from being fully voluntary to being a part of **collective bargaining** in the **labor market**, where the employers (as part of an agreement) have also promised to pay all or part of some **social security** expenditure. Finally, occupational welfare can be decided by the state, but the financing and implementation will be an obligatory duty for employers.

These three levels do not exhaust the ways in which welfare can be delivered, and they can be interwoven. One example is that many of the **pensions** provided in the occupational welfare systems are indirectly supported by tax relief, which is fiscal welfare, and they are also often supported by a direct public provision of a basic level of pension. This concept is useful for pointing to different routes to social security, as well as the varied ways to achieve goals in the **welfare state**.

SOCIAL EXCLUSION. This term describes a situation in which individuals in a society are not included in one or more aspects of society's life or do not participate in societal activities. In the literature, there does not seem to be one agreed upon definition of what social exclusion is. It seems to be the opposite of **integration** into society. Different definitions encompass different aspects of the concept. Some emphasize the relation with the **labor market**, whereas others take a broader approach. The **European Union's** observatory on social exclusion defines it as the absence of a "certain basic standard of living and participation in the major social and occupational opportunities in society." In this way, a person subject to social exclusion can be seen as not having the same **rights** as other citizens in the given society.

Social exclusion can be in relation to one or more aspects of societal life, but it can also encompass a broader interpretation of the individual's position in society. This means that the individual can be excluded from the labor market and participation in cultural activities, or not be integrated into local life and so forth.

The term was first developed in **France**. In the mid-1970s, it was used to describe groups or individuals not covered by the traditional **social security** system. Hence, they were excluded from certain social protection systems. Under such a definition, those excluded will change throughout time as the social security system changes. The term's origin also seems to stress the relationship between individuals in society and society's structure. Finally, it emphasizes the role of societal processes rather than considering this to be a necessarily permanent situation.

The term seems to have evolved from a broader concept, which was used to encompass the broader societal structure and development, rather than the narrower focus of such concepts as **equality, poverty,** and **justice.** As the term seems to be the antonym of integration, many policies with the aim of reducing social exclusion have focused on what could integrate people into society. As many **welfare-state** systems are based on labor market participation, research into social exclusion has primarily examined how labor market measures could help integrate people into society. Many ways of discussing social exclusion have been narrowed down to the consequences of **unemployment** and not being part of the labor market's core force (*see also* SEGMENTED LABOR MARKET). This is a limited version of the concept that does not integrate other types of social exclusion, for example, the elderly who do not want to be alone but are feeling lonely and, in this sense, are excluded from social life.

Although the term has different connotations, and there is no single way of defining it, it has influenced the debate about welfare-state policies. Researchers have concentrated on analyzing the situation of those who are **marginalized,** and not only those living off traditional income transfers. This approach emphasizes that income transfers are only one part of the welfare states' policy for a better-functioning society. *See also* GHETTO; RACISM; SOCIAL INCLUSION.

SOCIAL INCLUSION. The opposite of **social exclusion,** but it is often referred to as a set of policies with the explicit aim of getting individuals or groups of individuals **integrated** into society through different types of polices and initiatives. **Active labor market policy** is often looked upon as one measure that can be used to include people in society; however, this only counters one type of inclusion, that is, in the **labor market,** and not the **need** to be included in society in a broader sense. In several **welfare states,** various types of programs both in the public and **voluntary sectors** try to help integrate people who are otherwise on the margins of society or at risk of being socially excluded.

SOCIAL INDICATORS. Measures of welfare and **social change** in various countries. This is a relatively new concept that originated in the early 1950s and gradually developed in many Western countries because, among other things, it was expected that it would produce new types of information that were not previously collected by traditional economic measurements. In 1954, a **United Nations** report entitled "International Definition and Measurement of Standards and Levels of Living" was published and gave rise to the regular collection of data. This was followed by a 1973 Organization for Economic Cooperation and Development (OECD) agreement on 24 areas of fundamental social concern. Today it is used to a more limited extent, mainly due to problems with the definition; however, the OECD publishes social indicators, including many of the aforementioned elements. Still, in many areas, only a few data at a comparative level are available. Recent years have seen an increase in these types of data, for example, the OECD's study known as "How's Life" and various think tanks that report on **well-being, happiness**, and so forth. This also reflects a criticism of mainly using gross national product as an indicator of a society's level of welfare.

Social indicators have been developed by a process of defining welfare areas that may be of interest and then finding components that are generally able to describe the chosen areas. The social indicators thus reveal how different groups in society have access to certain **services**, or the average **life expectancy**. The indicators not only include components that can be measured in terms of money, they try to encompass a broader version of society's impact on individuals and their positions. This is the reason for including information on life expectancy, the infant mortality rate, and so on.

Unlike economic indicators, social indicators include nonmonetary aspects. Researchers have focused on such areas as **health, demography, education, housing**, safety, **employment** and work safety, recreation, consumption possibilities, and **democratic** participation.

Reports on social indicators have been a part of the general trend of publishing and making material available to analyze living standards in various countries. They reflect the economic and material perspectives and include a nonmaterial insight into daily living standards.

SOCIAL INHERITANCE. This refers to a situation in which children end up in similar sorts of jobs or facing similar types of problems as their parents. It is especially the negative type of social inheritance that is of interest in relation to **social policy**, that is, when the same **families** receive **social assistance** generation after generation. It needs to be clarified that this is not the case for all children, and that many children have a higher level of **education** than their parents. At the same time, it may be important for a society to be aware of how negative social inheritance can be reduced by, for example, improving education and ensuring education for everyone in the society.

SOCIAL INNOVATION. Innovation is a term often related to the development of production in the private sector. This is especially related to the production of goods and **services**. In recent years, the term has also entered the vocabulary of **welfare-state** development, to point to the fact that welfare services can also be organized, delivered, and structured in various ways. It is further seen as a way in which welfare states will be able to cope with the **demographic** transitions in coming years.

SOCIAL INSURANCE. A system in which the individual, in the event of a certain **contingency**, can receive a benefit without a **means test**, but the individual must fulfill the criteria for receiving the benefit, for example, by being sick or unemployed but still actively looking for a job. Social insurance is typically publicly organized, and membership can be compulsory but may also be voluntary. The compulsory nature of the system means that it is not possible for those offering the insurance to analyze individual risk. A social insurance system will therefore tend to be more equal than private insurance systems. The social insurance will often be paid for by those who are insured, but support from the state may be possible, often in the form of a guarantee in case of deficits. Social insurance systems are often used in the countries that have adopted the **continental welfare model**. *See also* HEALTH INSURANCE.

SOCIAL INTEGRATION. This term refers to whether the individual is an **integrated** part of society's way of functioning. It includes both economic and noneconomic aspects. It also refers to policies with the aim of integrating people into a society. *See also* SOCIAL EXCLUSION; SOCIAL INCLUSION.

SOCIAL INVESTMENT STATE. This is a specific paradigm to describe a certain type of **welfare state** having a focus on how the welfare state can support societal development in different ways. This includes how **work and family life** can be combined, enabling both adults to be in the **labor market**, but also how investment in **education** can make it possible for individuals and society to develop or, finally, ensure that the welfare state can help create jobs and manage overall economic development via social investment.

SOCIAL MOVEMENTS. A variety of groups or individuals who have in common one or more specific issues they want to pursue in society. Historically, they have been involved in different areas and have different views about which solution to find. The socialist movement is just one example. Given their different aims and goals, social movements can be increasing or decreasing in size and intensity based on changes in societies. A topic might be hot for a time, with many active participants, and then vanish. Today, social movements are of interest in the way that they point to and can have an impact on **welfare-state** policies. This can be done by creating pressure for changes in social structures or societal policies aimed at the weaker groups in society. An impact on welfare-state policies can also be the way in which they influence and form self-help groups to support one another. In recent times, social movements have also included various groups wanting changes in environmental policy or **social integration**. *See also* INTEREST GROUPS; PRESSURE GROUPS; TRADE UNION.

SOCIAL NETWORKS. This term describes the individual's way of having contact with other people in society. The network may include **families** or friends, but it can also be social workers and their clients. Social networks are seen as playing a central role in reducing **marginalization** and feelings of loneliness in the **welfare state**. The expectation is that social networks can reduce the pressure on the welfare state because they can support the individual and reduce the **need** for **benefits in-kind** or **benefits in cash**. Supporting social networks can be a way of increasing cohesion in a society. It can also be a way of reducing the need for public economic support in various areas, including the risk of crime; however, it is debatable whether state-supported networks have the same impact as the more voluntarily created ones. *See also* INTEGRATION; SOCIAL MOVEMENTS.

SOCIAL POLICY. This type of policy is included within the **welfare state**. It can be restricted to a very narrow area—for example, only the Ministry of Social Security—but will often be understood in a broader context, including the core areas of the welfare state, for example, **social security**, **education**, **health care**, and **housing**. Social policy is often investigated by **integrating** various disciplines in the analysis of how it has an impact, but this requires a multidisciplinary approach.

SOCIAL RIGHTS. These are the **rights** that individuals have in the **social security** system. How these rights are acquired and maintained is a specific element in the **welfare-state** systems of various countries. The issue of social rights is also often connected to **T. H. Marshall's** discussion of citizen rights.

SOCIAL SAFETY NET. The support individuals can receive in the case that a **contingency** occurs. It can sometimes be presented as the last type of support an individual can get; therefore, the size of this last benefit would have an impact on the number of people living in **poverty**.

SOCIAL SECURITY. The set of policies established to compensate for the economic consequences of a specific social **contingency**. Social security as a concept has been codified by **International Labour Organization** Convention No. 102 (1952). It covers nine areas, including medical **care** and benefits in relation to sickness, **unemployment**, old age, **industrial injury**, **family**, maternity, **invalidity**, and widowhood. It was originally described in EU Regulation 1408/71, and now with a broader scope in EU Regulation 883/2004. Industrial injury, which was one of the first social contingencies to be covered in most countries, is still the area that is most developed worldwide. The other types are developed and implemented differently in each country. They will also differ in relation to eligibility and level of benefits.

Social security is a narrower concept than **social policy**, as it does not include **services** and different types of policies with the intention of reducing the problems—that is, **preventive** measures. It also does not include measures and initiatives to avoid **poverty** and **social exclusion**. Still, social security does include many of the central elements in the **welfare-state** policies of many countries, in particular **pensions**, which are central and account for a large proportion of spending throughout the world.

SOCIAL SERVICES. Welfare states originally focused on income replacement when certain **contingencies** occurred; however, in recent years, the emphasis has also been on various kinds of social services that can be important for the welfare state to function. Social services include, by now, such central elements as **care** (for example, for children and the elderly) and **health**, including hospitals. Social services like **child care** and care for the frail elderly, which are provided by the welfare state, are examples of **needs** that earlier were taken care of by **civil society** but are now part of the responsibility of the state.

SOCIAL STRATIFICATION. This term is linked to the way a society is **stratified** along different lines. This can be by occupational position, **education**, and/or income.

SOCIAL UNREST INDEX. An index developed by the **International Labour Organization**. It is a composite indicator that provides an overview of global social **health**. Five variables are used in the index. The first is the confidence in **government** measuring people's satisfaction with the performance of their national government. The second is the actual living standard, which measures whether people's lives are getting better, including developments in **unemployment**. The third focus is on the local job **market** and how individuals perceive the **labor market**. The fourth element is the **freedom** one has in one's life; it measures people's perceptions of their **right** to choose how they want to live their lives. Finally, access to the Internet is included.

SOCIAL WELFARE. This concept can be approached from different angles. From a statistical perspective, social welfare is measured by examining real income and its **distribution** among groups or individuals. The other approach considers social welfare as the aggregate of the individual's **utilities**, which are a function of his or her access to various goods and **services**. Social welfare is a way of trying to evaluate a society's welfare by taking both production and distribution into consideration. Most of the analyses involve **normative** judgments and **interpersonal comparisons**, which often make the concept quite difficult to use as a basis for making recommendations. Still, making judgments based on different measures of **inequality**, and from this providing a description of social welfare, is a way of informing about society's welfare.

SOCIAL WELFARE FUNCTION. The sum of the individual **utilities** in a given society. Based upon this definition, it implicitly follows that if the utility of one person is increased, then society's total utility is increased. It can fulfill different criteria by emphasizing different elements, for example, the **distribution** between different individuals in society. This is mainly a theoretical concept that can be used to discuss the implications of different types of activities and intervention. It is not possible empirically to find a society's welfare function, as it requires that we possess full information about all individuals' welfare and utility, and that all individuals will be able to establish a ranking among various alternatives. Analytically, the principle is useful as a reminder that establishing priorities among scarce resources is necessary. *See also* ARROW'S IMPOSSIBILITY THEOREM.

SOCIAL WELFARE POLICY. This type of policy emerged out of the development of the **welfare state** in many countries after World War II and the rapid expansion of the **public sector**. It was—and still is—a policy in many countries with the general aim of making improvements in living standards for those in **need**, and it was originally and still is mainly achieved by state intervention. Economic demand management was expected to be the policy that would ensure full **employment** and continuous growth to **finance** the development of the welfare state.

During the economic crisis in the Western world after the first and second oil shocks in the 1980s, social welfare policy was increasingly questioned from different perspectives—both Right and Left. The Left criticized it for helping and maintaining the capitalist class, the Right for harming the dynamics of production. This led to suggestions for reducing the level of welfare, often presented as arguments about **retrenchment**, but also **privatization**.

Today, it seems that the period of rapid growth in spending on **social welfare** is over in the most mature welfare states, but that there is still considerable state involvement in social and welfare policies in many countries. Furthermore, it seems that we are witnessing **convergent** trends in social welfare. *See also* NEW LEFT; NEW RIGHT.

SOCIAL WORK. Work done by field workers and those in the administration dealing with social problems. Social workers are people who, as representatives of a statutory or nonstatutory body, deliver different types of **social services** (income and **benefits in-kind**) and advice to individuals. Generally speaking, these individuals have undergone a specific training to perform the work, and they know the social systems and how to communicate with the people concerned. They should also have a psychological understanding of processes and reasons for changes. Social workers are often the front-line workers in **social policy**, and thus the first contact of the user of the system. Some forms of social work are also labeled **street-level bureaucracy**.

SOCIALIZATION. The process by which people are **integrated** into society, either by learning or adaptation of **norms**, rules, and values in a specific society. Socialization often takes place within the **family** and the **educational** system.

SOLIDARITY. In its most general sense, solidarity is unity resulting from common interests or feelings. It is a collective responsibility between people who are dependent upon or related to one another; it can describe the population of the nation-state, the workers in a specific **trade union**, employees in a specific firm, people in a given **community**, members of an organization, and so on.

Solidarity is a central element of the **welfare state**. The willingness to contribute to the provision of a welfare state through **taxes** and duties can be seen as one type of solidarity. The macro solidarity, that is, the overall agreement of solidarity, may be different from micro solidarity, or the individual's willingness to support **families**, friends, and/or the local area. It can also be solidarity with other members of a trade union or employer organization to try to achieve common goals.

The degree of solidarity and interrelated level of welfare services differs among the welfare states. Different types of welfare states may have different levels of the aforementioned abstract, formalized form of solidarity. Emile Durkheim distinguished between two types of solidarity, mechanical and organic. These types refer to different commitments within the different states and models. Solidarity was a prime mover for the development of the welfare states that have emerged more recently, mainly in the 20th century.

Solidarity in the sense of willingness to pay for welfare-state activities, especially for the most vulnerable, seems to exist more generally in all welfare states. The willingness to pay for welfare-state activities seems to be dependent to a certain degree on the **legitimacy** of the welfare state. The willingness to pay for and accept activities has often been highest in relation to **pensions** and **health care**.

SOUTH AFRICA. South Africa's system has historically been influenced by the system in the **United Kingdom**, but its development was relatively late due to the fact that it was a colony. Furthermore, the long period of apartheid dampened the development of social programs. Some of the programs, when developed, actually excluded Asian, colored, and black employees. This was the case for **family allowances**, introduced in 1947. The **welfare state** started with the introduction of the **industrial injury** law in 1914. This was followed by old-age **pensions** in 1928. **Unemployment benefits** became available beginning in 1937. The **government** mainly pays for the system, although with some contributions from the insured and employers for unemployment benefits and industrial injury.

This system has low coverage and a strict **means test** for eligibility for a benefit. The breakdown of apartheid has changed this, but in the long run, change will depend on economic conditions. The relatively weak economic position of South Africa, with so many people living in **poverty**, makes it more difficult to develop a welfare state. This explains why it still has a more rudimentary coverage, with a high reliance on the **family**.

South Africa has experienced a period of rapid economic development, and it has been a member of the BRICS countries (**Brazil, Russia, India, China**, and South Africa) since 2011. Although **unemployment** and poverty have been reduced in recent years, they remain high. These are just some of the challenges for the development of welfare policy in South Africa. Social and welfare policies balance on and suffer from differences between ideals and reality.

SOUTHERN EUROPEAN WELFARE STATE MODEL. This model is also referred to as the Latin Rim model. It is a rudimentary **welfare-state** type due to its limited coverage of citizens in many areas. It is highly influenced by the Catholic way of thinking and is therefore often connected with the **subsidiarity** principle. This implies that the state's intervention in the field is rather limited and that the state primarily takes over only as a last resort.

The more influential role of the **church** in Southern Europe may also explain why the development of welfare-state systems started later than in other locations. This was partly due to greater reliance on the **family** structure, partially because needy people could get some help from the church. This reduced the scope of and **need** for **public-sector** involvement.

Southern European countries (here referring mainly to **Greece**, **Italy**, **Spain**, and **Portugal**) have what some would call a more dualistic welfare-state model. This is so because coverage largely depends on having a job. Those without a job or those having a job in the **hidden economy** will thus not be covered unless the family steps in. On the other hand, the **health care** sector is mainly **universal** for all citizens regardless of **class** and status in society. The consequence is that certain segments of the populations in these countries are highly protected, whereas the rest receive almost no coverage.

In the area of **pensions**, the system is generally well-developed; therefore, it is not just a rudimentary system. However, the core areas in **social security** are only developed to a limited degree, and with a compensation level below those in other European countries. This can, in part, be explained by lower economic possibilities.

Finally, this model has been connected with the principle of clientelism, under which the possibility of receiving a social benefit will depend on support for a specific political party or group. This has been the case, for example, in Italy, especially in the southern part. It also exists in the other Southern European welfare state types, but due to long periods under dictatorships, it has not been developed to the same degree.

SPAIN. Spain's **social policy** development has been strongly influenced by the civil war in the 1930s and the long period of dictatorship until the mid-1970s. As did other European countries, it introduced quite early on a law on **industrial injury** (1900), but it was only after World War I that laws covering old-age (**pension**) and **unemployment benefits** followed (both in 1919). **Sickness benefits** and **maternity benefits** came along in 1929, and **family allowances** were introduced in 1938. The system belongs to the **Southern European welfare state model**, with a large proportion of the system being **financed** by contributions. In relation to family allowances, a more general scheme has been developed.

Spain expanded its social policy in the 1980s and 1990s but still keeps the core of the old system intact. The gap in spending on social policy between Spain and Northern Europe is still considerable, although a lot of catching up has taken place, making it **converge** with other welfare states in Europe. Nonetheless, Spain has experienced dramatic economic problems in the wake of the recent **financial crisis** and a high level of **unemployment**, especially youth unemployment. Furthermore, to cope with the fiscal crisis, dramatic cuts in **public-sector** spending have been made, including changes in the pension system, and fewer people are employed in the public sector as part of the initiatives to reduce the public-sector deficit.

STATE, MARKET, AND CIVIL SOCIETY. This refers to the interaction and division of responsibilities in **welfare states** among three different actors: the state, the **market**, and the **civil society**. States have certain responsibilities in areas not taken care of by the market or civil society because of **market failure** or due to a wish to provide a higher degree of **equality**. The market delivers certain goods and **services** in areas where it is possible to create market conditions. The civil society provides other types of activities. Other names exist, for example, the welfare mix, referring to the impact of the three sectors, or the welfare-state triangle. Whatever name it is given, it is the interplay between the sectors that is the focus.

The balance among state, market, and civil society varies among welfare states and welfare-state types. The balance has changed throughout time, creating a different welfare mix in various countries. It will presumably continue to change in the future.

Within the triangle of state, market, and civil society, one can also distinguish between formal and informal provisions and for-profit and nonprofit activities. There are no clear-cut divisions among them—overlaps exist and will likely continue to do so—but as a way of thinking about different elements of providers and services in the welfare state, the formal/informal and for-profit/nonprofit distinctions among the actors are useful.

The division of responsibility varies among welfare-state types. The responsibility of the **family** is higher in the residual model, the market in the **liberal** model, and the state in the **social democratic model**. *See also* DEMOCRACY; GOVERNANCE.

STATUTORY RETIREMENT AGE. In many **welfare states**, this is the age when the **right** to a state **pension** becomes available. The formal age of retirement is different from the average age of retirement, which is often lower by using, for example, **early retirement** benefits. Recent years have seen a movement toward the same age of retirement for men and women (in many countries it had been earlier for women) as part of the equal treatment of men and women. Historically speaking, the intention has been to lower the age of retirement, partly as a response to the high level of **unemployment** after the first and second oil-price crises, but also as a way for those who have been working hard to retire during a time when they still have a possibility of a life where they can enjoy their free time. The increased wealth was thus not only used to increase consumption possibilities, but also for more leisure. In the last 20 to 30 years, in many countries, increased longevity has put pressure on the payment of pensions, whether they be state or occupational-based pensions, or **pay-as-you-go systems** or **funded systems**. This, accompanied by **demographic** changes, has resulted in a decreased labor supply, which has been the reason for an increase in the pension age, that is, when public pension is available, with the aim and expectation that people will stay in the **labor market** longer, at the same time reducing the pressure on **public-sector** spending given the demographic changes. This increase has been taking place throughout most of Europe during the last 10 to 15 years, and it started even before the **financial crisis**, but as part of the goal to reduce pressure on public-sector spending, it continued after the start of the financial troubles.

STIGMATIZATION. This refers to the phenomenon that takes place when individuals feel that they are looked negatively upon when receiving social benefits from the **welfare state**. This may reduce the individual's willingness to take up a benefit due to the negative psychological implications of receiving it. Stigmatization may derive from having to ask for a benefit, the risk that others will see that one is receiving a benefit, or a feeling that one is no longer able to take **care** of himself or herself. These elements may give rise to a sense of stigma, which can then contribute to **social exclusion**. Stigmatization will be different for different individuals and can also depend upon the prevailing **norms** in the individual's surroundings.

STRATIFICATION. This involves an understanding of how to classify people in a society based upon a set of specific criteria. Historically, there has been a focus on upper, lower, or middle **classes**. The concept is currently used to define and discuss different kinds of **welfare states** as related to different types of welfare regimes. Furthermore, the emphasis is more on occupational position than the classical class position. *See also* SOCIAL STRATIFICATION.

STREET-LEVEL BUREAUCRACY. This term refers to those individuals who are in direct contact with the clients within the **social security** system. They often have discretionary power to make decisions about whether an individual will receive a benefit and, in some countries, the size of the benefit. The power of street-level bureaucrats in some countries has led to criticism of their work. This is because a client who is unable to communicate well with the bureaucrat may have difficulty receiving the benefits he or she has a **right** to collect. On the other hand, it has been argued that by having street-level bureaucrats with discretionary power, it is possible to take a more holistic view of the clients' problems and help solve them. The ability to take a holistic view is greater when there is leeway for decisions than when the benefits are fixed. *See also* BUREAUCRACY; SOCIAL WORK.

SUBSIDIARITY. A concept that originated from Catholic thinking in the 20th century. Definitions today often quote Pope Pius XI in *Quadragesimo Anno* (1931): "It is wrong to withdraw from the individual and to commit to the **community** at large what private enterprise and endeavor can accomplish." Furthermore, it is stated in *Quadragesimo Anno* that what can be done at a lower level should not be taken over by the higher level. This implies that a **welfare-state** model building on this principle will be **individualistic** and **decentralized**. The individualistic approach is indicated in the sentence on withdrawing from the individual. The decentralized approach is based on the idea that any intervention should be undertaken at the lowest possible level. It can be argued that the individual level includes the **family**, which can be the firm ground upon which **social policy** is built. This has been a cornerstone of such welfare systems as the **Southern European welfare state model** and also in many Catholic countries.

The concept of subsidiarity has also influenced social policy in the **European Union (EU)** and the process for European **integration**. In the Maastricht Treaty of 1991, subsidiarity was directly stated in article 3b: "In areas which do not fall within its extensive competence, the community shall take action, in accordance with the principle of subsidiarity, only if and in so far as the objectives of the proposed action cannot be sufficiently achieved by the member states and can, therefore, by reason of the scale or effort, be better achieved by the community." Following the discussion of the concept of subsidiarity at the Edinburgh summit in 1992, this is understood to mean that the EU must be able to show that the action is necessary. Furthermore, it must add value to the community that action is taken on a higher level than that of the nation-states and regional or local authorities. Subsidiarity has since been integrated into all treaties in the EU. Admittedly, it can naturally be difficult at times to evaluate whether added value exists.

In the **United States**, the U.S. Constitution also—indirectly—uses the concept of subsidiarity by stating that the federal government should only step in if intervention cannot be undertaken in the different states or by the people themselves. In **Germany**, it is also stated that the Länder (Germany's regional units) should implement as many EU regulations as possible rather than having the federal government impose them.

The concept has therefore had a clear impact on the way welfare states have developed and been structured in many countries by proposing the sharing of competencies among different levels of society. It has also been used as an argument for rolling back the state's influence in society and reducing welfare-state spending by leaving a larger proportion of the activities to local and individual spending. The degree of centralization and decentralization varies markedly among welfare states, including a large diversity due to the existence of local differences. Differences in **services** may be greater than those in direct economic support.

SUBSIDIES. Forms of support intended to reduce the price the consumer would otherwise have to pay for a good. For example, they can be used to reduce the price of goods that are assumed to be important to people with a low income. Subsidies can therefore be a way of trying to alleviate **poverty**. They have also been used in many countries as a way of reducing the costs of **basic needs** for a **family**. Subsidies to ensure cheap **housing**, bread, and heating are elements that have reduced the need for **social assistance**, especially in former Eastern European countries. In this way, subsidies can be an alternative to other types of income transfers. They can also be a way, like **taxes** and duties, to provide **incentives** for the individual or family to spend more money on one specific good than on another good. With the increase in **health** problems due to growing obesity, the use of subsidies for, for example, vegetables may be a way of addressing the problem.

SUPPLEMENTARY PENSIONS. Pensions received in addition to the basic pension provided by the **welfare state**. Supplementary pensions may be either voluntary, to targeted groups, or based on **occupational welfare**. They can also be supported indirectly through the **tax** system (*see also* TAX EXPENDITURES). In many countries, supplementary pensions have been developed so that there is a broader variety of pensions and a possibility of a higher savings rate for people who need more than the level that the welfare state is able to cope with given its economic and **demographic** situation. Supplementary pensions have thus become an important pillar in the pension systems of several countries and broadened them from being mainly **pay-as-you-go systems** to **funded systems**.

SURVIVORS. People who survive the death of a relative. In several **welfare states**, there have historically been survivor **pensions** for women following the deaths of their husbands, mainly because the societies were built around the male **breadwinner** model.

SUSTAINABILITY. The term sustainable development was first related to environmental issues regarding the impact of the development and use of natural resources on the globe. In recent years, the term has also been used to refer to the way in which a society can develop while ensuring its ability to **finance** the **welfare state** in the long run and also reduce the risk of dramatic consequences of a possible new **financial crisis** of the welfare state.

SWEDEN. Sweden operates based on the **Scandinavian welfare state model**, with a **universal**, all-encompassing system, even though in recent years it has been under economic pressure and **marketization** has come more widely into use. The individual is covered as a citizen, although certain parts of the system rely on his or her being in the **labor market**. Sweden developed its system early, with the introduction of a **sickness benefit** in 1891, and a law on **industrial injury** in 1901. A law covering old-age **pensions** followed in 1913; **unemployment benefits** followed in 1934, and, in 1947, a law on **family allowances** was enacted.

The pension system, family allowances, and **health care** are universal and mainly paid for through general **taxes** and duties, although some of the money comes from obligatory **social security** contributions; however, these have many resemblances to general taxes and duties. **Unemployment** benefits are based on membership in an unemployment benefit fund, which is the case for approximately two-thirds of the Swedish **labor force**. The late development of unemployment benefits in Sweden may be a reason for the **active labor market policy (ALMP)**, which is intended to get people back into the labor market as soon as possible.

Aside from developing benefit systems after World War II, Sweden rapidly developed more comprehensive coverage in many **service** areas in the **welfare state**, including **child care** and **care** for the elderly. In addition, the Swedish welfare state was **decentralized**, with many decisions—and related **financing**—being dealt with at the local level (*see also* SUBSIDIARITY).

After a long period of time with rather few initiatives in **social policy**, when Sweden was ruled by **liberal governments**, the first Social Democratic government came to power in 1932, presumably as a consequence of rising unemployment. Welfare-state development in Sweden has since been inspired by the rule of the Social Democratic Party from 1932–1976. This was done in such a way that the farmers felt satisfied, and, in many ways, the developments were built on a consensus among different **classes** in Sweden. The compromise implied a capitalist production structure, but with state intervention and regulation to improve employment conditions and create a more equal society. The compromise and consensus strategy was also necessary, as the Social Democratic Party did not have a majority in parliament. It has also been labeled as an attempt to create a "people's home," implying that after political **democracy** was established, the time had come for social democracy, by building a welfare state with emphasis on the **rights** of citizens.

Only with the breakdown of the coalition between the middle class and the labor movement did the Swedish model run into problems.

Sweden has been inspired by **Bismarckian, Beveridgian,** and Keynesian ways of managing the economy. This continues to have an impact on the structure of the system by maintaining financing through taxes and duties, but also through social security contributions.

After World War II, in which Sweden was neutral, a rapid expansion of the welfare state took place. The ground had already been laid before the war, but with Swedish society becoming more affluent, many areas were expanded and improved upon, in relation to both services and income transfers. Until the late 1980s, ALMP and a very broad and generous coverage were the main elements of the Swedish welfare-state model. It has been further strengthened by a relatively large degree of stability in the labor market, despite the fact that since 1976, both liberal and conservative governments have run Sweden from time to time.

The increase in international competition, especially since the 1970s, has made it difficult for Sweden to continue to support one of the largest **public sectors** and highest levels of taxes and duties in Europe. Thus, it witnessed a series of **retrenchments** in the 1990s and early 2000s in several areas, and in some there is now less emphasis on universality. Still, Sweden's is a well-developed welfare state, with a high level of public spending on welfare, a high degree of **equality**, and a continued commitment to a full employment policy; however, the model does seem to have matured, and with a focus implying a slight shift away from the Scandinavian welfare state model.

SWITZERLAND. With about 7.5 million inhabitants, Switzerland has been neutral since the last century and is a relatively rich country. It is based on highly independent cantons. The Swiss welfare system developed relatively late. Laws on **industrial injury, sickness benefits,** and **maternity benefits** were adopted in 1911. **Unemployment** insurance followed in 1924, **pensions** in 1946, and, finally, **family allowances** in 1952. Some of the cantons had, at that time, already developed social programs, including family allowances.

The structure is primarily based on voluntary and compulsory insurance, with contributions from employers and employees. There is only limited state support, although there is some support for old-age pensions and sickness and maternity benefits, although the retirement age has been increased. In 2010, a reform of the unemployment insurance implied an increase in contributions, but also a **replacement rate** at 70 percent. The welfare state that has emerged in Switzerland can be characterized a **continental** and **conservative** type.

T

TAKE-UP RATE. The percentage of those eligible for benefits who actually receive them. A take-up rate of 100 percent means that all those who have a **right** to a certain benefit receive it. Reasons for **nontake-up** may be the feeling of **stigma** when receiving a benefit or lack of knowledge about the right to receive it. It is difficult to estimate take-up rates, as those eligible for a benefit but not claiming it may not be included in the statistics and also not be known to the **public sector**.

TARGETING. In **social policy**, this means directing benefits toward groups with specific **needs**. Targeting involves the selection of who receives the benefits, and it can thereby be used to reduce the economic pressure on the **welfare state**. Very specific targeting can make it possible that certain groups will not be covered by the system. Thus, the use of targeting can result in **marginalization** of these groups.

TAX COMPLIANCE. Having a **tax** system and rules on how to pay and collect taxes and duties is important in the way **welfare states** are **financed**; however, compliance with the rules is central in getting the revenue from individuals and companies. The degree of tax compliance refers to how many pay the taxes they should. Use of tax havens is a way to reduce tax payment and thus part of why compliance is not achieved, but a lack of control can explain the level of compliance. Finally, the activities in the **hidden economy** are an element that reduce the level of compliance in different countries.

TAX EXPENDITURES. These expenditures are a way to give, redistribute, or allocate resources in society. A **government** may use tax expenditures to have an impact on the **distribution** of welfare. **Richard Titmuss** labeled tax expenditures **fiscal welfare**. Tax expenditures are defined as a departure from the generally accepted or benchmark structure, which produces a favorable **tax** treatment. This can be for either individuals or certain groups in society.

Measuring and calculating tax expenditures is quite difficult. They can be calculated by the use of revenue forgone, revenue gained, or the outlay equivalence method. Most empirical studies use revenue forgone, as this can be calculated by looking at the different favorable tax treatments and their impact on revenue. Both the revenue gained and outlay equivalence methods raise additional problems and further questions, for example, in relation to the consequences of the dynamic changes in an economy.

Tax expenditures are not only used in the field of **social policy** or **welfare-state** expenditure, as they are also utilized in broader areas. They have an impact on the distribution and redistribution of resources in the welfare state. By using tax expenditures, it is possible to give certain groups better conditions than others or provide **incentives** to promote savings/investments and so on.

The advantage of tax expenditures in relation to social policy is the ability to reach targeted groups quite easily through the tax system. This can result in a high **take-up rate**, as all those qualified for the benefit will have easy access to it and do not have to make a special application and go through other formalities. Furthermore, tax expenditures can be targeted at those groups with the lowest income by, for example, giving a specific tax reduction to income groups below a certain ceiling.

The disadvantage of tax expenditures is that they are mainly based on income statistics, which may be inaccurate. Moreover, if the individual has to claim them when sending in tax returns, some will not receive them. Furthermore, they may hide the size of the welfare state since information on the macro level is rarely available. Because of their general characteristics, tax expenditures often have an upside-down effect, meaning that they mainly benefit the middle **class** and groups in society with higher income levels. In many countries, it is not possible to get information on the size of tax expenditures, which makes it difficult to assess the distributional and social impact of their use.

TAXES AND TAX BASE. Taxes are the legislated amount of private income, company earnings, and value of real estate or other properties. Furthermore, they can be levied on goods and **services**. The individual or company will have to pay into **government**, regional, or local authorities without any **right** to receive anything specific back. In principle, taxes can be imposed anywhere in the economic system. They can be a fixed amount or as a percentage of the tax base. They can be proportional, progressive, or regressive in their impact.

The tax base is the value of everything that is subject to taxes. The base varies with the items defined as taxable and the valuation (or assessment) of those items. The trend has been to broaden the tax base as a way of reducing marginal taxes and duties, thereby reducing the possible **disincentives** arising from taxes and duties. *See also* INCENTIVE; TAX COMPLIANCE; TAX EXPENDITURES.

THIRD SECTOR. That part of society that lies outside the state and the **market**. Some prefer to describe the third sector as activities lying within the welfare triangle of **state, market, and civil society**. The third sector includes voluntary organizations, nonprofit organizations, private nonprofit organizations, philanthropic bodies, foundations of charities, charitable trusts, self-help groups, and other activities related to and between individuals outside the public and private sectors. The size of the third sector can be difficult to measure and can also vary between different types of **welfare states**. Still, in all welfare states, third-sector activities are important elements in the society's total activities.

THIRD WAY. The welfare policy advocated by Tony Blair of the Labour Party in the **United Kingdom**. The idea in third way politics has been to try to combine traditional social **democracy** with the challenges of a more **globalized** world. Elements in third way politics include activation and **labor market** policies to increase **equality, residual welfare**, social responsibility and individual obligations, **targeting** of benefits, and more effective **government** services.

THREE WORLDS OF WELFARE. The title of a book by Gøsta Esping-Andersen, published in 1990, that continues research on comparative **welfare state** issues by and with the use of the concept of **decommodification** and divides welfare states into three different regime types (**continental, liberal**, and **social democratic**).

TITMUSS, RICHARD MORRIS (1907–1973). Titmuss was one of the key figures in research and writings on **social policy** in the 20th century. From 1950 until his death in 1973, he was professor of social administration at the London School of Economics. He wrote on **poverty, social exclusion**, and the **welfare state**, and was also the first to introduce the distinction among **public welfare, fiscal welfare**, and **occupational welfare**.

TRADE UNION. A collection of individuals who have the same interests and either the same type of **education** or same type of jobs, who have come together to improve their own pay and conditions of work. In some countries, trade unions are divided along religious or political lines. Thus, there might be a Catholic or Protestant affiliation. Political lines have been related to **communist**, social democratic, or conservative understanding.

In many countries, trade unions have been a major factor, acting as **pressure groups** and urging the development of a **welfare state** by emphasizing the need for coverage and support in case of specific **contingencies**, for example, **industrial injury**. The trade unions still play a role in many **social security** issues, and in many countries they actively participate in shaping **collective agreements**, which have an impact on the level of wages and coverage for **pensions** and **sickness benefits** or **health insurance**.

Trade unions often play a central role in **integrating** the social partners in decision making and participate in **tripartite** negotiations. Such social partnerships as a way of developing societies can be found in many welfare states. Trade unions are integrated in the development of **labor market policy**, including **active labor market policy** and other policies related to, for example, work and safety in the workplace.

In the **United Kingdom**, regarding the number of members, the Trades Union Congress (founded in 1867) is the central body, or where appropriate, the Scottish Trades Union Congress or the Irish Congress of Trade Unions. In the United Kingdom, the miners strike in 1984 and 1985, by Arthur Scargill, from the National Union of Mineworkers, is one instance of a conflict where the trade unions lost, and after that, the Conservative-led **government** reduced the trade unions' options and influence.

In **Germany**, the most important labor organization is the German Confederation of Trade Unions, having more than 6 million members. The German system, which resembles a **corporatist** system, implies that the trade union still plays a central role.

An example of a trade union also having had a strong political impact is Solidarity in **Poland**, which was established in 1980, at the Gdansk Shipyard, under the leadership of Lech Walesa. It was the first trade union not controlled by the Communist Party in a Warsaw Pact country, and it was also involved in several strikes. Solidarity reached 9.5 million members before its September 1981 Congress. In the 1980s, Solidarity was a broad social movement with a focus on workers' **rights** and **social change**. In December 1990, Walesa was elected president of Poland. Since then, the organization has become a more traditional, **liberal** trade union.

In the Nordic countries, the Confederations of Trade Unions have had a strong influence on the development of the welfare state, including working conditions; however, more recently, they have had a more weakened position.

TRANSACTION COSTS. This refers to the fact that all types of activities cost something, either directly in money or time for the organization. When entering a new contract, for example, there is a **need** to find out what the price of the contract should be, find someone to enter into the contract, and make and write the contract. Employing a new person also has such transaction costs as advertising, reading applications, holding interviews, and so forth. Thus, in relation to the **welfare state**, using private providers can imply a new type of cost for the **public sector**, which one needs to take into account to find out whether the use of a private provider is cheaper or more expensive than producing the service within the public sector. *See also* PRIVATIZATION.

TRANSFER. Welfare states transfer money or **vouchers** to individuals so that they may either have a sufficient amount of money to avoid living in **poverty** or to help individuals and **families** in certain circumstances.

TRANSFERABILITY. Individuals working and/or living in different countries or moving when retired may need to be able to take social benefits with them; therefore, in the **European Union**, for example, there is a **right** to take certain **social security** benefits from one country to another. When retiring and having worked in different countries, it is often the case that individuals will get a partial **pension** depending upon the number of years worked in these different countries. Having worked for 10 years in four countries, for instance, the person will receive 10/40, or a quarter of a pension, from each of the four countries. These elements have been introduced to reduce the possible negative impact for migrant workers.

TRIPARTITE. This describes participation by three parties in discussions and decision making, especially in relation to **labor market policy**, but in the most developed tripartite structures, for example, **corporatism**, and also in relation to economic policy in a broader sense. The three parties participating are normally understood to be the state, the employers, and the employees. In corporatist states, these three parties are central actors in relation to core elements of welfare policy. *See also* INTERNATIONAL LABOUR ORGANIZATION (ILO).

TRUST. This concept has gained importance in analyzing **welfare states** in recent years, as there has been greater focus on trust in the delivery of welfare **services** and the relationship between provider and user in many countries. Trust in this connection is central to **prevent free rides** and avoid, for example when using **vouchers**, the service provider engaging in **cream-skimming**. Trust can vary and is a highly individual element. It is often stated that it takes a long time to build trust, but that it can be lost in a few seconds.

U

UKRAINE. Ukraine was part of the former **Union of Soviet Socialist Republics (USSR)**, during which time it had a **communist** type of welfare system. The country has been independent since 1991, and it has approximately 45 million inhabitants. Ukraine's **welfare state** policy was, to a large extent, developed in the former USSR with, until 1991, a strong emphasis on guaranteed work as a core of the welfare system. After independence, a new law on social assistance was enacted in 1992.

The first **social welfare** legislation dates from 1912, and concerns **industrial injury, sickness benefits**, and **maternity benefits**. A law on **unemployment** followed in 1921, and one on **pensions** in 1922. In 1944, the **family allowance** system was adopted. These laws have been reformulated and changed since independence. The current system is chiefly a **social insurance** system, although it provides **universal** coverage for **family** allowances and **health care**. Employers pay a large proportion of the cost through a 37 percent **tax** on payroll. Employees also pay a small percentage based on their earnings. A new pension reform in 2011 raised the retirement age to 60 for women and 62 for men who work in public **service**. It also increased the insurance qualifying period to 30 years for women and 35 years for men.

UNDERCLASS. *See* CLASS.

UNDEREMPLOYMENT. This term is used to describe the situation in which individuals are unable to get as much work as they would like to have. Workers are underemployed when they are willing to supply more hours of work than their employers are willing to offer. In principle, this can be as low as zero, thereby eventually being nonemployment. In times of **financial crisis** and high levels of **unemployment**, there is a particularly high risk of underemployment. This implies that when economic growth starts, the labor supply can be increased. There may thus be a vacant labor supply for the **welfare states** if the economies begin growing again after a period of slow economic growth.

UNEMPLOYMENT. The state of being without a job but actively looking for work. Unemployed individuals should be both able and willing to take up a vacant job. The unemployment rate describes the percentage of the **labor force** that is unemployed. Different types of and explanations for unemployment exist, including classical unemployment, **Marxist** unemployment, and Keynesian unemployment. Some focus more on the reasons behind unemployment, which can be structural, voluntary, weather conditions, seasonal, technological, and the business cycle.

In **classical economic** theory, unemployment is explained by inadequate flexibility in real wages; that is, if the wages of those searching for a job were entirely flexible, full employment would prevail. In Keynesian economic theory, a lack of demand in the economy explains the level of unemployment. Thus, a change in the overall demand for labor would help ensure a balance between demand and supply. This could, for example, be achieved by public works similar to those used in many countries during the 1930s, including Franklin D. Roosevelt's New Deal in the **United States**. In Marxist theory, the explanation is that there is too low a profit level.

The different theories suggest various remedies to change the level of unemployment. In **welfare states**, the level of unemployment and the consequences for the individual and **families** have had an impact on the creation of unemployment schemes and policies to increase **employment** and hopefully also reduce unemployment. Unemployment has been seen as one of the major explanations of **poverty, inequality**, and **social exclusion**. This largely depends on the level of **unemployment benefits** and the length of time unemployment benefits are available. In welfare states with low levels of unemployment benefits, the risk of poverty is greater, and at the same time, the figures in relation to the level of unemployment may be misleading, as fewer people may register for unemployment benefits if the level is low.

Historically, the level of unemployment has varied worldwide. It was high during the economic crisis in the 1930s, was high again after the first and second oil shocks in the 1970s, and has increased considerably in many countries since the **financial crisis** of 2008. During the most recent crisis, young people have had the highest incidence of unemployment in some countries, and in Southern Europe and Eastern Europe, every second young person is unemployed. The rate of employment for most OECD countries is presented in appendix F. Whether the world will return to a substantially lower level of unemployment depends upon the possibility of increasing economic growth in the developed world; however, the rapid aging of Western societies, with more elderly individuals leaving the **labor market** than young entering it, implies that a reduction should be possible in the long run. In the Third World, reduction will be highly dependent upon economic growth. From a welfare perspective, a long-term spell of unemployment implies a risk that many individuals will never reenter the labor market, leaving these people with the potential to be dependent on welfare benefits. *See also* HIDDEN ECONOMY; LABOR MARKET POLICY; UNDEREMPLOYMENT.

UNEMPLOYMENT BENEFIT. A benefit that can be received when the social **contingency** of **unemployment** occurs. Different countries have different systems for delivering these benefits, as well as various criteria for receiving them. In most systems, the individual must be a member of an unemployment insurance fund, have paid contributions for a certain period of time, and be actively seeking a job while unemployed. In some systems, the newly educated can get benefits that they may be ineligible for in other programs. For those having been unemployed for some time, often about a year, the unemployment benefit is no longer available, and the individual must rely on **social assistance**. Depending upon the system, it may then be difficult to again become eligible for a benefit, and the person will have often to work for a certain amount of time before gaining the **right** to the **service**. Thus, those working on the fringe of the **labor market** are often less protected than others.

Furthermore, the level of the unemployment benefits is subject to a ceiling, and the time period to receive is limited. The level may also be **means-tested**, and it may vary for young, educated people and those who have only been in the labor market for a few years. The systems may also vary from a **social insurance** system to a fully actuarial insurance system. The **financing** can vary from a purely individual system to a system in which employees, employers, and the state participate in financing it. Given the difference in risk of becoming unemployed, this is an argument for a collective unemployment insurance system, as for some it would otherwise involve a prohibitively high price to pay to be covered.

UNION OF SOVIET SOCIALIST REPUBLICS (USSR). A now dissolved union of countries in Europe and Asia build upon a **communist** legacy of jobs and a duty to work for everyone in a centrally planned economy, including state ownership of buildings, production, shops, and so forth, implying that, for example, **housing** costs and the price of bread were low. Thus, the development of classical **social security** systems was also not carried out to the same degree as in other countries. *See also* RUSSIA.

UNITED KINGDOM. The first elements of **social policy** in the United Kingdom were the **Poor Laws**. These changed in 1834, to take account of industrialization and the new risks that arose as a consequence thereof. Poor relief was at such a low level that the income was below that of those working in the factories. A workhouse test was introduced, which meant that individuals not able to support themselves could be put in a workhouse, where they received just enough food to survive.

In the period between 1830–1880 many voluntary organizations were established, with the aim of self-help. They included friendly societies, building societies, and **trade unions**. They tried to **prevent** people from falling into **poverty** and being forced into workhouses. The combination of continuous bad working and living conditions as a consequence of the Industrial Revolution and the growth of new political groups is a major explanation for the emergence of new initiatives in social policy legislation. **Industrial injury** was the first area to be covered, in 1897; followed by a **universal** old-age **pension** in 1908; **unemployment benefits** and **sickness benefits** in 1911; and, finally, **family allowances** in 1945.

The changes from 1908 onward were brought about by a **liberal government**, elected in 1906. It was committed to a policy in which those who were poor or unemployed for good reasons would be covered to a certain degree. It seems obvious that the British government—although it did not use the insurance principle—was inspired by Otto von Bismarck's reforms and, in this way, was trying to reduce social unrest.

Reforms were not undertaken during World War I, and only in relation to unemployment benefits was radical change made during the interwar period. A reform of 1934 was, in fact, an amalgamation of poor relief acts and the unemployment benefit system. This was forced through because the unemployment benefit systems were no longer able to pay for themselves and needed public support. Between World War I and World War II, a situation emerged in which voluntary groups played an important role in the system. At the same time, a complicated system that still did not cover all risks had been developed.

Because of these changes and the social consciousness that developed during World War II, the Beveridge Commission was established. The Beveridge Report had a profound influence on British social policy. Furthermore, the ideas of **John Maynard Keynes** on economic demand management influenced the decision-making process.

The Beveridge Report pointed out that the system was "conducted by a complex of disconnected administrative organs, proceeding on different principles." The proposal for reform was to pool risks by individuals having access to a **social insurance** system through paying a flat-rate contribution and with a possibility of receiving a **flat-rate benefit**. This was the cornerstone of the report's recommendations. The report's main recommendation was implemented through a new National Insurance Act in 1946, the National Insurance

Injuries Act in 1946, and the National Assistance Act in 1948. The levels of benefits were set very low, presumably lower than those envisaged by Beveridge. In 1948, a new national **health** service was introduced by act of parliament. The general consensus supporting the reforms can be seen as one of the reasons why the system lasted nearly 35 years without any radical changes.

Still, more general systems and **services** developed and grew until the end of the 1970s, when the Conservative Party, under Margaret Thatcher, took over. The system continued to build on flat-rate contributions and a low level of benefits. Other elements were gradually introduced. These included a state earnings-related pension in 1975, which was a break from the tradition of **flat-rate benefits**. It was put on top of the flat-rate pension. Thatcher dismantled the scheme by making it possible to opt out, and it was replaced by private insurance—supported by **tax** grants.

The Thatcher era saw a tightening of eligibility conditions and periods when unemployment benefits could be received. **Means tests** for benefits were introduced in several areas with the Social Security Act of 1980 and the Social Security and Housing Benefit Act of 1982. There was greater reliance on the **market** for social provisions (either individually or as occupational systems), which, to a certain degree, could be supported by tax allowances. Finally, voluntary organizations were again playing a pivotal role in the social system. It was argued that additional voluntary contributions could help the British system continue to give the dependent a decent living standard.

The British **welfare state** is, therefore, no longer as universal as was the intention of the Beveridge Report, and it has many characteristics that more closely resemble the liberal approach to the welfare state. In 1990s and early 2000s, the United Kingdom moved to what the Labour Party called a **third way** in social policy. The third way, it is argued, is somewhere between the liberal approach and the more **social democratic** approach, emphasizing both the use of market forces and the state's social responsibility. Conservative prime minister David Cameron, who was elected in 2010, has since promoted, after strong cuts in welfare spending, what has been labeled the **Big Society** program. The intention is to more actively involve citizens in the development and provision of welfare services. Still, the British welfare state, compared to other welfare states, places less emphasis on direct delivery of **care**, especially for children, and is nearly a fully private market solution.

UNITED NATIONS (UN). Established in 1945, with the purpose of helping to create and maintain peace, and further encourage international cooperation and the ability to find solutions for economic, social, and cultural problems, this is the most important international organization. Most countries in the world today are members in the UN.

The UN system has many important institutions, including the **International Labour Organization (ILO)**, World Health Organization (WHO), United Nations Children's Fund (UNICEF), United Nations Educational, Scientific, and Cultural Organization (UNESCO). The WHO helps especially poor countries with a food program and vaccinations for various diseases, whereas UNICEF deals with children's daily lives, and UNESCO with **education**. The Economic and Social Council (ECOSOC) has as its goals improving living standards throughout the world and promoting full **employment**. In 2004 and 2005, for example, the UN helped the victims of the tsunami in Southeast Asia through a large relief program and by coordinating the assistance from the many donor countries.

UNITED STATES OF AMERICA. Generally speaking, the United States has been a latecomer in the development of **social security** and social policies, and even today it lags behind the European notion of what a **welfare state** is. The late development of federal systems does not mean that no social security existed due to the federal structure of the United States. At the local level, several types of poor relief existed that changed throughout time as economic conditions and possibilities changed. Some—mainly white veterans— also received state **pensions**, although not as part of a general pension system.

In the period after World War I, the strategy seems to have been to move away from the more European types of welfare state. To an even greater extent than the **Bismarckian** welfare state, the United States relied on **occupational welfare**, that is, company-related benefits and pension plans that were sometimes supported by **tax** incentives. Still, the development of federal legislation was slow until 1935.

Workers compensation was introduced in several states. In 1915, approximately 30 percent of the workforce was covered. Pensions were generally introduced in 1935, and in the same year, **unemployment benefits** were introduced as part of the New Deal. **Sickness benefits** and **maternity benefits** were first introduced in 1965, and **health insurance** for the disabled came in 1972.

The New Deal, the reforms implemented by Franklin D. Roosevelt in two rounds, in 1933–1935 and 1935–1939, were cornerstones of later U.S. welfare systems. The first round mainly focused on the creation of jobs in the aftermath of the collapse of the financial **markets** in 1929 and the Depression. The second round focused on social security and introduced new legislation, with a broader scope and perspective than had ever been witnessed before in the United States. The New Deal included a state **unemployment** insurance program and a federal grant program to help dependent children, the blind, and the elderly. Matching grants for vocational rehabilitation, infant and maternal health, and aid to crippled children were introduced. Finally, it included the aforementioned old-age program. These new initiatives were **financed** out of payroll **taxation**, and a large part of the programs relied on the individual states to follow up and undertake local initiatives.

In contrast to Western European welfare states, only limited changes took place after World War II in the United States, and it can still be regarded as a laggard compared to Europe in relation to **social policy**. Part of the explanation is that there was no real pressure from **trade unions**, and the balance of power between federal and state authorities has made it difficult to implement general and more **universal** systems. Furthermore, the historically **individualistic** approach in the country emphasized a preference for solutions based on nonstate organizations. The United States still does not have a comprehensive **health care** system. Only in the 1960s, during the John F. Kennedy administration, was there any intention to initiate new social programs, but few modifications actually occurred.

The current system consists of two main areas—an insurance-based system and public assistance. The insurance system is for the employed and is therefore biased in favor of the middle **class**. Public assistance is **targeted** and **means-tested**, so only the poorest individuals can receive the benefits. Compared to Europe, there is a great reliance on private **charity** organizations to provide welfare in relation to children and health care. This means that there is a much broader scope for **nongovernmental organizations** and less impact from direct public provision. There does not seem to be any change underway in this respect, and it seems that the best chance for the poor is a flexible **labor market policy** and creation of new jobs in the service sector.

In general, the model can be described as a **liberal** market-based system in which only those who have a job are covered. The rest of the population is only covered to a limited extent, and often only if they can afford to take out insurance. As a result, the most vulnerable have a relatively low living standard because they have to rely upon Temporary Assistance for Needy Families, which has eliminated individual **entitlement** and instead focuses on work and personal responsibility. The law further limits the number of months for receiving **social assistance** during a lifetime to 60. The absence of any guaranteed minimum income explains why the U.S. model is sometimes described as a **working poor** model. In 2010, a new health care reform was enacted, widening the scope and coverage of health care. *See also* OBAMA CARE.

UNIVERSALISM. This is often interpreted as access to **social security** for all citizens of a given society as long as they fulfill certain criteria for eligibility for the specific benefit, for example, being sick, having had an **industrial**

injury, or reaching a certain age. It often characterizes the **institutional welfare state model** and has been primarily used in the northern part of Europe.

The basic arguments for universalism are, first, that a society's development has resulted in individuals needing more help, and that as societies have developed (industrialization, more complex societies, etc.), it has been a collective responsibility to help those in **need** after these changes. Second, is the idea that all of us, as human beings, have basic **rights**. A narrower definition of universalism is that it should only apply to individuals who are in similar conditions and have the same rights. This principle can involve a distinction between those who through no fault of their own need help and those who, due to their own way of living, need help. (*see also* DESERVING AND UNDESERVING).

In many **welfare states**, the distinction between universalism and particularism has had an impact on the way the systems have been fashioned. The more universal systems have been based on citizens' rights (*see also* T. H. MARSHALL), thereby reducing the scope for individual solutions. Even with universal rights, some welfare systems mainly guarantee a minimum protection, and those wishing for a higher level of protection will have to find individual solutions, for example, by taking out private insurance. Treatment at hospitals, is, in most welfare states, a prime example of a universal service.

UTILITARIANISM. A theoretical framework within which society's overall aim is to maximize the total **utility** of the citizens. If total utility is the most important goal, resources have to be increased for one citizen even at the cost of another. A utilitarian will chiefly argue for a free **market**, given that the individual is seen as the best one to know exactly what to choose in all areas, which can be done in the market under the condition that no **market failure** exists. In principle, it is the individual's pleasure when using a resource that results in what is best for society.

Utilitarianism has been used to try to define a society's welfare function based on the addition of individual preferences. This concept can also be labeled **methodological individualism** due to its emphasis on the individual. Utilitarianism would also prescribe intervention to increase **equality**, as this would be in line with the moral and political philosophy behind the theory, emphasizing that society should take into account and maximize all individuals' **happiness**, this despite that fact that subjective and **normative** elements are involved in such a procedure.

UTILITY. In **welfare economics**, utility describes the individual's satisfaction in having or consuming a specific combination of goods and **services**. In classical descriptions (Jeremy Bentham, John Stuart Mill), utility is defined as **happiness** and pleasure. According to **classical economists**, the individual will try to maximize his or her utility given the constraints, for example, of production possibilities, wealth, and income.

An individual's choice will be based on the highest utility level that can be achieved. It is not only absolute utility that is of interest. The marginal utility, which refers to the extra utility one person gets from an extra unit of a good, has been an influential concept in the debate on **justice** and **inequality**, indicating, for example, that a rich person will at some point have a decreasing utility from the consumption of extra units of a specific good. Society's overall welfare function—if measured as the total utility—could then be increased if redistribution from the rich to the poor took place.

The main problem with the concept of utility is the difficulty in measuring it. When it is not possible to measure utility in a way that everyone can agree on, its use in concrete policy making is more difficult. Furthermore, the utilities one person derives from a good may be very different from what another derives from the same good due to diverse preferences. This means that utility can be a difficult concept to use systematically.

UTOPIA. An ideal state described by Thomas More (1478–1535) in a book published in 1516. The name is of a place that does not exist. In **welfare-state** and philosophical discussions, Utopia is seen as an ideal that one could move toward but presumably never reach. At the same time, utopian approaches have been seen as ways to formulate ideas and hypotheses that can be used in debates about the development of the welfare state, including discussion on how to balance **rights** and duties.

V

VERTICAL EQUITY. This term describes the consequences of redistribution from wealthier to poorer groups in society. This redistribution can be in terms of income, wealth, buying power, or access to different types of **services**. How this redistribution takes place does not influence the principle, but when measuring **inequality**, it may have an impact on whether the redistribution is first to those who have the lowest income or, for example, to someone at the top or to someone just below the middle in the income **distribution**. Both types of redistribution would achieve a higher degree of vertical equity, but the overall change in the level of inequality would be different.

VOLUNTARY SECTOR. Those who are willing to perform functions in society for the benefit of people other than themselves and their closest relatives. The voluntary sector can be found in most **welfare states**, but it is more developed in some than others. Voluntary action is not only directly related to **social policy**, it is also tied to the area of sports and leisure activities, especially for children and young individuals. The voluntary sector is based on—as the words say—voluntary activities by individuals who will often receive support directly or indirectly from the welfare state; however, there is a conflict in being a voluntary organization and yet receiving state support to carry out activities, since receiving state support may reduce the independence of the organization.

In the debate about the welfare state, the quality and ability of the voluntary sector to support the vulnerable has been questioned by those who think that individuals should not run the risk of becoming dependent on **charity**, and that there is a risk that discretionary judgment by those performing the **voluntary work** will not provide access to social benefits in a just way. Furthermore, voluntary work may have a tendency to concentrate in specific areas, leaving other areas of the welfare state with less support. In most welfare states, the voluntary sector supplements state involvement in welfare policies. *See also* NONGOVERNMENTAL ORGANIZATION (NGO); PRESSURE GROUPS.

VOLUNTARY WORK. A term for a person doing work on a voluntary basis and therefore without getting a wage income for the work. Being voluntary also implies that the individual has the **right** to stop when he or she wishes to do so, suggesting that voluntary work may not be as stable as paid work. In **welfare states**, it is argued that voluntary work is necessary because the state cannot afford to pay for all activities and, furthermore, that some activities are outside the scope of the welfare state, for example, ensuring social relations. Voluntary work has existed in various forms and in various sectors in most welfare states for centuries. It is often seen as a supplement to state activities. Voluntary work consists of visiting lonely people or helping in **child care** institutions or sports clubs. It can also include making food or helping to collect money for voluntary activities.

VOUCHERS. Coupons that are connected with certain **rights** to buy a given **service** or good. Vouchers have been used, among other things, to provide lunches for school children. They are also a way to give citizens rights as consumers in relation to teaching, **child care**, and **care** for the elderly. The use of vouchers offers the possibility of creating something that resembles a **market** within the **public sector** in the **welfare state**. In the **United States**, for example, vouchers have been issued in the form of food stamps/cards, giving the individual a right to get food. An argument for using vouchers has been that it is thereby known what the individual gets from the public economic support. Vouchers are also used in different welfare states as part of **marketization** of welfare services and a way of creating more competition within the public sector. A risk with vouchers is that **cream-skimming** will occur, and that a more **segregated** society will emerge.

WEBER, MAX (1864–1920). One of the most outstanding theorists of the 20th century, Weber published works in many different fields of the social sciences (philosophy, theology, sociology, economics, and political science). With respect to **welfare-state** analysis, his work is of particular interest in that it focuses on two elements: **bureaucracy** and the understanding of human behavior.

Bureaucracy in a Weberian sense is an effective administrative body that knows exactly what to do and will do it in the most efficient way. The reason for this efficiency can be seen in the clear rules and hierarchical order of the administrative system; therefore, those who are employed will know what to do and when to do it. The individuals will act in a rational way, and the system will be rational and effective. The understanding of human behavior refers to an analysis of how and to what degree individuals interact. It has the intention of learning and accepting why they are acting as they are. Learning about individual behavior could then lead to understanding actions.

Weber's ideas have been challenged by some who have argued that his work on bureaucracy and political systems was a **legitimization** of fascism and a demand for a strong political leader. Others see Weber as a founder of modern sociology and claim that he merely wanted to develop an analytical way of looking at modern society that would be open to debate and better ways of understanding social processes.

Weber's research on the Protestant work ethic has been influential in the discussion about the organization of society and production. In this way, his ideas have influenced many scholars, who have tried to understand what is behind the welfare state and how it can be understood. *See also* RATIONALITY.

WELFARE ECONOMICS. A theory that is concerned with how to maximize society's welfare function and find ways to improve welfare in a society. Furthermore, it tries to analyze whether different types of intervention will increase or decrease society's welfare. It is often based on using the individual's value judgment of welfare as a condition for comparing different situations. Changes in the individual's welfare will always be seen as an improvement if one person's situation is improved without any other person's situation being worsened (the **Pareto** criteria). This analysis is quite difficult in practice; therefore, other types of criteria have been developed. The Kaldor-Hicks compensation principle is one of the most famous. This states that it is still a welfare improvement if those gaining by the change can compensate the losers and still have a surplus. Today, welfare economics is merely a broad term describing analysis of the **welfare state** and **welfare society** by using economic theory based on rational behavior in various situations and involving various decisions in society.

WELFARE SOCIETY. This is a broader term than **welfare state**, as it includes wider and more elaborate viewpoints on **democracy** and nonmonetary items; however, as the two concepts are frequently used interchangeably, in this book, the main presentation and discussion comes under the concept of the welfare state. Welfare society can sometimes also be understood in a broader context by including **nongovernmental organizations**, **voluntary work**, **occupational welfare**, and the welfare created in **families**. The concept thereby emphasizes that welfare is produced not only by the state, but also to a large extent by other actors in various societies.

WELFARE STATE. This term has been defined in various ways throughout time, and there is still no consensus about what a welfare state is. According to Flora et al., the term was introduced by Archbishop Temple in 1941, as an answer to the aggression and power of **Germany**. It could be argued that the rise of the welfare state after World War II—at least in the **United Kingdom**—was especially due to the vision of William Beveridge on administration and **John Maynard Keynes** with regard to having a commitment to full **employment** and economic stability. Others claim that the term was coined by Alfred Zimmern of Oxford in 1934, but made more popular by Archbishop Temple in *Citizen and Churchman*, from 1940.

The concept may be seen as a contrast to the **laissez-faire** state, and also as a way to interpret the state's role in more than political terms. It develops the **rights** of individual citizens as part of the state's role in society. Again, it may further be seen in contrast to a power state.

Different definitions of the term *welfare state* can be found in various dictionaries. They are as follows:

> *Oxford English Dictionary* (1955): "A polity so organized that every member of the **community** is assured of his due maintenance with the most advantageous conditions possible for all."

Oxford Paperback Dictionary (1988): "A country seeking to ensure the welfare of all its citizens by means of **social services** operated by the state."

Encyclopedia Americana (1968): "A form of **government** in which the state assumes responsibility for minimum standards of living for every person."

International Encyclopedia of the Social Sciences (1968): "The institutional outcome of the assumption by a society of legal and therefore formal and explicit responsibility of the basic **well-being** of all its members."

Encyclopedia Britannica (1974): "A concept of government in which the state plays a key role in the protection of the economic and **social welfare** of its citizens."

These definitions center on the way in which the state makes and develops **social security** for its citizens.

A definition often quoted comes from **Asa Briggs** (1969): "A welfare state is a state in which organized power is deliberately used in an effort to modify the play of **market** forces." This definition emphasizes the questions of how and why a welfare state intervenes in society. Deliberate intervention is a core problem when discussing welfare-state issues. It is often interpreted as state intervention, but state intervention is sometimes not, at least deliberately, used to modify the play of market forces, although the intervention will have an impact. An example is **education**, which does not directly aim at intervention in the market; however, it may, in the long run, have an impact on the market forces' ability to function.

Briggs suggested that the modification of the market should take place in at least three ways:

1. By guaranteeing minimum income
2. By the narrowing of insecurity
3. By all citizens having a right to the best standards available

The last point refers to what in the welfare-state debate has been labeled **universalism** versus selectivism. An instrument that should guarantee all citizens—within certain defined limits—rights is a universal principle, which could mean that many states will not be regarded as welfare states.

Still, even if this is agreed upon as being a good definition of a welfare state, there is and will be many problems in measuring it. When is a state deliberately trying to modify the play of market forces? Is it when declaring rhetorically that it is doing so, or is it when we can see direct intervention in the economy? Or should we examine the laws passed in the legislature that have an impact on the individual firms? Or should we be more interested in the way the **financing** of the state has an impact on individual households, firms, or markets? The Briggs definition is thus mainly a starting point for a discussion of what a welfare state is.

Economists focus on the economic impact of the state on society, political scientists focus on the decision-making process, and sociologists focus on who has responsibility for the individual in society. **Social policy** and social workers focus more on how society is organized and how the interaction between social workers and society and the client should be.

From different theoretical perspectives, it is still difficult to find out when we are really dealing with a welfare state. How great should the state's involvement in society be before we can talk about a welfare state? What will we include in our measurement of the welfare state? The reason for asking these types of questions is clearly that some of the state's expenditures do not belong to expenditures in the area of a welfare state. This is the case, for example, with expenditures on military service, foreign policy, and at least part of the administration. Expenditures on internal security, control of mergers, and other legal areas would normally also be outside the scope of a welfare state. This gives rise to further problems about how to analyze the concept and which expenditures should be included when analyzing it.

Should we focus on expenditures from the Department of Social Security, or should we take a broader view, including the Department of Labor or Department of Housing, and how should we draw the boundaries? There are no straightforward answers to these questions. They will largely depend upon the purpose of the analysis. Furthermore, it is often not enough to just examine legal intervention and the legal rules, as economic rules in the **tax** system may have an impact and, moreover, **collective bargaining** either directly or indirectly supported by the government could have an impact on the welfare state.

Using the Organization for Economic Cooperation and Development, International Monetary Fund, Eurostat, or other central statistical sources is another way to describe the size of the welfare state that may yield different results; therefore, it is necessary to be aware of, and investigate how, these entities have defined different areas before using the data for an interpretation of the welfare state's development. In addition, the data may be skewed, as they do not include **tax expenditures**, which means that those parts of the welfare state that are provided for by the tax system are not reflected in the figures used for analytical purposes.

These difficulties in analyzing the nature of the welfare state also indicate why the literature has been so full of attempts to find typologies able to describe different types of welfare states, for instance, the **Beveridgian model, Bismarckian model, Confucian model, conservative model, liberal model, Scandinavian welfare state model, social democratic welfare model,** and **Southern European welfare state model.** This large variety of models indicates why the welfare state is so challenging to describe and define.

The measurement of the welfare state often focuses on the level of expenditure as a proportion of **gross domestic product,** the way the welfare state is financed, and the organization of the welfare state (private/public delivery). But this is insufficient; one also has to examine the welfare state in its historical context. This is due to the fact that both the historical reasons for the development of various welfare states and the chosen strategies differ, and the chosen solutions will therefore also presumably differ despite that **convergence** has also taken place.

The introduction in many countries of programs that can be seen as forerunners to welfare-state programs is related to the political and economic situation in those countries. In **Germany,** for example, the intention of Chancellor Otto von Bismarck's programs was to reduce, or eliminate, unrest in the working population by providing **social insurance** programs. In other countries, the introduction of welfare-state programs was a response to the changing **need** for protection in the population in the wake of the Industrial Revolution.

The new needs first and foremost had to do with the fact that due to the Industrial Revolution, many workers were not covered in case of accidents and sickness, and **families** were dependent on the income of one person when they moved to the cities. This created a need for new types of organization and structures in society. In many countries, the state was involved in fulfilling these needs, because the market, left to itself, did not provide these types of security.

Along with the first kinds of protection (accidents and sickness), there was an increased need for support in relation to **pensions,** education, **housing,** and spouses. Likewise, the systems gradually developed support for people living in **poverty,** income supplements for low-income earners, housing benefits, and so on.

Today, the welfare state can be found in many different forms, from the all-encompassing "cradle to the grave," to a more minimalist system in which only minor benefits are provided by the **public sector** and the rest by the private sector. They differ in the way they are financed, from universal tax systems to systems mainly based upon individual contributions and private insurance. There is also a range of systems, where the emphasis varies from focusing on specific **contingencies** to living standards for individuals, and from systems in which a large portion of the benefit consists of income support and mainly public income transfers to systems that largely rely on **benefits in-kind** or provision of **care**, for example, in the form of care for the elderly by providing homes for them.

In Europe, a slight tendency toward convergence seems to be taking place through the emphasis on certain minimum standards to be provided by the state. In addition, occupational benefits or private sources will supplement that support. This has a historical connection with the **continental model**, but it is a more mixed model, in which universal **entitlement** and universal delivery are also included. History indicates that welfare states have often taken a long time to develop and mature, and even then changes may continuously be taking place. These changes can involve **retrenchment**, but they may also be coverage of new areas, improving levels of benefits, and so forth. No clear trends can be perceived when analyzing the development of different welfare states, and even looking at activity during a span of a few years may be misleading, as a change can be temporary in nature. Some of the changes are related to the general economic climate, but in some countries, the **aging of societies** has also had an impact on welfare-state development in the past 10 to 15 years and may perhaps continue do so in the coming years.

Still, the main issue in most countries in relation to welfare states is the ability to guarantee basic economic security and protect individuals and families from various types of **market failures**. The following definition in *New Ways of Steering and Managing in the Welfare State* (Greve, 2002) is based on analysis of the various regimes and approaches to welfare: "By a welfare state is understood an institutionalized system where the actors the **state, market, and civil society** interact in various relations with the purpose of maximizing society's welfare function and where the degree of public involvement is sufficiently high to be able to counteract the consequences of market failure, including ensuring a guaranteed minimum income." *See also* MEASUREMENT OF WELFARE; WELFARE STATE TRIANGLE.

WELFARE STATE TRIANGLE. This term refers to the relationship among the **state, market, and civil society**, and how they interact with one another.

WELL-BEING. The simple understanding of the concept is that a person is well and has a good life. It can broadly be defined from two different angles. One is the absence of negative conditions, and the other as the existence of positive elements in life. Some objective elements are included, for example, average **life expectancy**, but subjective elements can also be incorporated. Well-being can further be seen as current contentment with life or the overall fulfillment of satisfaction with life; there may be both a short-term and long-term understanding of the concept.

Subjective well-being can be defined as the individuals' evaluation of his or her quality of life. The concept has been used to include three components: an assessment of whether one's life is good, whether one has a positive level of feelings, and that there are relatively few moments spent in negative moods. Well-being is thus a concept that tries to encompass the individuals' perceptions of his or her own life, but also, as in the issue of **social indicators**, to find out how to have a good life looking at it from both an objective and subjective perspective. The concept of well-being is therefore also related to such issues as **poverty** and **deprivation**. *See also* HAPPINESS.

WOMEN. *See* FEMINISM; GENDER.

WORK AND FAMILY LIFE. This has, to an increasing degree, been seen as an important aspect in ensuring **well-being** for individuals and **families**. It has also been part of guaranteeing that **gender equality** can be achieved in a society. There are various ways in which **welfare states** can help in achieving the goal of having a satisfactory work and family life, a prime example being the existence of affordable and high-quality **child care**; however, it also involves how working time is organized and whether it enables parents to work in such a way that they can both be parents and have a family life, and also be in the **labor market**.

WORKFARE. This term describes welfare systems with a strong emphasis on people receiving welfare benefits, for example, **social assistance** and **unemployment benefits**, fulfilling certain work requirements. It can be debated how much this differs from the early **Poor Laws**, and it can therefore also be questioned whether this is actually new. For some, workfare has a negative connotation of putting pressure on individuals to work even if they are unable to do so; for others, the positive connotation lies in the attempt to **integrate** or reintegrate individuals into the **labor market**.

WORKING POOR. When a person is working full-time or close to full-time and still has a disposable income below the **poverty** line, then this person is argued to be part of the working poor. The concept is used as a way of describing poverty so as to also include those who are in the **labor market** but who are unable to earn a sufficiently high level of income.

Appendix A

GDP per Head, U.S. Dollars, Constant Prices, Constant PPPs

	2002	*2005*	*2010*	*2011*	*2012*
Australia	32,737	34,888	36,582	37,257	—
Austria	32,306	33,637	35,322	36,131	36,278
Belgium	30,824	32,204	32,915	33,230	32,909
Canada	33,358	35,106	35,223	35,753	—
Chile	11,099	12,690	14,557	15,273	—
China	3,097	4,102	6,804	—	—
Czech Republic	18,390	21,268	23,625	24,102	23,771
Denmark	31,807	33,196	32,388	32,611	32,336
Estonia	13,118	16,531	16,741	18,126	18,718
EU (27 countries)	25,654	26,886	27,562	27,925	27,759
Euro area (17 countries)	28,524	29,314	29,814	30,153	29,898
Finland	28,336	30,708	31,310	32,036	31,819
France	28,668	29,554	29,636	30,081	29,939
Germany	30,659	31,117	33,573	34,581	34,754
Greece	21,758	24,348	23,997	22,287	—
Hungary	14,897	16,975	16,972	17,301	17,053
Iceland	30,395	34,992	32,758	33,598	33,968
Indonesia	2,875	3,207	3,916	—	—
Ireland	35,758	38,795	36,128	36,506	36,744
Israel	21,944	23,210	26,222	26,929	27,286
Italy	28,254	28,280	27,059	27,053	26,350
Japan	28,955	30,446	30,886	30,761	—
Korea	20,598	22,783	26,774	27,554	—
Luxembourg	63,688	68,211	68,605	68,143	66,801
Mexico	11,780	12,461	13,001	13,396	—
Netherlands	33,894	35,111	36,933	37,119	36,635
New Zealand	23,742	25,222	24,976	25,052	—
Norway	45,043	47,640	46,776	46,734	47,545
OECD	27,926	29,590	30,156	30,565	—
Poland	12,137	13,786	17,194	17,968	18,299
Portugal	21,439	21,369	21,780	21,414	20,813
Russian Federation	9,546	11,822	14,136	14,731	—
Slovak Republic	13,799	16,175	20,159	20,932	21,324
Slovenia	21,061	23,472	25,032	25,133	24,500
South Africa	7,887	8,601	9,508	9,730	—

	2002	2005	2010	2011	2012
Spain	26,095	27,392	26,899	26,981	26577
Sweden	30,067	32,701	34,124	35,123	35,130
Switzerland	35,586	36,648	39,267	39,600	39,683
Turkey	9,484	11,394	12,521	13,445	—
United Kingdom	30,475	32,952	32,814	32,890	32,714
United States	39,889	42,448	41,940	42,385	—

Source: Organization for Economic Cooperation and Development, http://stats.oecd.org/.

Appendix B

Government Spending as Percentage of GDP

	2000	*2005*	*2010*	*2011*
Australia	35.6	33.9	—	—
Austria	51.9	50.0	52.6	50.6
Belgium	49.1	51.9	52.5	53.3
Brazil	—	—	—	—
Canada	41.1	39.3	44.1	—
Chile	—	—	—	—
China	—	—	—	—
Czech Republic	41.6	43.0	44.1	43.4
Denmark	53.7	52.8	57.8	58.0
Estonia	36.1	33.6	40.6	38.2
EU (27 countries)	—	—	—	—
Finland	48.3	50.3	55.8	54.8
France	51.7	53.6	56.6	56.0
Germany	45.1	46.9	47.5	45.3
Greece	47.1	44.6	50.2	50.1
Hungary	47.8	50.1	49.5	48.8
Iceland	41.9	42.2	51.6	46.1
India	—	—	—	—
Indonesia	—	—	—	—
Ireland	31.2	33.8	66.8	48.7
Israel	51.3	49.4	45.0	—
Italy	45.9	47.9	50.5	49.9
Japan	—	36.4	40.8	—
Korea	22.4	26.6	30.1	—
Luxembourg	37.6	41.5	42.4	42.0
Mexico	—	19.1	23.3	—
Netherlands	44.2	44.8	51.2	49.8
New Zealand	37.8	37.8	—	—
Norway	42.3	41.8	45.5	44.5
OECD	—	—	—	—
Poland	41.1	43.4	45.4	43.6
Portugal	41.6	46.6	51.3	48.9
Russian Federation	—	34.2	—	—
Slovak Republic	52.1	38.0	40.0	38.2
Slovenia	46.5	45.3	50.0	50.2
South Africa	—	—	—	—

	2000	2005	2010	2011
Spain	39.2	38.4	45.7	44.1
Sweden	55.1	53.9	52.5	51.3
Switzerland	35.6	35.2	33.8	—
Turkey	—	—	39.0	—
United Kingdom	36.8	43.8	50.3	48.7
United States	33.9	36.3	42.5	—

Source: Organization for Economic Cooperation and Development, www.oecd
.org/publications/factbook/.

Appendix C

Government Debt as Percentage of GDP

	1997	*2000*	*2005*	*2010*
Australia	18.5	11.4	6.3	11.0
Austria	59.2	61.2	62.1	65.8
Belgium	109.9	99.5	91.8	96.8
Canada	52.7	40.9	30.2	36.1
Chile	13.2	13.6	7.3	9.2
Czech Republic	9.6	13.2	23.2	36.6
Denmark	69.1	54.8	39.3	39.6
Estonia	—	3.3	2.1	3.2
Finland	65.0	48.0	38.2	41.7
France	45.6	47.4	53.3	67.4
Germany	24.3	38.4	40.8	44.4
Greece	105.2	108.9	110.6	147.8
Hungary	60.9	54.1	58.1	73.9
Iceland	46.2	33.8	19.4	81.3
Ireland	57.3	34.8	23.5	60.7
Israel	102.8	83.4	92.1	74.7
Italy	111.0	103.6	97.7	109.0
Japan	76.7	106.1	164.5	—
Korea	10.0	16.7	27.6	31.9
Luxembourg	3.7	3.2	0.8	12.6
Mexico	23.5	21.2	20.3	27.5
Netherlands	53.9	44.1	43.0	51.8
New Zealand	36.2	32.1	22.1	30.5
Norway	24.7	19.3	17.2	26.1
Poland	43.0	35.8	44.8	49.7
Portugal	56.2	52.1	66.2	88.0
Slovak Republic	20.8	23.9	33.1	39.1
Slovenia	—	—	26.9	36.0
Spain	55.3	49.9	36.4	51.7
Sweden	74.1	56.9	46.2	33.8
Switzerland	25.3	25.6	28.1	20.2
Turkey	32.9	38.2	51.1	42.9
United Kingdom	—	42.2	43.5	85.5
United States	45.4	33.9	36.1	61.3

Source: Organization for Economic Cooperation and Development, http://www
.oecd.org/publications/factbook/.

Appendix D

Tax Revenue as Percentage
of GDP in Selected Years

	1965	1970	1980	1990	2000	2005	2010	2011
Australia	20.6	21.1	26.2	28.0	30.4	30.0	25.6	—
Austria	33.9	33.9	39.0	39.7	43.0	42.1	42.0	42.1
Belgium	31.1	33.8	41.2	41.9	44.7	44.5	43.5	44.0
Canada	25.7	30.9	31.0	35.9	35.6	33.2	31.0	31.0
Chile	—	—	—	17.0	18.9	20.7	19.6	21.4
Czech Republic	—	—	—	—	34.0	36.1	34.2	35.3
Denmark	30.0	38.4	43.0	46.5	49.4	50.8	47.6	48.1
Estonia	—	—	—	—	31.0	30.6	34.2	32.8
Finland	30.4	31.6	35.8	43.7	47.2	43.9	42.5	43.4
France	34.2	34.2	40.2	42.0	44.4	44.1	42.9	44.2
Germany	31.6	31.5	36.4	34.8	37.5	35.0	36.1	37.1
Greece	18.0	20.2	21.8	26.4	34.3	32.1	30.9	31.2
Hungary	—	—	—	—	39.3	37.3	37.9	35.7
Iceland	26.2	27.4	29.6	30.9	37.2	40.7	35.2	36.0
Ireland	24.9	28.2	30.7	32.8	31.0	30.1	27.6	—
Israel	—	—	—	—	36.8	35.6	32.4	32.6
Italy	25.5	25.7	29.7	37.6	42.0	40.6	42.9	42.9
Japan	17.8	19.2	24.8	28.6	26.6	27.3	27.6	—
Korea	—	—	17.1	19.5	22.6	24.0	25.1	25.9
Luxembourg	27.7	23.5	35.7	35.7	39.1	37.6	37.1	37.1
Mexico	—	—	14.8	15.8	16.9	18.1	18.8	—
Netherlands	32.8	35.6	42.9	42.9	39.6	38.4	38.7	—
New Zealand	23.9	25.9	30.5	36.9	33.2	36.6	31.5	31.7
Norway	29.6	34.5	42.4	41.0	42.6	43.2	42.9	43.2
OECD	25.5	27.5	30.9	33.0	35.2	34.9	33.8	—
Poland	—	—	—	—	32.8	33.0	31.7	—
Portugal	15.9	17.8	22.2	26.8	30.9	31.1	31.3	—
Slovak Republic	—	—	—	—	34.1	31.5	28.3	28.8
Slovenia	—	—	—	—	37.3	38.6	37.5	36.8
Spain	14.7	15.9	22.6	32.5	34.3	36.0	32.3	31.6
Sweden	33.3	37.8	46.4	52.3	51.4	48.9	45.5	44.5
Switzerland	17.5	19.2	24.6	24.9	29.3	28.1	28.1	28.5
Turkey	10.6	9.3	13.3	14.9	24.2	24.3	25.7	25.0
United Kingdom	30.4	36.7	34.8	35.5	36.4	35.4	34.9	35.5
United States	24.7	27.0	26.4	27.4	29.5	27.1	24.8	25.1

Source: Organization for Economic Cooperation and Development, http://stats.oecd.org/.

Appendix E

Employment Rate in Percentage of Total Population

	2000	2005	2010	2011	2012
Australia	50.3	51.9	53.8	54.0	—
Austria	48.3	49.0	51.1	51.3	51.5
Belgium	43.3	44.5	—	—	—
Canada	51.8	53.8	54.5	54.4	54.3
Czech Republic	50.5	50.6	50.1	50.1	50.0
Denmark	53.4	53.1	52.4	51.5	—
Finland	50.4	50.3	50.2	50.2	50.1
France	46.0	46.1	45.9	45.9	—
Germany	48.1	49.6	51.0	51.7	51.7
Hungary	40.3	41.7	42.6	42.9	43.9
Ireland	46.6	49.3	48.3	47.6	47.1
Italy	41.5	42.1	41.6	41.6	42.4
Luxembourg	61.6	68.8	74.7	75.2	—
Netherlands	51.0	52.4	52.9	—	—
New Zealand	50.0	52.6	53.6	54.0	53.9
Norway	52.3	51.9	53.2	53.1	—
Poland	45.5	45.1	—	—	—
Portugal	50.8	52.8	52.8	52.5	—
Slovak Republic	48.4	49.1	—	—	—
Spain	44.9	48.1	50.1	50.1	49.9
Turkey	36.7	33.5	—	—	—
United Kingdom	48.8	50.6	51.1	51.2	51.4
United States	51.0	51.0	50.2	49.7	—

Source: Organization for Economic Cooperation and Development, http://stats.oecd.org/.

Appendix F

Rate of Unemployment as Percentage of Civilian Labor Force

	2000	2005	2010	2011	2012
Australia	6.3	5.0	5.2	5.1	5.2
Austria	3.6	5.2	4.4	4.2	4.3
Belgium	7.0	8.4	8.3	7.1	7.5
Canada	6.8	6.8	8.0	7.4	7.2
Czech Republic	8.9	8.0	7.3	6.7	7.0
Denmark	4.6	5.0	7.6	7.8	—
Finland	9.8	8.4	8.4	7.8	7.7
France	8.3	8.7	9.2	9.1	—
G7	5.6	6.2	8.2	7.6	—
Germany	7.8	11.2	7.1	5.9	5.5
Greece	11.2	9.6	11.8	16.3	23.6
Hungary	6.5	7.3	11.2	11.0	10.9
Iceland	2.3	2.6	7.6	7.1	6.0
Ireland	4.6	4.8	13.9	14.6	15.0
Italy	10.7	7.8	8.5	8.5	10.8
Japan	4.7	4.4	5.0	4.6	4.3
Korea	4.4	3.7	3.7	3.4	3.2
Luxembourg	1.8	3.1	4.2	4.2	—
Mexico	2.6	3.5	5.2	5.2	4.9
Netherlands	2.7	4.7	4.5	4.4	5.3
New Zealand	6.2	3.8	6.5	6.5	6.9
Norway	3.5	4.6	3.6	3.3	—
OECD	6.1	6.6	8.3	7.9	—
Poland	16.1	17.7	9.6	9.6	10.1
Portugal	4.0	7.7	10.8	12.8	15.7
Slovak Republic	18.8	16.2	14.4	13.5	13.9
Spain	13.9	9.2	20.1	21.7	25.1
Sweden	5.9	7.8	8.6	7.8	8.0
Switzerland	2.5	4.2	4.2	3.8	3.9
Turkey	6.5	10.6	11.9	9.8	9.2
United Kingdom	5.5	4.7	7.8	7.9	7.9
United States	4.0	5.1	9.6	8.9	8.1

Source: Organization for Economic Cooperation and Development, http://stats.oecd.org/.

Appendix G
Indicators of Well-Being

	Housing	Income	Jobs				Education	Health		Life Satisfaction	Work–Life Balance	
	Dwellings without Basic Facilities	Household Net Adjusted Disposable Income	Employment Rate	Job Security	Long-Term Unemployment Rate	Personal Earnings	Educational Attainment	Life Expectancy	Self-Reported Health	Life Satisfaction	Employees Working Long Hours	Time Devoted to Leisure and Personal Care
Australia	1.2	28,884	73	12.4	0.96	43,908	73	82.0	85	7.2	14.13	14.41
Austria	1.2	28,852	72	9.5	1.07	43,688	82	81.1	69	7.4	8.76	14.46
Belgium	1.4	26,874	62	7.4	3.45	44,321	70	80.5	73	6.9	4.43	15.71
Brazil	6.7	10,225	68	14.0	3.02	10,905	41	73.5	69	6.7	12.5	14.84
Canada	0.2	28,194	72	11.3	1.0	42,253	88	81.0	88	7.4	3.91	14.25
Chile	9.4	11,039	61	10.5	2.94	15,820	71	78.3	59	6.5	16.32	13.66
Czech Republic	0.7	16,957	66	6.7	2.8	19,312	92	78.0	59	6.3	7.58	14.34
Denmark	0.6	24,682	73	12.9	1.85	45,802	76	79.9	70	7.5	1.97	16.06
Estonia	9.6	12,800	65	10.7	7.06	17,323	89	76.3	51	5.4	4.1	14.2
Finland	0.7	25,739	69	14.5	1.75	36,468	83	80.6	69	7.4	3.89	14.89
France	0.6	28,310	64	9.3	3.83	37,505	71	82.2	67	6.6	8.96	15.33
Germany	0.9	28,799	73	8.3	2.84	39,593	86	80.8	64	6.7	5.41	15.31
Greece	0.9	20,440	56	4.7	8.75	28,011	65	80.7	76	5.1	5.23	14.65
Hungary	4.7	13,858	56	7.8	5.36	19,437	81	75.0	55	4.7	3.1	14.9
Iceland	0.4	21,201	79	10.8	1.97	37,290	67	82.4	77	7.6	13.45	14.06
Ireland	0.2	24,104	60	6.9	8.52	50,109	73	80.6	83	7.0	3.94	15.18
Israel	3.8	19,120	61	10.5	1.13	28,629	82	81.8	82	7.1	17.58	13.81
Italy	0.4	24,216	57	6.9	4.36	33,947	55	82.7	64	5.8	4.07	14.89
Japan	6.4	24,147	70	10.5	1.78	35,143	92	82.7	30	6.0	31.7	13.96

Country												
Korea	4.2	17,337	64	24.3	0.01	35,406	80	81.1	37	6.0	27.66	14.63
Luxembourg	0.1	35,517	65	5.4	1.41	52,847	78	81.1	72	7.0	2.62	15.05
Mexico	4.2	12,732	60	21.4	0.11	9,885	36	74.2	66	7.3	28.63	12.66
Netherlands	0	25,493	75	8.8	1.49	44,321	73	81.3	76	7.5	0.66	15.66
New Zealand	0.2	21,892	73	10.5	0.59	30,420	73	81.2	89	7.2	13.02	14.87
Norway	0.3	31,459	75	7.9	0.38	43,990	81	81.4	73	7.7	2.83	15.56
OECD	2.2	23,047	66	10.5	3.14	34,466	74	79.8	69	6.6	8.76	14.87
Poland	4	15,371	60	8.1	3.05	19,806	89	76.9	57	5.9	7.24	14.2
Portugal	1.2	19,366	64	8.7	6.14	24,384	32	80.8	49	5.0	8.5	14.71
Russian Federation	2.8	15,286	68	10.5	2.17	19,719	91	69.8	37	5.6	0.16	14.84
Slovak Republic	1.4	16,682	59	5.0	8.65	19,335	91	76.1	62	5.9	6.38	14.78
Slovenia	0.5	19,119	64	7.7	3.61	32,480	83	80.1	60	6.1	5.55	14.62
Spain	0	22,847	58	10.9	8.99	34,769	53	82.4	75	6.3	6.34	15.85
Sweden	0	26,242	74	13.9	1.29	37,094	87	81.9	80	7.6	1.23	15.11
Switzerland	0.1	30,060	79	8.4	1.57	50,323	86	82.8	81	7.8	5.87	14.78
Turkey	12.7	13,044	48	25.8	2.59	19,032	31	74.6	67	5.3	46.13	11.73
United Kingdom	0.1	26,904	70	6.8	2.62	44,743	75	81.1	77	6.8	12.06	14.83
United States	0	38,001	67	11.4	2.8	54,450	89	78.7	90	7.0	11.13	14.27

Source: Organization for Economic Cooperation and Development, http://stats.oecd.org/.

Appendix H

Gini Coefficient on Disposable Income, Post-Taxes, and Transfers in Selected Years

	1990	1995	2000	2005	2009	2010	2011
Australia	—	0.309	0.317	—	—	0.334	—
Austria	—	—	—	0.26	0.268	0.267	—
Belgium	—	—	—	0.269	0.262	0.262	—
Canada	0.287	0.289	0.318	0.317	0.32	0.32	—
Chile	—	—	—	—	0.508	—	0.501
Czech Republic	—	—	—	0.259	0.254	0.256	—
Denmark	0.226	0.215	0.227	0.232	0.238	0.252	—
Estonia	—	—	—	0.337	0.314	0.319	—
Finland	—	0.218	0.247	—	0.255	0.26	—
France	—	—	0.287	0.288	0.293	0.303	—
Germany	0.256	0.266	0.264	—	0.288	0.286	—
Greece	—	—	—	0.34	0.331	0.337	—
Hungary	—	0.294	0.293	0.291	0.272	—	—
Iceland	—	—	—	0.269	0.266	0.244	—
Ireland	—	—	—	0.315	0.331	—	—
Israel	0.329	0.338	0.347	0.378	0.373	0.376	—
Italy	—	0.326	0.321	—	0.312	0.319	—
Japan	—	0.323	0.337	—	0.336	—	—
Korea	—	—	—	—	0.314	0.31	0.311
Luxembourg	—	—	—	0.277	0.276	0.27	—
Mexico	—	—	0.507	—	—	0.466	—
Netherlands	0.292	0.297	0.292	0.284	0.283	0.288	—
New Zealand	0.318	0.335	0.339	—	0.317	—	—
Norway	—	0.243	0.261	—	0.245	0.249	—
Poland	—	—	—	0.326	0.304	0.305	—
Portugal	—	—	—	0.373	0.339	0.344	—
Russian Federation	—	—	—	—	—	—	—
Slovak Republic	—	—	—	0.275	0.261	0.261	—
Slovenia	—	—	—	0.245	0.247	0.246	—
Spain	—	—	—	0.324	0.333	0.338	—
Sweden	—	0.211	0.243	—	0.269	0.269	—
Switzerland	—	—	—	—	0.298	—	—
Turkey	—	—	—	—	0.411	—	—
United Kingdom	0.355	—	0.352	0.335	0.345	0.341	—
United States	0.349	0.361	0.357	0.38	—	0.38	—

Source: Organization for Economic Cooperation and Development, http://stats.oecd.org/.

Appendix I

Public Sector Spending on
Social Protection as Percentage of GDP

	1980	1985	1990	1995	2000	2005	2010	2011	2012
Australia	10.3	12.2	13.2	16.2	17.3	16.5	17.9	18.1	18.7
Austria	22.4	23.7	23.8	26.5	26.6	27.1	28.8	27.9	28.3
Belgium	23.5	26	24.9	26.2	25.3	26.5	29.5	29.6	30.0
Canada	13.7	17.0	18.1	18.9	16.5	16.9	18.6	18.3	18.2
Chile	—	—	9.9	11.1	12.8	10.1	9.8	9.5	—
Czech Republic	—	—	15.3	17.4	19.1	18.7	20.8	20.9	20.6
Denmark	24.8	23.2	25.1	28.9	26.4	27.7	30.1	30.0	30.5
Estonia	—	—	—	—	13.9	13.1	20.1	18.8	18.4
Finland	18.1	22.4	24.1	30.7	24.2	26.2	29.4	28.6	29.0
France	20.8	26.0	25.1	29.3	28.6	30.1	32.2	32.1	32.1
Germany	22.1	22.5	21.7	26.6	26.6	27.3	27.1	26.2	26.3
Greece	10.3	16.1	16.6	17.5	19.3	21.1	23.3	23.5	23.1
Hungary	—	—	—	—	20.7	22.5	22.6	21.8	21.1
Iceland	—	—	13.7	15.2	15.2	16.3	18.0	17.8	16.4
Ireland	16.5	21.1	17.3	18.1	13.4	16.0	23.7	23.5	23.1
Israel	—	—	—	17.4	17.2	16.3	16.0	15.8	15.8
Italy	18.0	20.8	19.9	19.8	23.1	24.9	27.8	27.6	28.1
Japan	10.2	11.1	11.1	14.1	16.3	18.5	—	—	—
Korea	—	—	2.8	3.2	4.8	6.5	9.2	9.2	9.3
Luxembourg	20.6	20.2	19.1	20.8	20.9	22.8	23	22.5	23.3
Mexico	—	1.7	3.3	4.3	5.3	6.9	8.1	7.7	—
Netherlands	24.8	25.3	25.6	23.8	19.8	20.7	23.5	23.7	24.3
New Zealand	17.0	17.6	21.5	18.6	19.0	18.1	21.2	21.5	22.0
Norway	16.9	17.8	22.3	23.4	21.3	21.6	23.0	22.6	22.1
OECD	15.5	17.2	17.6	19.5	18.9	19.7	22.0	21.7	21.7
Poland	—	—	14.9	22.6	20.5	21.0	21.8	20.7	20.4
Portugal	9.9	10.1	12.5	16.5	18.9	23.0	25.6	25.2	25.0
Slovak Republic	—	—	—	18.8	17.9	16.3	19.0	18.0	17.6
Slovenia	—	—	0	0	21.8	21.1	23.5	24.0	23.7
Spain	15.5	17.8	19.9	21.4	20.2	21.1	26.5	26.0	26.3

	1980	1985	1990	1995	2000	2005	2010	2011	2012
Sweden	27.1	29.5	30.2	32.0	28.4	29.1	28.3	27.6	28.2
Switzerland	13.8	14.7	13.5	17.5	17.8	20.2	20.0	20.2	20.3
Turkey	3.2	3.1	5.7	5.6	—	9.9	—	—	—
United Kingdom	16.5	19.4	16.7	19.9	18.6	20.5	23.7	23.9	23.9
United States	13.2	13.2	13.6	15.5	14.5	16.0	19.9	19.7	19.4

Source: Organization for Economic Cooperation and Development, http://stats.oecd.org/.

Appendix J

Public Expenditure as a Percentage of GDP on Labour Market Policy in 2010

Programs	10: PES and Administration	20: Training	30: Job Rotation and Sharing	40: Employment Incentives	50: Supported Employment and Rehabilitation	60: Direct Job Creation	70: Start-Up Incentives	80: Out-of-Work Income Maintenance and Support	90: Early Retirement	100: Total	100: Total	100: Total
										100: Total	110: Active Measures (10–70)	120: Passive Measures (80–90)
Australia	0.17	0.03	0	0.01	0.07	0.03	0.01	0.51	0	0.82	0.31	0.51
Austria	0.18	0.52	0	0.06	0.03	0.04	0.01	1.23	0.17	2.24	0.84	1.4
Belgium	0.22	0.16	0	0.6	0.13	0.36	0	1.53	0.74	3.75	1.48	2.27
Canada	0.14	0.13	0	0	0.01	0.02	0.01	0.81	0	1.15	0.33	0.81
Chile	0.02	0.35	0	0.02	0	0.05	0	0.19	0	0.64	0.44	0.19
Czech Republic	0.11	0.04	0	0.05	0.08	0.04	0	0.37	0	0.7	0.33	0.37
Denmark	0.51	0.42	0	0.32	0.66	0	0	1.2	0.37	3.48	1.91	1.57
Estonia	0.09	0.06	0	0.06	0	0	0.02	0.87	0	1.1	0.23	0.87
Finland	0.18	0.53	0.05	0.08	0.1	0.09	0.02	1.48	0.3	2.82	1.04	1.78
France	0.3	0.38	0	0.11	0.07	0.22	0.05	1.45	0.01	2.59	1.14	1.46
Germany	0.38	0.31	0	0.1	0.03	0.05	0.08	1.28	0.05	2.28	0.94	1.34
Greece	—	0.02	0	0.11	0	0	0.1	0.71	0	—	—	0.71
Hungary	0.09	0.05	0	0.08	0	0.39	0.01	0.72	0	1.34	0.62	0.72
Ireland	0.18	0.46	0	0.06	0.01	0.26	0	2.94	0.05	3.96	0.96	2.99
Israel	0.02	0.07	0	0.02	0.03	0	0	0.66	0	0.8	0.15	0.66
Italy	0.11	0.18	0	0.14	0	0.01	0.02	1.35	0.1	1.91	0.46	1.45
Japan	0.05	0.07	0	0.1	0	0.05	0	0.35	0	0.63	0.28	0.35
Korea	0.01	0.07	0	0.02	0.03	0.28	0	0.34	0	0.76	0.42	0.34

Luxembourg	0.05	0.04	0	0.32	0.01	0.13	0	0.64	0.16	1.35	0.54	0.8
Mexico	0	0.01	0	0	0	0	0.01	0	0	0.01	0.01	0
Netherlands	0.43	0.13	0	0.01	0.48	0.17	0	1.75	0	2.97	1.22	1.75
New Zealand	0.12	0.14	0	0.02	0.05	0.01	0	0.46	0	0.79	0.34	0.46
Norway	—	0.22	0	0.06	0.18	0.04	0	0.47	0	—	—	0.47
OECD	0.16	0.17	0	0.12	0.09	0.09	0.02	0.95	0.09	1.72	0.66	1.03
Poland	0.09	0.04	0	0.21	0.21	0.04	0.1	0.23	0.11	1.04	0.69	0.34
Portugal	0.14	0.4	0	0.1	0.03	0.05	0	1.29	0.1	2.11	0.72	1.39
Slovak Republic	0.1	0.01	0	0.1	0.03	0.01	0.08	0.24	0.36	0.94	0.33	0.61
Slovenia	0.11	0.07	0	0.09	0	0.13	0.06	0.73	0	1.19	0.45	0.73
Spain	0.17	0.2	0.01	0.26	0.04	0.1	0.12	3.1	0.04	4.03	0.89	3.14
Sweden	0.34	0.09	0	0.45	0.24	0	0.02	0.73	0	1.87	1.14	0.73
Switzerland	0.13	0.22	0	0.08	—	0	0.01	0.82	0	—	—	0.82
United Kingdom	—	—	0	—	—	—	0	0.3	0	—	—	0.3
United States	0.04	0.04	0	0.01	0.03	0.01	0	0.76	0	0.9	0.14	0.76

Source: Organization for Economic Cooperation and Development. http://stats.oecd.org/.

Appendix K

Spending on Health Care as Percentage of GDP

	2000	2005	2010	2011	2012
Australia	7.6	8.0	8.5	—	—
Austria	9.4	9.9	10.4	10.2	—
Belgium	8.1	10.0	10.5	10.5	—
Canada	8.5	9.3	10.8	10.6	10.7
Chile	—	6.5	7.1	7.2	—
Czech Republic	6.0	6.7	7.2	7.4	—
Denmark	8.3	9.3	10.7	—	—
Estonia	5.2	5.0	6.3	5.8	—
Finland	6.9	8.0	9.1	8.6	8.7
France	9.8	10.6	11.3	11.2	—
Germany	10.0	10.4	11.1	11.0	—
Greece	7.6	9.3	9.4	9.0	—
Hungary	6.9	8.2	7.8	7.7	7.6
Iceland	9.3	9.4	9.3	9.0	8.9
Ireland	5.7	7.2	9.0	8.5	—
Israel	7.3	7.6	—	—	—
Italy	7.5	8.4	8.9	8.7	8.7
Japan	7.3	8.0	9.5	—	—
Korea	4.1	5.3	6.9	7.0	7.2
Luxembourg	6.2	7.1	—	—	—
Mexico	4.9	5.6	—	—	—
Netherlands	7.6	10.1	11.2	11.1	11.6
New Zealand	—	8.4	10.2	10.3	—
Norway	7.8	8.5	9.1	8.9	9.0
Poland	5.3	5.8	6.5	6.4	—
Portugal	8.6	9.8	10.2	9.7	9.4
Slovak Republic	5.4	6.7	8.5	7.6	—
Slovenia	—	8.0	8.6	8.5	8.5
Spain	7.0	8.0	9.4	9.1	—
Sweden	7.8	8.7	9.0	8.9	—
Switzerland	9.9	10.9	10.9	11.0	—
Turkey	4.7	5.1	—	—	—
United Kingdom	6.7	7.9	9.1	9.1	—
United States	13.0	15.2	17.0	17.0	—

Source: Organization for Economic Cooperation and Development, http://stats.oecd.org/.

Bibliography

CONTENTS

I. INTRODUCTION

The following sections list books, articles, websites, and so forth related to the welfare state. While this bibliography is not exhaustive, it does encompass as many different authors and viewpoints as possible. More specific and detailed descriptions of the subjects referred to in this dictionary can be found in the 31 sections given here. More information can also be found on the debate about the welfare state, welfare state models, and historical developments. The literature supplements the dictionary for those who want more detailed descriptions and additional discussion of and elaboration on theoretical elements of the welfare state debate.

Sections XXIX to XXXII include sources covering data on individual countries or groups of countries about such topics as spending in various areas, institutional structures, and individuals who are unemployed. They include an overview of important and useful websites that can be used to locate updated and new information on welfare state policies. The overview contains mainly websites with international information.

Aside from the websites included in the overview, many countries have websites in English, making it possible for people who are unfamiliar with the national language to get information seen from the government's perspective. These national websites often have the information spread throughout a variety of ministries, for example, the Ministry of Social Security, Ministry of Labor, Ministry of Health Care, and so forth. The diverse institutional structures in different countries imply that no uniform structure or system can be expected. In addition, the structure of the social insurance systems found in numerous countries implies that the information can be found on the sites of the individual social insurance companies. In addition, many international organizations give essential information on welfare state issues, as do several nongovernmental organizations. Examples of websites are given in section XXXI, but be aware that sites sometimes change their name and address, which means that some of the information given here may not be fully updated.

It is difficult to point to just a few central books that analyze the welfare state and related concepts. Analysis and research on the welfare state have been and presumably always will be interdisciplinary; therefore, it will not only appear in books or articles dealing with welfare state issues in such disciplines as economics, sociology, political science, law, and history, but also in works that combine approaches. Nevertheless, several important topics can be highlighted, and the topics covered here integrate the various core areas so that the debates and knowledge regarding concepts, theories, and individual countries will supplement the entries in the dictionary.

Central to a description of the historical development of many welfare states are the works of Peter Flora. These include Peter Flora, ed., *Growth to Limits: The Western European Welfare States since World War II*, volumes 1 through 4 (1986), as well as Peter Flora and A. J. Heidenheimer, eds., *The Developments of Welfare States in Europe and America* (1981). There is also G. Rimlinger's *Welfare Policy and Industrialization in Europe, America, and Russia* (1971). A good overview of key historical contributions to welfare state analysis can be found in Christopher Pierson and Francis G. Castles, eds., *The Welfare State Reader* (2006). These works can be used to compare the various welfare states and their development.

Books of value for gaining a historical understanding of the origins of and changes in the welfare state are *Social Insurance and Allied Services* (1942), by Lord William Beveridge ("The Beveridge Report"); *The General Theory of Employment, Interest, and Money* (1933), by John Maynard Keynes; and *Essays on the Welfare State* (1958), by Richard M. Titmuss.

Understanding and presentation of the classical elements of welfare economics, including theoretical aspects, can be found in J. R. Hicks, "The Foundation of Welfare Economics" (1939), in the *Economic Journal*; Kenneth J. Arrow, *Social Choice and Individual Values* (1951); Amartya K. Sen, *Collective Choice and Social Welfare* (1970); and Amartya K. Sen, *Choice, Welfare, and Measurement* (1982).

The debate about and analysis of different types of welfare state models are covered in Gøsta Esping-Andersen, *The Three Worlds of Welfare Capitalism* (1990). For an overview, see Bent Greve, ed., *The Routledge Handbook of the Welfare State* (2013).

The standard works about financing the welfare state and public-sector economics are by Richard A. Musgrave, *The Theory of Public Finance* (1959), and Paul A. Samuelson, "Pure Theory of Public Expenditure" (1954), in the *Review of Economics and Statistics*.

Central works on poverty are *Poverty: A Study of Town Life* (1901) and *Poverty and Progress* (1941), both by B. Seebohm Rowntree, and *Poverty and the Welfare State* (1951), by B. Seebohm Rowntree and G. R. Lavers.

Discussion of the crisis of the welfare state can be found in James O'Connor's *The Fiscal Crisis of the State* (1973) and Ramesh Mishra's *The Welfare State in Crisis: Social Thought and Social Change* (1984). Several older books that have been crucial to historical understanding and research in the area are also included in the bibliography.

The bibliography covers the central areas of the analysis of the welfare state and its historical development. Developing this organizational structure has not been an easy task, as many books could be placed under more than one category. Each work has been included only once. Hence, difficult decisions had to be made about where to put each title. Each subject area in the bibliography may provide a starting point for further reading, and by using the resources presented here—and also the literature listed in these sources—a full picture of the welfare state can be obtained. Furthermore, using databases for searches has become easier, so it should be possible for a reader to find more information about any particular topic.

The literature on the welfare state is expanding rapidly, including numerous new journals. The journals often cover many of the areas for which literature has been listed in this bibliography. They are listed in section XXX. These journals provide regular and updated information on the development of welfare states, and many are written from a comparative perspective, enabling the reader to get the most recent information on a number of countries.

II. GENERAL HISTORY OF THE WELFARE STATE'S DEVELOPMENT

Ashford, D. E. *The Emergence of the Welfare State*. London: Basil Blackwell, 1986.
Baldwin, Peter. *The Politics of Social Solidarity: Class Bases of the European Welfare State, 1875–1975*. Cambridge, UK: Cambridge University Press, 1990.

Beveridge, William. *Full Employment in a Free Society.* London: Allen & Unwin, 1944.

——. *The Pillars of Security.* London: Allen & Unwin, 1943.

——. *Social Insurance and Allied Services.* London: His Majesty's Stationery Office, 1942.

Birch, R. C. *The Shaping of the Welfare State.* London: Longman, 1974.

Briggs, Asa. "Welfare State." In P. P. Wiener, ed., *The Dictionary of the History of Ideas*, vol. 4, 1–18. New York: Scribner, 1973–1974.

——. "The Welfare State in a Historical Perspective." In C. Schottland, ed., *The Welfare State*, 29–45. New York: Harper & Row, 1969.

Bruce, M. *The Coming of the Welfare State.* London: Batsford, 1961.

Clarke, J. "The Problem of the State after the Welfare State." *Social Policy Review* 8 (1996): 13–39.

Dostaler, G., D. Ethier, and L. Lepage, eds. *Gunnar Myrdal and His Works.* Montreal, Quebec, Canada: Harvest House, 1992.

Durkheim, E. *De la division du travail social.* Paris: Felix Alcan, 1893.

Evans, Eric J. *Social Policy, 1830–1914: Individualism, Collectivism, and the Origins of the Welfare State.* London: Routledge and Kegan Paul, 1978.

Flora, Peter, ed. *Growth to Limits: The Western European Welfare States since World War II*, vols. 1–4. Berlin, Germany: De Gruyter, 1986.

Flora, Peter, and A. J. Heidenheimer, eds. *The Developments of Welfare States in Europe and America.* London: Transaction Books, 1981.

Henriques, Ursula. *Before the Welfare State.* London: Longman, 1979.

McEvedy, C., and R. Jones. *Atlas of World Population History.* Harmondsworth, England: Penguin, 1978.

Pierson, Christopher, and Francis G. Castles, eds. *The Welfare State Reader.* Cambridge, UK: Polity, 2006.

Roberts, D. *Victorian Origins of the Welfare State.* New Haven, Conn.: Yale University Press, 1960.

Roof, M. *A Hundred Years of Family Welfare.* London: Michael Joseph, 1972.

Saville, J. "The Welfare State: A Historical Approach." *New Reasoner* 1, no. 3 (1957): 5–25.

Schottland, Charles I., ed. *The Welfare State: Selected Essays.* New York: Harper Torchbooks, 1967.

Thane, Pat. *The Foundations of the Welfare State.* London: Longman, 1982.

Titmuss, Richard M. *The Irresponsible Society.* London: Allen & Unwin, 1960.

Williams, G. *The Coming of the Welfare State.* London: Allen & Unwin, 1967.

III. HISTORY OF THE WELFARE STATE AFTER WORLD WAR II

Ashford, Douglas. *The Emergence of the Welfare State.* Oxford, UK: Basil Blackwell, 1986.

Berkowitz, E., and K. McQuaid. *Creating the Welfare State: The Political Economy of Twentieth-Century Reform.* New York: Praeger, 1980.

Marshall, Thomas H. *Social Policy in the Twentieth Century*. London: Hutchinson Educational, 1975.

Myrdal, Gunnar. *Beyond the Welfare State*. London: Duckworth, 1958.

Palmer, Geoffrey, ed. *The Welfare State Today*. Wellington, New Zealand: Fourth Estate Books, 1977.

IV. ECONOMICS AND THE WELFARE STATE

Arrow, Kenneth J. *Social Choice and Individual Values*. New York: Wiley, 1951.

Asimakopulos, A., R. D. Cairns, and C. Green, eds. *Economic Theory, Welfare, and the State: Essays in Honour of John C. Weldon*. Basingstoke, England: Macmillan, 1990.

Bardhan, Pranab, and John E. Roemer, eds. *Market Socialism: Current Debate*. New York: Oxford University Press, 1993.

Barr, Nicholas A. *The Economics of the Welfare State*. Oxford, UK: Oxford University Press, 1998.

Baumol, William, and Charles Wilson. *Welfare Economics*. Cheltenham, England: Edward Elgar, 2001.

Boadway, Robin W., and Neil Bruce. *Welfare Economics*. London: Basil Blackwell, 1984.

Gelauff, G. M. M. *Modeling Welfare State Reform*. Amsterdam, Netherlands: North-Holland, 1994.

Gough, Ian. *The Political Economy of the Welfare State*. London: Macmillan, 1979.

Harris, R. *Choice in Welfare*. London: Institute of Economic Affairs, 1971.

Harris, R., and A. Seldon. *Overruled on Welfare*. London: Institute of Economic Affairs, 1979.

Harsanyi, John. "Cardinal Individualist Ethics, and International Comparisons of Utility Economics and in the Theory of Risktaking." *Journal of Political Economy* 3 (1955): 309–21.

Hicks, Alexander M., and Thomas Janoski. *The Comparative Political Economy of the Welfare State*. Cambridge, UK: Cambridge University Press, 1994.

Hicks, John R. "The Foundation of Welfare Economics." *Economic Journal* 49 (1939): 696–712.

Hills, J. *Changing Tax: How the Tax System Works and How to Change It*. London: Child Poverty Action Group, 1988.

Janoski, Thomas. *The Comparative Political Economy of the Welfare State*. Cambridge, UK: Cambridge University Press, 1994.

Johansson, P. O. *An Introduction to Modern Welfare Economics*. Cambridge, UK: Cambridge University Press, 1991.

Judge, K. *Rationing Social Services*. London: Heinemann, 1987.

Keynes, John Maynard. *Essays in Persuasion*. London: Macmillan, 1931.

——. *The General Theory of Employment, Interest, and Money*. London: Macmillan, 1933.

——. *How to Pay for the War: A Radical Plan for the Chancellor of the Exchequer*. London: Macmillan, 1940.

Le Grand, Julian, and Saul Estrin, eds. *Market Socialism*. Oxford, UK: Clarendon, 1989.

Le Grand, Julian, and R. Robinson. *The Economics of Social Problems*. London: Macmillan, 1984.

——, eds. *Privatisation and the Welfare State*. London: Allen & Unwin, 1984.

Lindbeck, Assar. *The Selected Essays of Assar Lindbeck. Volume 1: Macroeconomics and Economic Policy*. Aldershot, England: Edward Elgar, 1993.

——. *The Selected Essays of Assar Lindbeck. Volume 2: The Welfare State*. Aldershot, England: Edward Elgar, 1993.

Little, I. M. D. *A Critique of Welfare Economics*, 2nd ed. Oxford, UK: Clarendon Press, 1957.

McKenzie, G. W. *Measuring Economic Welfare: New Methods*. Cambridge, UK: Cambridge University Press, 1983.

Ng, Y.-K. *Welfare Economics*. London: Macmillan, 1979.

Pierson, Christopher. *Beyond the Welfare State? The New Political Economy of the Welfare State*. Cambridge, UK: Polity, 1991.

Pigou, A. C. *The Economics of Welfare*. London: Macmillan, 1920.

——. *Wealth and Welfare*. London: Macmillan, 1912.

Rowley, C. K., and A. T. Peacock. *Welfare Economics: A Liberal Restatement*. Oxford, UK: Martin Robertson, 1975.

Salannié, Bernard. *The Economics of Taxation*. Cambridge, Mass.: MIT Press, 2003.

Samuelson, Paul A. *Foundations of Economic Analysis*. Cambridge, Mass.: Harvard University Press, 1947.

Sen, Amartya K. *Collective Choice and Social Welfare*. San Francisco, Calif.: Holden Day, 1970.

Sen, Amartya K., and B. Williams, eds. *Utilitarianism and Beyond*. Cambridge, UK: Cambridge University Press, 1982.

Sinn, H. W. "A Theory of the Welfare State." *Scandinavian Journal of Economics* 97, no. 4 (1995): 495–526.

Smith, Adam. *The Wealth of Nations*. London: J. M. Den & Sons, 1970.

Sugden, Robert. *The Economics of Rights, Welfare, and Cooperation*. Oxford, UK: Blackwell, 1986.

V. IDEOLOGY AND THE WELFARE STATE

Abel-Smith, Brian. "Whose Welfare State?" In Norma Mackenzie, ed., *Conviction*, 55–73. London: MacGibbon and Kee, 1959.

Alber, J. "Continuities and Changes in the Idea of the Welfare State." *Politics and Society* 16, no. 4 (1988): 451–57.

Bean, P., J. Ferris, and D. Whynes, eds. *In Defense of Welfare*. London: Tavistock, 1985.

Beland D. "The Politics of Social Policy Language." *Social Policy and Administration* 45, no. 1 (2011): 1–18.

Borchert, J. "Welfare-State Retrenchment: Playing the National Card." *Critical Review* 10, no. 1 (1996): 63–94.

Bradshaw, Jonathan. "A Taxonomy of Social Need." *New Society* 496 (1972): 640–43.

Brown, Martin K. *Remaking the Welfare State*. Philadelphia, Pa.: Temple University Press, 1988.

Bulmer, Martin, Jane Lewis, and David Piachaud, eds. *The Goals of Social Policy*. London: Unwin Hyman, 1989.

Castles, Francis G. *The Working Class and Welfare*. Wellington, New Zealand: Allen & Unwin, 1985.

Cutler, Antony, Karel Williams, and John Williams. *Keynes, Beveridge, and Beyond*. London: Routledge and Kegan Paul, 1986.

Deacon, Alan. *Perspectives on Welfare: Ideas, Ideologies, and Policy Debates*. Buckingham, England: Open University Press, 2002.

Deakin N., C. J. Finer, and B. Mathews, eds. *Welfare and State: Critical Concepts in Political Science*. London: Routledge, 2004.

Douglas, J. D. *The Myth of the Welfare State*. Brunswick, N.J.: Transaction Books, 1989.

Doyal, L., and Ian Gough. "A Theory of Human Needs." *Critical Social Policy* 10 (1990): 6–33.

Esping-Andersen, Gøsta, and R. Friedland. "Class Coalitions in the Making of West European Economics." *Political Power and Social Theory* 3 (1982): 1–52.

Evers, Adablert, Helga Nowotny, and Helmut Wintersbeger. *The Changing Face of Welfare*. Aldershot, England: Gower, 1987.

Farr J. "Understanding Conceptual Change Politically." In T. Ball, J. Farr, and R. L. Hanson, eds, *Political Innovation and Conceptual Change*, 24–49. Cambridge, UK: Cambridge University Press, 1989.

Freeman, Roger A. *The Wayward Welfare State*. Stanford, Calif.: Hoover Institution Press, 1981.

Friedman, Milton. *Capitalism and Freedom*. Chicago: University of Chicago Press, 1962.

Furniss, Norman, ed. *Futures for the Welfare State*. Bloomington: Indiana University Press, 1986.

Furniss, Norman, and T. Tilton. *The Case for the Welfare State*. Bloomington: Indiana University Press, 1979.

George, Vic. *Major Thinkers in Welfare: Contemporary Issues in Historical Perspective*. Bristol, UK: Policy Press, 2012.

George, Vic, and Paul Wilding. *Welfare and Ideology*. Hemel Hempstead, England: Harvester Wheatsheaf, 1994.

Giddens, Anthony. *The Third Way: The Renewal of Social Democracy*. Oxford, UK: Polity, 1998.

Gilbert, N. *Capitalism and the Welfare State*. New Haven, Conn.: Yale University Press, 1983.

Ginsburg, N. *Class, Capital, and Social Policy*. London: Macmillan, 1979.

Glennerster, Howard. *The Future of the Welfare State*. London: Heinemann, 1983.

Glennerster, Howard, and James Midgley, eds. *The Radical Right and the Welfare State: An International Assessment*. Hemel Hempstead, England: Harvester Wheatsheaf, 1991.

Golding, P., and S. Middleton. *Images of Welfare*. Oxford, UK: Martin Robertson, 1982.

Goodin, Robert. *Reasons for Welfare*. Princeton, N.J.: University of Princeton Press, 1988.

Gregg, P. *The Welfare State*. London: George G. Harrap & Co., 1967.

Hall, P., H. Land, R. Parker, and A. Webb. *Change, Choice, and Conflict in Social Policy*. London: Heinemann, 1975.

Hills, John. *The Future of Welfare: A Guide to the Debate*. York, England: Joseph Rowntree Foundation, 1993.

Johnson, Norman. *Reconstructing the Welfare State*. Hemel Hempstead, England: Harvester Wheatsheaf, 1990.

———. *The Welfare State in Transition: The Theory and Practice of Welfare Pluralism*. Hemel Hempstead, England: Harvester Wheatsheaf, 1987.

Jordan, B. *Rethinking the Welfare State*. Oxford, UK: Blackwell, 1987.

———. *Welfare and Well-Being: Social Value in Public Policy*. Bristol, UK: Policy Press, 2008.

Kaufmann, Franz-Xaver. *European Foundations of the Welfare State*. New York: Berghahn Books, 2012.

Kim, Sung Ho. *Max Weber's Politics of Civil Society*. Cambridge, UK: Cambridge University Press, 2004.

Klein, R., and M. O'Higgins, eds. *The Future of the Welfare State*. Oxford, UK: Basil Blackwell, 1985.

Marshall, Thomas H. *The Right to Welfare and Other Essays*. London: Heinemann, 1981.

Morel, Nathalie, Bruno Palier, and Joakim Palme, eds. *Toward a Social Investment State? Ideas, Policies, and Challenges*. Bristol, UK: Policy Press, 2012.

Murray, Charles. *Losing Ground*. New York: Basic, 1984.

Nozick, Robert. *Anarchy, State, and Utopia*. Oxford, UK: Basil Blackwell, 1974.

Offe, Claus. "Advanced Capitalism and the Welfare State." *Politics and Society* 2, no. 4 (1972): 479–88.

———. *Disorganized Capitalism*. Cambridge, Mass.: MIT Press, 1985.

Pierson, Paul. *The New Politics of the Welfare State*. Oxford, UK: Oxford University Press, 2001.

Pinker, R. *The Idea of Welfare*. London: Heinemann, 1979.

Pius XI. *Quadragesimo Anno: Papal Encyclical*. Vatican City, 1931.

Robson, W. *Welfare State and Welfare Society*. London: Allen & Unwin, 1976.

Room, Graham. *The Sociology of Welfare*. Oxford, UK: Blackwell, 1979.

Sen, Amartya K. "Rational Fools." *Philosophy and Public Affairs* 6, no. 4 (1977): 317–44.

Sleeman, J. F. *The Welfare State: Its Aims, Benefits, and Costs.* London: Allen & Unwin, 1973.

Spicker, Paul. "The Principle of Subsidiarity and the Social Policy of the European Community." *Journal of European Social Policy* 6, no. 1 (1991): 3–14.

———. *Principles of Social Welfare: An Introduction to Thinking about the Welfare State.* London: Routledge, 1988.

———. *Social Policy: Themes and Approaches.* Hemel Hempstead, England: Harvester Wheatsheaf, 1995.

Taylor-Gooby, Peter. *Social Change, Social Welfare, and Social Science.* Hemel Hempstead, England: Harvester Wheatsheaf, 1991.

Taylor-Gooby, Peter, and J. Dale. *Social Theory and Social Change.* London: Longman, 1981.

Taylor-Gooby, Peter, and Stafan Svallfors. *The End of the Welfare State? Responses to State Retrenchment.* London: Routledge, 1999.

Therborn, Gøran. "Karl Marx Returning: The Welfare State and Neo-Marxist, Corporatist, and Statist Theories." *International Political Science Review* 7, no. 2 (1986): 131–64.

Titmuss, Richard M. *The Gift Relationship.* London: Allen & Unwin, 1971.

———. *The Philosophy of Welfare.* London: Allen & Unwin, 1987.

Urry, John. *The Anatomy of Capitalist Societies: The Economy, Civil Society, and the State.* London: Macmillan, 1981.

Walker, Alan. *Social Planning.* Oxford, UK: Blackwell, 1984.

Webb, A., and G. Wistow. *Planning, Need, and Scarcity.* London: Allen & Unwin, 1986.

Wilensky, Harold, and C. Lebeaux. *Industrial Society and Social Welfare.* New York: Russell Sage, 1958.

VI. TYPOLOGIES OF THE WELFARE STATE

Arts, Will, and John Gelissen. "Models of the Welfare State." In Francis G. Castles, Stephan Leibfried, Jane Lewis, Herbert Obinger, and Christopher Pierson, eds., *The Oxford Handbook of the Welfare State*, 569–83. Oxford, UK: Oxford University Press, 2010.

———. "Three Worlds of Welfare Capitalism or More?" *Journal of European Social Policy* 12, no. 2 (2002): 137–58.

Aspalter, Christian. "The Development of Ideal-Typical Welfare Regime Theory." *International Social Work* 54, no. 6 (2011): 735–50.

Bazant, Ursula, and Klaus Schubert. "European Welfare Systems: Diversity beyond Existing Categories." In Klaus Schubert, Simon Hegelich, and Ursula Bazant, eds, *The Handbook of European Welfare Systems*, 513–34. Oxford, UK: Routledge, 2009.

Castles, Francis G., ed. *Families of Nations: Patterns of Public Policy in Western Democracies.* Aldershot, England: Dartmouth, 1993.

———. *The Future of the Welfare State*. Oxford, UK: Oxford University Press, 2004.

Castles, Francis G., and Deborah Mitchell. "The Three Worlds of Welfare Capitalism or Four?" Discussion Paper 21, Australian National University, 1993.

Collier D., and J. E. Mahon Jr. "Conceptual 'Stretching' Revisited: Adapting Categories in Comparative Analysis." *American Political Science Review* 87, no. 4 (1993): 845–55.

Cook, Linda J. "Eastern Europe and Russia." In Francis G. Castles, Stephan Leibfried, Jane Lewis, Herbert Obinger, and Christopher Pierson, eds., *The Oxford Handbook of the Welfare State*, 671–86. Oxford, UK: Oxford University Press, 2010.

Esping-Andersen, Gøsta. *Social Foundations of Postindustrial Economies*. Oxford, UK: Oxford University Press, 1999.

———. *The Three Worlds of Welfare Capitalism*. Cambridge, UK: Polity, 1990.

———, ed. *Welfare States in Transition: National Adaptions in Global Economies*. London: Sage, 1996.

Ferrera, Maurizio. "The 'Southern' Model of Welfare in Social Europe." *Journal of European Social Policy* 6, no. 1 (1996): 17–37.

Greve, Bent. *Vouchers – nye styrings- og leveringsmåder i velfærdsstaten* (*New Ways of Steering and Managing in the Welfare State*). Copenhagen, Denmark: DJØF's forlag, 2002.

———, ed. *The Routledge Handbook of the Welfare State*. Oxford, UK: Routledge, 2013.

Hall, Peter A., and David Soskice, eds. *Varieties of Capitalism: The Institutional Foundations of Comparative Advantage*. Oxford, UK: Oxford University Press, 2001.

Huber, Evelyne, and Juan Bogliaccini. "Latin America." In Francis G. Castles, Stephan Leibfried, Jane Lewis, Herbert Obinger, and Christopher Pierson, eds., *The Oxford Handbook of the Welfare State*, 644–55. Oxford, UK: Oxford University Press, 2010.

Kolberg, J. E. *The Study of Welfare-State Regimes*. Armonk, N.Y.: M. E. Sharpe, 1990.

Leibfried, Stephan. *Toward a European Welfare State? On Integrating Poverty Regimes in the European Community*. Bremen, Germany: University Bremen, ZeS — Arbeitspapier Nr. 2/91, 1991.

———. "Toward a European Welfare State? On Integrating Poverty Regimes into the European Community." In Zsuzsa Ferge and Jon Eivind Kolberg, eds, *Social Policy in a Changing Europe*, 245–79. Frankfurt am Main, Germany: Campus, 1992.

Meltzer, Allan H., and Scott E. Richard. "A Rational Theory of the Size of Government." *Journal of Political Economy* 89, no. 5 (1981): 914–27.

Peng, Ito, and Joseph Wong. "East Asia." In Francis G. Castles, Stephan Leibfried, Jane Lewis, Herbert Obinger, and Christopher Pierson, eds., *The Oxford Handbook of the Welfare State*, 656–70. Oxford, UK: Oxford University Press, 2010.

Powell, Martin, and Armando Barrientos. "An Audit of the Welfare Modeling Business." *Social Policy and Administration* 45, no. 1(2011): 69–84.

Room, Graham, ed. *Toward a European Welfare State?* Bristol, UK: School for Advanced Urban Studies, 1991.

Sainsbury, Diana. "Analyzing Welfare State Variations: The Merits and Limitations of Models Based on the Residual-Institutional Distinction." *Scandinavian Political Studies* 14, no. 1 (1991): 1–30.

Schubert, Klaus, Simon Hegelich, and Ursula Bazant. "European Welfare Systems: Current State of Research and Some Theoretical Considerations." In Klaus Schubert, Simon Hegelich, and Ursula Bazant, eds., *The Handbook of European Welfare Systems*, 3–28. Oxford, UK: Routledge, 2009.

Scruggs, Lyle, and James P. Allan. "Welfare-State Decommodification in 18 OECD Countries: A Replication and Revision." *Journal of European Social Policy* 16, no. 1 (2006): 55–72.

Titmuss, Richard M. "Review of Wilensky and Lebeaux." *British Journal of Sociology* 9, no. 3 (1958): 293–95.

Wilensky, Harold L., and Charles N. Lebeaux. *Industrial Society and Social Welfare: The Impact of Industrialization on the Supply and Organization of Social Welfare Services in the United States.* New York: Free Press, 1958, 1965.

VII. POVERTY AND INEQUALITY

Abel-Smith, Brian, and Peter Townsend. *The Poor and the Poorest.* London: Bell, 1965.

Abrahamson, Peter. "Poverty and Welfare in Denmark." *Scandinavian Journal of Social Welfare* 1, no. 1 (1992): 20–27.

——. "Welfare and Poverty in Europe of the 1990s: Social Progress or Social Dumping?" *International Journal of Health Services* 21, no. 2 (1991): 237–64.

Alcock, Pete, Howard Glennerster, Ann Oakley, and Adrian Sinfield, eds. *Welfare and Wellbeing: Richard Titmuss's Contribution to Social Policy.* Bristol, UK: Policy Press, 2001.

Atkinson, A. B. "Horizontal Equity and the Distribution of the Tax Burden." In H. J. Aaron and M. J. Boskin, eds., *The Economics of Taxation*, 3–18. Washington, D.C.: Brookings Institution, 1980.

——. "Income Distribution and Social Change Revisited." *Journal of Social Policy* 4, no. 1 (1975): 57–68.

——. "On the Measurement of Inequality." *Journal of Economic Theory* 2, no. 3 (1970): 244–63.

——. *Poverty and Social Security.* London: Harvester Wheatsheaf, 1989.

Atkinson, A. B., B. Cantillon, E. Marlier, and B. Nolan. *Social Indicators: The EU and Social Inclusion.* Oxford, UK: Oxford University Press, 2002.

Ben-Ami, Daniel. *Ferraris for All: In Defense of Economic Progress.* Bristol, UK: Policy Press, 2012.

Blackorby, C., and D. Donaldson. "Measures of Inequality and Their Meaning in Terms of Social Welfare." *Journal of Economic Theory* 18 (1978): 59–80.

Bradshaw, Jonathan, and Alan Deacon. *Reserved for the Poor.* Oxford, UK: Martin Robertson, 1984.

Bryson, Luis. *Welfare and the State: Who Benefits?* London: Macmillan, 1992.

Deacon, Alan. *In Search of Scrounger*. London: Bell, 1976.
——. "The Scrounging Controversy." *Social and Economic Administration* 12, no. 2 (1978): 120–32.
Dorling, Danny. *Injustice: Why Social Inequality Persists*. Bristol, UK: Policy Press, 2010.
Friedmann, J. "Rethinking Poverty: Empowerment and Citizen Rights." *International Social Science Review* 48, no. 2. (1996): 161–72.
Hills, John, Tom Sefton, and Kitty Stewart. *Toward a More Equal Society*. Bristol, UK: Policy Press, 2009.
Giddens, A., and Patrick Diamon, eds. *The New Egalitarianism*. Cambridge, UK: Polity, 2005.
Joseph, Sir K., and J. Sumption. *Equality*. London: John Murray, 1979.
Kangas, Olli, and Joakim Palme. "Does Social Policy Matter? Poverty Cycles in OECD Countries." *International Journal of Health Services* 30, no. 2 (2000): 335–52.
Korpi, Walther. "Social Policy and Distributional Conflict in the Capitalist Democracies." *West European Politics* 3, no. 3 (1980): 296–316.
Le Grand, J. *The Strategy of Equality*. London: Allen & Unwin, 1982.
Millar, Jane. *Poverty and the Lone Parent: The Challenge to Social Policy*. Aldershot, England: Avebury, 1989.
Novak, T. *Poverty and Social Security*. London: Pluto, 1984.
——. *Poverty and the State*. Milton Keynes, England: Open University Press, 1988.
Rodgers, B. *The Battle against Poverty. Volume 1: From Pauperism to Human Rights*. London: Routledge, 1969.
——. *The Battle against Poverty. Volume 2: Toward a Welfare State*. London: Routledge, 1969.
Rowntree, B. Seebohm. *Poverty: A Study of Town Life*. London: Macmillan, 1901.
——. *Poverty and Progress*. London: Longman, 1941.
Rowntree, B. Seebohm, and G. R. Lavers. *Poverty and the Welfare State*. London: Longman, 1951.
Saunders, Peter. *Down and Out: Poverty and Exclusion in Australia*. Bristol, UK: Policy Press, 2011.
——. *Welfare and Inequality*. Cambridge, UK: Cambridge University Press, 1994.
Sen, Amartya K. *Choice, Welfare, and Measurement*. Cambridge, Mass.: MIT Press, 1982.
——. *Commodities and Capabilities*. Amsterdam, Netherlands: North-Holland, 1985.
——. *Inequality Reexamined*. Oxford, UK: Clarendon Press, 1992.
——. *On Economic Inequality*. Oxford, UK: Clarendon Press, 1973.
——. *Poverty and Famines*. Oxford, UK: Clarendon Press, 1981.
Sinfield, Adrian, ed. *Poverty, Inequality, and Justice*. Edinburgh, Scotland: New Waverly Papers, 1993.
Smeeding, Tim, M. O'Higgins, and Lee Rainwater, eds. *Poverty, Inequality, and Income Distribution in Comparative Perspective*. Hemel Hempstead, England: Harvester Wheatsheaf, 1990.
Stiglitz, Joseph E. *The Price of Inequality*. New York: W. W. Norton, 2013.

Tawney, R. M. *Equality*. London: Allen & Unwin, 1931.

Titmuss, Richard M. *Income Distribution and Social Change*. London: Allen & Unwin, 1962.

Townsend, Peter. *The International Analysis of Poverty*. London: Harvester Wheatsheaf, 1993.

————, ed. *The Concept of Poverty*. London: Heinemann, 1970.

Townsend, Peter, and David Gordon. *Breadline Europe: The Measurement of Poverty*. Bristol, UK: Policy Press, 2000.

Walker, R., R. Lawson, and P. Townsend. *Responses to Poverty: Lessons from Europe*. London: Heinemann, 1984.

Weale, A. *Equality and Social Policy*. London: Routledge and Kegan Paul, 1978.

Webb, A. L. *Income Redistribution and the Welfare State*. London: Allen & Unwin, 1971.

VIII. LIBERTY AND JUSTICE

Berlin, Sir I. *Four Essays on Liberty*. London: Oxford University Press, 1969.

Brian, B. A. *Treatise on Social Justice*. London: Harvester Wheatsheaf, 1989.

Campbell, T. *Justice*. London: Macmillan, 1988.

Dorling, Daniel. *Injustice: Why Social Justice Persists*. Bristol, UK: Policy Press, 2010.

Glyn, A., and D. Miliband, eds. *Paying for Equality: The Economic Cost of Social Injustice*. London: IPPR/Rivers Oram Press, 1994.

Hamlin, A. *Ethics, Economics, and the State*. Brighton, England: Harvester Wheatsheaf, 1986.

Hayek, Friedrik. *The Constitution of Liberty*. London: Routledge and Kegan Paul, 1960.

————. *The Mirage of Social Justice*. London: Routledge and Kegan Paul, 1976.

Hindess, Barry. *Freedom, Equality, and the Market: Arguments on Social Policy*. London: Tavistock, 1987.

Le Grand, Julian. *Equity and Choice*. Bristol, UK: University of Bristol/HarperCollins Academic, 1990.

Le Grand, Julian, and Robert Goodin. *Not Only the Poor: The Middle Class and the Welfare State*. London: Allen & Unwin, 1987.

Millar, D. *Social Justice*. Oxford, UK: Clarendon Press, 1976.

Rawls, John. *A Theory of Justice*. Oxford, UK: Clarendon Press, 1972.

Walzer, M. *Spheres of Justice*. Oxford, UK: Martin Robertson, 1983.

IX. UNITED KINGDOM

Atkinson, Anthony B. *Incomes and the Welfare State: Essays on Britain and Europe*. Cambridge, UK: Cambridge University Press, 1996.

Castles, Francis G., and Christopher Pierson. "A New Convergence: Recent Policy Developments in the United Kingdom, Australia, and New Zealand." *Policy and Politics* 24, no. 3 (1996): 233–45.

Edgerton D. *Warfare State, Britain, 1920–1970.* Cambridge, UK: Cambridge University Press, 2006.

Farnsworth, Kevin, and Zöe Irving. *Social Policy in Challenging Times: Economic Crisis and Welfare Systems.* Bristol, UK: Policy Press, 2011.

Finlayson, Geoffrey. *Citizen, State, and Social Welfare in Britain, 1830–1990.* Oxford, UK: Clarendon Press, 1994.

Freeden, M. *Liberalism Divided: A Study in British Political Thought, 1914–1939.* Oxford, UK: Oxford University Press, 1986.

Glennester, Howard. *British Social Policy since 1945.* Oxford, UK: Blackwell, 2000.

Gregg, Pauline. *The Welfare State: An Economic and Social History of Great Britain from 1945 to the Present Day.* Amherst: University of Massachusetts Press, 1967.

Harris, J. *William Beveridge: A Biography.* Oxford, UK: Clarendon Press, 1997.

Heidenheimer, A. J. "Secularization Patterns and the Westward Spread of the Welfare State: Two Dialogues about How and Why Britain, the Netherlands, and the United States Have Differed." *Comparative Social Research* 6 (1983): 3–38.

Hennessy, P. *Never Again: Britain, 1945–1951.* London: Vintage, 1992.

Hennock, P. *British Social Reform and German Precedents: The Case of Social Insurance, 1880–1914.* Oxford, UK: Oxford University Press, 1987.

Lowe, R. *The Welfare State in Britain since 1945.* London: Palgrave, 2005.

Mommsen, W. J., ed. *The Emergence of the Welfare State in Britain and Germany: 1850–1950.* London: Croom Helm, 1983.

Norman, E. R. *Church and Society in England, 1770–1970: A Historical Study.* Oxford, UK: Oxford University Press, 1976.

Peacock, Alan, and Jack Wiseman. *The Growth of Public Expenditure in the UK.* Oxford, UK: Oxford University Press, 1961.

Pedersen, S. *Family, Dependence, and the Origins of the Welfare State: Britain and France, 1914–1945.* Cambridge, UK: Cambridge University Press, 1993.

Richardson, Joanna, ed. *From Recession to Renewal. The Impact of the Financial Crisis on Public Services and Local Government.* Bristol, UK: Policy Press, 2011.

Timmins, Nicholas. *The Five Giants: A Biography of the Welfare State.* London: HarperCollins, 1995.

Walker, Robert, and Michael Wiseman. *The Welfare We Want? The British Challenge for American Reform.* Bristol, UK: Policy Press, 2003.

X. GERMANY

Abelshauser, W., ed. *Die Weimarer Republik als Wohlfahrtsstaat.* Stuttgart, Germany: Franz Steiner, 1987.

Brunner, O., W. Conze, and R. Koselleck, eds. *Geschichtliche Grundbegriffe, Historisches Lexikon zur politisch-sozialen Sprache in Deutschland.* Stuttgart, Germany: Klett-Cotta, 1972–1997.

Conrad C. "Die Sprachen des Wohlfahrtsstaates." In S. Lessenich, ed., *Wohlfahrtssta-atsliche Grundbegriffe. Historische und aktuelle Diskurse*, 55–69. Frankfurt, Germany: Campus Verlag, 2003.

———. "Wohlfahrt, Wohlfahrtsstaat II." In J. Ritter, K. Gründer, and G. Gabriel, eds., *Historisches Wörterbuch der Philosophie*, Band 12, 999–1,000. Darmstadt, Germany: Wissenschaftliche Buchgesellschaft, 2005.

Crew, D. F. *Germans on Welfare: From Weimar to Hitler*. Oxford, UK: Oxford University Press, 1998.

Gneist, R. *Der Rechtsstaat*. Berlin, Germany: Verlag von Julius Springer, 1872.

———. *Der Rechtsstaat und die Verwaltungsgerichte in Deutschland*. Berlin, Germany: Verlag von Julius Springer, 1879.

Götz, N. *Ungleiche Geschwister: Die Konstruktion von nationalsozialistischer Volksgemeinschaft und Schwedischen Volksheim*. Berlin, Germany: Nomos, 2011.

Hahn, E. "Rudolf Gneist and the Prussian Rechtsstaat." *Journal of Modern History* 49, no. 4 (1977): 1,361–81.

Huber, E. R. *Deutsche Verfassungsgeschichte seit 1789, band VI, Die Weimarer Reichsverfassung*. Stuttgart, Germany: Duncker und Humblut, 1981.

Kaufmann, F-X. "Der Begriff Sozialpolitik und seine wissenschaftliche Bedeutung." In *Geschichte der Sozialpolitik in Deutschland seit 1945, Band I. Bundesministerium für Arbeit Sozialordnung und Bundesarchiv*. Baden-Baden, Germany: Nomos, 2001.

Lambrecht, L. "Karl Nauwerck (1810–1892): *Ein 'unbekannter' und 'vergessener' Radikaldemokrat?*'" In H. Bleiber, W. Schmidt, S. Schötz, eds., *Akteure eines Umbruchs, Männer und Frauen der Revolution von 1848/49*, 431–62. Berlin, Germany: Fides, 2003.

Mommsen, W. J., ed. *The Emergence of the Welfare State in Britain and Germany: 1850–1950*. London: Croom Helm, 1983.

Ritter, E. *Die katholisch-soziale Bewegung Deutschlands im neunzehnten Jahrhundert und der Volksverein*. Cologne, Germany: J. P. Bachem, 1954.

Ritter, G. A. *Machtstaat und Utopie*. Munich, Germany: Oldenbourg, 1940.

———. *Der Sozialstaat. Entstehung und Entwicklung im internationalen Vergleich*. Munich, Germany: Oldenbourg, 1991.

Sachße, C., and F. Tennstedt. *Der Wohlfahrtsstaat im Nationalsozialismus. Gescichte der Armenfürsorge in Deutschland*, vol. 3. Stuttgart, Germany: Kohlhammer, 1992.

XI. UNITED STATES

Axinn, J., and H. Levin. *Social Welfare: A History of the American Response to Need*. New York: Dodd, Mead, 1975.

Blank, R., and R. Haskins. *The New World of Welfare*. Washington, D.C.: Brookings Institution, 2001.

Levine, Daniel. *Poverty and Society: The Growth of the American Welfare State in International Comparison*. New Brunswick, N.J.: Rutgers University Press, 1988.

Marmor, T. R., T. L. Mashaw, and P. L. Harvey. *America's Misunderstood Welfare State*. New York: Basic, 1990.

Myrdal, Gunnar, and Sissela Bok. *An American Dilemma: The Negro Problem and Modern Democracy*. London: Harper & Row, 1962.

Patterson, J. *The Welfare State in America*. Durham, England: British Association of American Studies, 1981.

Peck, J. *Workfare States*. New York: Guildford Press, 2001.

Quadagno, Jill. *The Transformation of Old-Age Security: Class and Politics in the American Welfare State*. Chicago: University of Chicago Press, 1988.

Solow, Robert. *Work and Welfare*. Princeton, N.J.: Princeton University Press, 1998.

Trattner, Walter I. *From Poor Law to Welfare State: A History of Social Welfare in America*. New York: Free Press, 1979.

Weil, Alan, and Kenneth Finegold, eds. *Welfare Reform: The Next Act*. Washington, D.C.: Urban Institute Press, 2002.

Weir, M., A. S. Orloff, and T. Skocpol. *The Politics of Social Policy in the United States*. Princeton, N.J.: Princeton University Press, 1988.

XII. SCANDINAVIAN COUNTRIES

Allardt, Erik. *Having, Loving, and Being: Welfare in the Nordic Countries*. Lund, Sweden: Lund Universitetsforlag, 1975.

Blomqvist, Paula. "Privatization of Swedish Welfare Services." *Social Policy and Administration* 38, no. 2 (2004): 139–56.

Castles, Francis G. *The Social Democratic Image of Society: A Study in the Achievements and Origins of Scandinavian Social Democracy in Comparative Perspective*. London: Routledge and Kegan Paul, 1978.

Cox, Robert. "Why Scandinavian Welfare States Remain Distinct." *Social Policy and Administration* 38, no. 2 (2004): 204–19.

Eriksen, R., E. J. Hansen, S. Ringen, and H. Usitalo, eds. *The Scandinavian Model: Welfare States and Welfare Research*. Armonk, N.Y.: M. E. Sharpe, 1987.

Greve, Bent. "Denmark: Universal or Not So Universal Welfare State." *Social Policy and Administration* 38, no. 2 (2004): 156–69.

———. "Denmark a Nordic Welfare State: Are the Active Labour Market Policy Withering Away?" *Open Social Science Journal* 5 (2012): 15–23

———, ed. *The Scandinavian Model in a Period of Change*. Basingstoke, England: Macmillan, 1996.

Hansen, Erik Jørgen, ed. *Welfare Trends in the Scandinavian Countries*. Armonk, N.Y.: M. E. Sharpe, 1993.

Kangas, O., and J. Kvist. "Nordic Welfare States." In B. Greve, ed., *The Routledge Handbook of the Welfare State*. Oxford, UK: Routledge, 2013.

Kautto, Mikko, Matti Heikkila, Bjorn Hvinden, Staffan Marklund, and Niels Ploug. *Nordic Social Policy: Changing Welfare States*. London: Routledge, 1999.

———. *Nordic Welfare States in the European Context*. London: Routledge, 2001.

Kosonen, Pekko. "Flexibilization and the Alternatives of the Nordic Welfare States." In Bob Jessop, Hans Kastendiek, Klaus Nielsen, and Ove Kaj Pedersen, eds., *The Politics of Flexibility: Restructuring States and Industry in Britain, Germany, and Scandinavia*, 263–81. Aldershot, England: Edward Elgar, 1991.

Olsson-Hort, Sven Erik. *Social Policy and Welfare State in Sweden*. Stockholm, Sweden: Arkiv, 1990.

———. "Welfare Policy in Sweden." In Thomas P. Boje and Sven Erik Olsson-Hort, eds., *Scandinavia in a New Europe*, 74–86. Oslo, Norway: Scandinavian University Press, 1993.

Palme, Joakim, et al. "Welfare Trends in Sweden: Balancing the Books for the 1990s." *Journal of European Social Policy* 12, no. 4 (2002): 329–46.

Sipilä, Jorma. *Social Care Services: The Key to the Scandinavian Welfare Model*. Alsderhot, England: Avebury, 1997.

Zetterberg, Hans L. *Before and Beyond the Welfare State: Three Lectures*. Stockholm, Sweden: City University Press, 1995.

XIII. OTHER COUNTRIES

Aspalter, C., ed. *Discovering the Welfare State in East Asia*. Westport, Conn.: Praeger, 2002.

———. *Welfare Capitalism around the World*. Hong Kong, China: Casa Verde Publication, 2003.

Deacon, Bob, et al. *The New Eastern Europe: Social Policy, Present and Future*. London: Sage, 1992.

Dimitri, A., Ileana Neamtu Sotiropoulos, and Maya Stoyanova. "The Trajectory of Post-Communist Welfare State Development: The Cases of Bulgaria and Romania." *Social Policy and Administration* 37, no. 6 (2003): 656–73.

Dixon, J., and R. P. Scheurell, eds. *Social Welfare in Developed Market Countries*. London: Routledge and Kegan Paul, 1989.

Farnsworth, Kevin, and Zöe Irving. *Social Policy in Challenging Times: Economic Crisis and Welfare Systems*. Bristol, UK: Policy Press, 2011.

George, V., and N. Manning. *Socialism, Social Welfare, and the Union of Soviet Socialist Republics (USSR)*. London: Routledge and Kegan Paul, 1980.

Goodman, R, G. White, and H. J. Kwon, eds. *The East Asian Welfare Model: Welfare Orientalism and the State*. London: Routledge, 1998.

Gough, Ian, Geof Wood, Armando Barrientos, Philippa Bevan, Peter Davis, and Graham Room. *Insecurity and Welfare Regimes in Asia, Africa, and Latin America*. Cambridge, UK: Cambridge University Press, 2004.

Lee, Min-kvan. *Chinese Occupational Welfare in Market Transition: Beyond the Iron Rice Bowl*. New York: St. Martin's Press, 2000.

Lee, P., and C. Raban. *Welfare Theory and Social Policy: Reform or Revolution*. London: Sage, 1988.

Madison, B. *Social Welfare and the Union of Soviet Socialist Republics*. Stanford, Calif.: Stanford University Press, 1968.

Matsaganis, Manos, Maurizio Ferrera, Luís Capucha, and Luis Moreno. "Mending Nets in the South: Antipoverty Policies in Greece, Italy, Portugal, and Spain." *Social Policy and Administration* 37, no. 6 (2003): 639–55.

McAuley, A. *Economic Welfare in the Union of Soviet Socialist Republics.* London: Allen & Unwin, 1979.

Peterson, W. C. *The Welfare State in France.* Lincoln: University of Nebraska Press, 1960.

Pfaller, A., I. Gough, and G. Therborn, eds. *Can the Welfare State Compete? A Comparative Study of Five Advanced Capitalist Countries.* Basingstoke, England: Macmillan, 1991.

Rhodes, Martin. "Southern European Welfare States: Identity, Problems, and Prospects for Reform." *Southern European Society and Politics* 1, no. 3 (1996): 1–22.

Springer, B. *The Social Dimension of 1992: Europe Faces a New EC.* New York: Praeger, 1992.

Széman, Zsuzsa. "The Welfare Mix in Hungary as a New Phenomenon." *Social Policy and Society* 2, no. 2 (2003): 101–8.

Tang, K. L., ed. *Social Welfare Development in Asia.* Dordrecht, Netherlands: Kluwer 2000.

XIV. COMPARATIVE ANALYSIS OF THE WELFARE STATE

Bouget, Denis. "Convergence in Social Welfare Systems in Europe: From Goal to Reality." *Social Policy and Administration* 37, no. 6 (2003): 674–93.

Bradshaw, Jonathan, et al. *The Employment of Lone Parents: A Comparison of Policy in 20 Countries.* London: Family Policy Studies Centre, 1996.

———. *Support for Children: A Comparison of Arrangements in Fifteen Countries.* HMSO Research Report No. 21. London: Department of Social Security, 1993.

Bradshaw, Jonathan, Mary Daly, and Jane Lewis. "The Concept of Social Care and the Analysis of Contemporary Welfare States." *British Journal of Sociology* 51, no. 2 (2001): 281–98.

Faist, Thomas. *Ethnicization and Racialization of Welfare State Politics in Germany and the USA.* Bremen, Germany: Zentrum für Sozialpolitik, Universität Bremen, 1994.

Ferge, Zzusa, and Jon Kolberg, eds. *Social Policy in a Changing Europe.* Frankfurt, Germany: Campus Verlag, and Boulder, Colo.: Westview Press, 1992.

Friedmann, R., N. Gilbert, and M. Shere, eds. *Modern Welfare States: A Comparative View of Trends and Prospects.* Brighton, England: Harvester Wheatsheaf, 1987.

Gordon, M. *Social Security Policies in Industrial Countries: A Comparative Analysis.* Cambridge, UK: Cambridge University Press, 1988.

Gough, Ian, A. Pfaller, and Gøran Therborn, eds. *Can the Welfare State Compete: A Comparative Study of Five Advanced Capitalist Countries.* London: Macmillan, 1991.

Greve, Bent. "Indication of Social Policy Convergence in Europe." *Social Policy and Administration* 30, no. 4 (1996): 348–67.

——. *Social Policy in Europe: Latest Evolution and Perspectives for the Future*. Copenhagen, Denmark: Danish National Institute of Social Research, 1992.

Hantrais, L. *Social Policy in the European Union*. Houndsmills, England: Macmillan, 1995.

Higgins, J. *States of Welfare: Comparative Analysis in the Social Policy*. Oxford, UK: Blackwell/Martin Robertson, 1981.

Johnson, Norman. *Mixed Economies of Welfare. A Comparative Perspective*. Hemel Hempstead, England: Prentice Hall, 1999.

Jones, Catherine. *New Perspectives on the Welfare State in Europe*. London: Routledge, 1993.

Kennett, Patricia. *Comparative Social Policy*. Buckingham, England: Open University Press, 2001.

Leibfried, Stephan, and Paul Pierson, eds. *European Social Policy: Between Fragmentation and Integration*. Washington, D.C.: Brookings Institution, 1995.

Millar, J., and A. Warman. *Family Obligations in Europe*. London: Family Policy Studies Centre, 1996.

Mishra, Ramesh. *The Welfare State in Capitalist Society: Politics of Retrenchment and Maintenance in Europe, North America, and Australia*. Hemel Hempstead, England: Harvester Wheatsheaf, 1990.

Oyen, Else, ed. *Comparing Welfare States and Their Futures*. London: Gower, 1986.

Rimlinger, G. *Welfare Policy and Industrialization in Europe, America, and Russia*. New York: Wiley, 1971.

Rose, R., and R. Shiratori. *The Welfare State East and West*. Oxford, UK: Oxford University Press, 1986.

Spicker, Paul. "Social Policy in a Federal Europe." *Social Policy and Administration* 30, no. 4 (1996): 293–304.

Taylor-Gooby, Peter. "Introduction: Open Markets versus Welfare Citizenship: Conflicting Approaches to Policy Convergence in Europe." *Social Policy and Administration* 37, no. 6 (2003): 539–54.

Wilensky, Harold. "Comparative Social Policy: Theories, Methods, Findings." In M. Dierkes and A. Antal, eds., *Comparative Policy Research: Learning from Experience*, 381–458. Aldershot, England: Gower, 1987.

XV. PUBLIC-SECTOR ECONOMICS

Boadway, R. *Public Sector Economics*. London: Basil Blackwell, 1984.

Culyer, A. J. *The Political Economy of Social Policy*. Oxford, UK: Martin Robertson, 1980.

Glennerster, Howard. *Paying for Welfare: The 1990s*. New York: Harvester Wheatsheaf, 1992.

Musgrave, Richard A. *The Theory of Public Finance*. New York: McGraw-Hill, 1959.

Musgrave, Richard A., and Peggy B. Musgrave. *Public Finance in Theory and Practice*. London: McGraw-Hill, 1989.

Samuelson, Paul A. "Pure Theory of Public Expenditure." *Review of Economics and Statistics* 36, no. 4 (1954): 387–89.

Stiglitz, Joseph E. *Economics of the Public Sector*. New York: W. W. Norton, 1986.

Tiebout, C. "A Pure Theory of Local Expenditures." *Journal of Political Economy* 64, no. 5 (1956): 416–24.

Wagner, A. "Finanzwissenschaft (1883)." Reproduced partly in Richard A. Musgrave and Alan Peacock, eds., *Classics in the Theory of Public Finance*, 1–15. London: Macmillan, 1962.

Walker, Alan, ed. *Public Expenditure and Social Policy*. London: Heinemann, 1982.

Wilensky, Harold. *The Welfare State and Equality: Structural and Ideological Roots of Public Expenditures*. Berkeley: University of California Press, 1975.

XVI. PUBLIC CHOICE

Borcherding, Thomas E. *Budgets and Bureaucrats: The Sources of Government Growth*. Durham, N.C.: Duke University Press, 1977.

Buchanan, James M., and Robert Tollison, eds. *The Theory of Public Choice II*. Ann Arbor: University of Michigan Press, 1984.

Friedman, Milton, and Rose Friedman. *Free to Choose*. Harmondsworth, England: Penguin, 1981.

Harris, R., and A. Seldon. *Welfare without the State: A Quarter-Century of Suppressed Public Choice*. London: Institute of Economic Affairs, 1987.

Mueller, Dennis C. *Public Choice*. Cambridge, UK: Cambridge University Press, 1979.

———. *Public Choice III*. Cambridge, UK: Cambridge University Press, 2003.

Niskanen, W. A., Jr. *Bureaucracy and Representative Government*. Chicago: Aldine-Atherton, 1971.

XVII. THE CRISIS OF THE WELFARE STATE

Alber, J. F. "Is There a Crisis?" *European Sociological Review*, 4, no. 3 (1988): 181–207.

Block, Fred L., Richard A. Cloward, Barbara Ehrenreich, and Frances Fox Piven. *The Mean Season: The Attack on the Welfare State*. New York: Pantheon, 1987.

Carr, E. H. *The Twenty Years' Crisis, 1919–1939: An Introduction to the Study of International Relations*. London: Papermac,1935, 1995.

Culpitt, I. *Welfare and Citizenship: Beyond the Crisis of the Welfare State?* London: Sage, 1992.

Esping-Andersen, Gøsta, Martin Rein, and Lee Rainwater, eds. *Stagnation and Renewal in Social Policy: The Rise and Fall of Policy Regimes*. Armonk, N.Y.: M. E. Sharpe, 1987.

Habermas, Jürgen. *Legitimation Crisis*. London: Heinemann, 1976.

Halsey, A. H., ed. *The Welfare State in Crisis*. Paris: OECD, 1981.

Mishra, Ramesh. *The Welfare State in Crisis: Social Thought and Social Change*. Brighton, England: Harvester Wheatsheaf, 1984.

Munday, Brian, ed. *The Crisis in Welfare: An International Perspective on Social Service and Social Work*. Hemel Hempstead, England: Harvester Wheatsheaf, 1989.

O'Connor, James. *The Fiscal Crisis of the State*. New York: St. Martin's Press, 1973.

Offe, Claus. *Contradictions of the Welfare State*. London: Hutchinson, 1984.

Pierson, P. *Dismantling the Welfare State? Reagan, Thatcher, and the Politics of Retrenchment*. Cambridge, UK: Cambridge University Press, 1994.

Therborn, G., and J. Roebroek. "The Irreversible Welfare State." *International Journal of Health Services* 16, no. 3 (1986): 319–38.

Whynes, David, ed. *In Defense of Welfare*. London: Tavistock, 1985.

Wicks, M. *A Future for All: Do We Need the Welfare State?* Harmondsworth, England: Penguin, 1987.

Wilding, P., ed. *In Defense of the Welfare State*. Manchester, England: Manchester University Press, 1986.

XVIII. VOLUNTARY ACTIVITIES

Baine, S., J. Benington, and J. Russell. *Changing Europe: Challenges Facing the Voluntary and Community Sectors in the 1990s*. London: NCVO Publications and Community Development Foundation, 1992.

Beveridge, William. *Voluntary Action*. London: Allen & Unwin, 1948.

Kramer, R. *Voluntary Agencies in the Welfare State*. Berkeley: University of California Press, 1981.

Morris, Mary. *Voluntary Work in the Welfare State*. London: Routledge and Kegan Paul, 1969.

XIX. POLITICAL SCIENCE AND THE WELFARE STATE

Buchanan, James M. *The Political Economy of the Welfare State*. Stockholm, Sweden: Almqvist & Wiksell, 1988.

Cohn G., J. A. Hill, and E. J. James. "A History of Political Economy." *Annals of the American Academy of Political and Social Science* 4, suppl. 6 (1894): 1–142.

Deakin, Nicolas. *The Politics of Welfare: Continuities and Change*. Hemel Hempstead, England: Harvester Wheatsheaf, 1994.

Esping-Andersen, Gøsta. *Politics against Markets*. Princeton, N.J.: Princeton University Press, 1985.

——. "Power and Distributional Regimes." *Politics and Society* 14, no. 2 (1985): 223–56.

Gutmann, A., ed. *Democracy and the Welfare State*. Princeton, N.J.: Princeton University Press, 1988.

Hadley, R., and S. Hatch. *Social Welfare and the Failure of the State*. London: Allen & Unwin, 1981.

Hancock, M. D. *Politics in the Post-Welfare State: Responses to the New Individualism*. New York: Columbia University Press, 1972.

Harris, D. *Justifying State Welfare*. Oxford, UK: Blackwell, 1987.

Hills, J., ed. *The State Welfare*. Oxford, UK: Clarendon Press, 1990.

Hirschman, A. *Shifting Involvement: Private Interest and Public Action*. Oxford, UK: Martin Robertson, 1972.

Kemshall, Hazel, ed. *Crime and Social Policy*. West Sussex, England: Wiley-Blackwell, 2013.

Korpi, Walter. *Class, Power, and State Autonomy in Welfare State Development*. Stockholm: Swedish Institute for Social Research, 1987.

——. *The Democratic Class Struggle*. London: Routledge and Kegan Paul, 1983.

——. *The Working Class in Welfare Capitalism*. London: Routledge and Kegan Paul, 1979.

Loney, Martin. *The Politics of Greed: The New Right and the Welfare State*. London: Pluto, 1986.

Luhmann, Niclas. *Political Theory in the Welfare State*. Berlin, Germany: De Gruyter, 1990.

McCarthy, M., ed. *The New Politics of Welfare*. Basingstoke, England: Macmillan, 1989.

Morgan, Kimberly J., and Andrea Louise Campell. *The Delegated Welfare State: Medicare, Markets, and the Governance of Social Policy*. Oxford, UK: Oxford University Press, 2012.

Oakley, A., and A. Susan Williams, eds. *The Politics of the Welfare State*. London: UCL Press, 1994.

Pampel, F. C., and J. B. Williamson. *Age, Class, Politics, and the Welfare State*. Cambridge, UK: Cambridge University Press, 1989.

Taylor-Gooby, Peter. *Public Opinion, Ideology, and State Welfare*. London: Routledge and Kegan Paul, 1985.

Weale, A. *Political Theory and Social Policy*. London: Macmillan, 1983.

XX. SPECIFIC BENEFITS

Espina, A. "Reform of Pension Schemes in the OECD Countries." *International Labour Review* 135, no. 2 (1996): 181–206.

Evandrou, M., J. Falkingham, J. Hills, and J. Le Grand. *The Distribution of Welfare Benefits in Kind*. London: London School of Economics Welfare State Programme, 1991.

Gough, I., Jonathan Bradshaw, John Ditch, Tony Eardley, and Peter Whiteford. "Social Assistance in OECD Countries." *Journal of European Social Policy* 7, no. 1 (1997): 17–43.

Myles, John. *Old Age in the Welfare State: The Political Economy of Public Pensions*. Lawrence: University Press of Kansas, 1989.

Palme, Joakim. *Pension Rights in Welfare Capitalism: The Development of Old-Age Pensions in 18 OECD Countries, 1930 to 1985.* Edsbruk, Sweden: Swedish Institute for Social Research, 1990.

Wilson, T., ed. *Pensions, Inflation, and Growth: A Comparative Study of the Elderly in the Welfare State.* London: Heinemann Educational Books, 1974.

XXI. THE LABOR MARKET

Atkinson, Anthony B., and Gunnar Viby Mogensen, eds. *Welfare and Work Incentives: A North European Perspective.* Oxford, UK: Clarendon Press, 1993.

Brittan, S. *Beyond the Welfare State: An Examination of Basic Incomes in a Market Economy.* Aberdeen, Scotland: Aberdeen University Press, 1990.

Gershuny, John. *Social Innovation and the Division of Labour.* Oxford, UK: Oxford University Press, 1983.

Mogensen, Gunnar Viby, ed. *Work Incentives in the Danish Welfare State: New Empirical Evidence.* Århus, Netherlands: Århus University Press, 1995.

Scharpf, Fritz, and Vivian Schmidt. *From Vulnerability to Competitiveness: Welfare and Work in the Open Economy.* Oxford, UK: Oxford University Press, 2000.

Sinfield, Adrian. "The Necessity for Full Employment." In H. Glennerster, ed., *The Future of the Welfare State: Rethinking Social Policy,* 61–78. London: Heinemann, 1983.

———. *What Unemployment Means.* Oxford, UK: Martin Robertson, 1981.

Sinfield, Adrian, and Neil Fraser. *The Real Cost of Unemployment.* Newcastle, England: BBC North-East, 1985.

Teague, Paul. *The European Community—The Social Dimension: Labour Market Policies for 1992.* London: Kogan Page, 1992.

XXII. SOCIAL DIVISION OF WELFARE

Adema, W., P. Fron, and M. Ladaique. "Is the European Welfare State Really More Expensive? Indicators on Social Spending, 1980–2012; and a Manual to the OECD Social Expenditure Database (SOCX)." OECD Social, Employment, and Migration Working Papers No. 124. Paris: OECD, 2011.

Alcock, Pete, Howard Glennerster, Ann Oakley, and Adrian Sinfield, eds. *Welfare and Wellbeing: Richard Titmuss's Contribution to Social Policy.* Bristol, UK: Policy Press, 2001.

Brewer, Mike, Luke Sibieta, and Liam Wren-Lewis. *Racing Away? Income Inequality and the Evolution of High Incomes.* IFS Briefing Note No. 76. London: Institute for Fiscal Studies, 2008

Ervik, R. and S. Kuhnle. "The Nordic Welfare Model and the European Union." In Bent Greve, ed. *Comparative Welfare Systems: The Scandinavian Model in a Period of Change,* 87–107. Basingstoke, England: Macmillan, 1996.

Faricy, Christopher. "The Politics of Social Policy in America: The Causes and Effects of Indirect versus Direct Social Spending." *Journal of Politics* 73, no. 1 (2011): 74–83.

Ginn, J., D. Street, and S. Arber, eds. *Women, Work, and Pensions: International Issues and Prospects*. Buckingham, England: Open University Press, 2001.

Greve, Bent. "The Hidden Welfare State, Tax Expenditure, and Social Policy." *Scandinavian Journal of Social Welfare* 3, no. 4 (1994): 203–11.

Hacker, Jacob S. *The Divided Welfare State: The Battle over Public and Private Social Benefits in the United States*. Cambridge, UK: Cambridge University Press, 2002.

Howard, C. *The Hidden Welfare State: Tax Expenditures and Social Policy in the United States*. Princeton, N.J.: Princeton University Press, 1997.

Hughes, G., and Adrian Sinfield. "Financing Pensions by Stealth." In G. Hughes and J. Stewart, eds., *Reforming Pensions in Europe: The Evolution of Pension Financing and Sources of Retirement Income*, 163–92. Cheltenham, England: Edward Elgar, 2004.

Kvist, J., and Adrian Sinfield. *Comparing Tax Routes to Welfare in Denmark and the United Kingdom*. Copenhagen, Denmark: Danish National Institute of Social Research, 1996.

———. "Comparing Tax Welfare States." In M. May, E. Brunsdon, and G. Craig, eds., *Social Policy Review*, 249–75. London: SPA, 1997.

McDaniel, P. R., and S. S. Surrey, eds. *International Aspects of Tax Expenditures: A Comparative Study*. Deventer, Netherlands: Kluwer, 1985.

Minarik, Joe. *Tax Expenditures in OECD Countries*. Paris: OECD, 2010.

Sinfield, Adrian. "Analysis in the Social Division of Welfare." *Journal of Social Policy* 7, no. 2 (1978): 129–56.

Stebbing, Adam, and Ben Spies-Butcher. "Universal Welfare by 'Other Means'? Tax Expenditures and the Australian Welfare State." *Journal of Social Policy* 39, no. 4 (2010): 585–606.

Surrey, S. S. *Pathways to Tax Reform*. Cambridge, Mass: Harvard University Press, 1973.

Titmuss, Richard M. *Commitment to Welfare*. London: Allen & Unwin, 1968.

———. *Essays on the Welfare State*. London: Allen & Unwin, 1958.

World Bank. "Why Worry about Tax Expenditures?" *PREMnotes* 77 (2003): 1–4.

XXIII. SOCIAL SECURITY AND SOCIAL POLICY

Aaron, H. J. *Economic Effects of Social Security*. Washington, D.C.: Brookings Institution, 1982.

Ashford, D. E., and E. W. Kelly, eds. *Nationalizing Social Security in Europe and America*. London: JAI Press, 1986.

Atkinson, Anthony B. *Poverty and Social Security*. Hemel Hempstead, England: Harvester Wheatsheaf, 1989.

Clasen, Jochen, ed. *Comparative Social Policy: Concepts, Theories, and Methods.* Oxford, UK: Blackwell, 1999.

———. *Social Insurance in Europe.* Bristol, UK: Policy Press, 1997.

———. *What Future for Social Security? Debates and Reforms in National and Cross-National Perspective.* Bristol, UK: Policy Press, 2001.

Dean, H. *Social Security and Social Control.* London: Routledge and Kegan Paul, 1990.

Ebbinghaus, Bernhard. *The Varieties of Pension Governance: Pension Privatization in Europe.* Oxford, UK: Oxford University Press, 2011.

Glazer, N. *The Limits of Social Policy.* Cambridge, Mass.: Harvard University Press, 1988.

Glennerster, Howard, and John Hills, eds. *The State of Welfare: The Economics of Social Spending.* Oxford, UK: Oxford University Press, 1998.

Goodin, Robert. *Protecting the Vulnerable.* Chicago: University of Chicago Press, 1985.

Greve, Bent. *Choice: Challenges and Perspectives for the European Welfare States.* Sussex, England: Wiley-Blackwell, 2010.

———. "Economics and Social Security in Europe." In Danny Pieters, ed., *Social Security in Europe: Miscellanea of the Erasmus-Programme Social Security in the E.C.,* 191–216. Bruylant, Belgium: Maklu, 1991.

Hill, Michael. *Social Policy: A Comparative Analysis.* London: Harvester Wheatsheaf, 1996.

Hill, Michael, and G. Bramley. *Analyzing Social Policy.* Oxford, UK: Blackwell, 1986.

Jones, Catherine. *Patterns of Social Policy: An Introduction to Comparative Analysis.* London: Tavistock, 1985.

Kemshall, Hazel. *Risk, Social Policy, and Welfare.* Buckingham, England: Open University Press, 2002.

Le Grand, Julian, and Will Bartlett. *Quasi-markets and Social Policy.* Basingstoke, England: Macmillan, 1993.

Madison, B. Q. *The Meaning of Social Policy.* London: Croom Helm, 1980.

Marshall, T. H. *Social Policy.* London: Hutchinson, 1961.

Martin, G. T. *Social Policy in the Welfare State.* Englewood Cliffs, N.J.: Prentice Hall, 1990.

Mishra, Ramesh. *Society and Social Policy: Theories and Practice of Welfare.* London: Macmillan, 1977.

Morris, R., ed. *Testing the Limits of Social Welfare.* London: Brandeis University Press, 1981.

Organization for Economic Cooperation and Development. *The Future of Social Protection.* OECD Social Policy Studies No. 6. Paris: OECD, 1988.

Pennings, Frans. "Social Security." In Bent Greve, ed., *The Routledge Handbook of the Welfare State.* Oxford, UK: Routledge, 2013.

Pinker, R. *Social Theory and Social Policy.* London: Heinemann Educational Books, 1971.

Plant, R., H. Lesser, and P. Taylor-Gooby, eds. *Political Philosophy and Social Welfare*. London: Routledge and Kegan Paul, 1980.

Rein, Martin. *Social Policy: Issues of Choice and Change*. New York: Random House, 1970.

Silburn, R. *The Future of Social Security*. London: Fabian Society, 1985.

Smith, G. *Social Needs: Policy Practice and Research*. London: Routledge, 1988.

Sullivan, M. *The Politics of Social Policy*. Hemel Hempstead, England: Harvester Wheatsheaf, 1992.

——. *Sociology and Social Welfare*. London: Allen & Unwin, 1987.

Titmuss, Richard. *Problems of Social Policy*. London: His Majesty's Stationery Office and Longmans, Green, 1950.

Townsend, Peter. *Sociology and Social Policy*. London: Allan Lane, 1975.

Vrooman, J. C. *Rules of Relief: Institutions of Social Security and Their Impact*. The Hague: Netherlands Institute for Social Research, 2009.

Walker, C. *Changing Social Policy*. London: Bedford Square Press, 1983.

Williams, F. *Social Policy: A Critical Introduction: Issues of Race, Gender, and Class*. Cambridge, UK: Polity, 1989.

Wilson, Thomas, and Dorothy Wilson, eds. *The State and Social Welfare*. Harlow, England: Longman, 1991.

XXIV. ADMINISTRATION AND THE WELFARE STATE

Adler, Michael, and S. Asquith. *Discretion and Welfare*. London: Heinemann, 1981.

Appleby, P. H. *Public Administration for a Welfare State*. London: Asia Publishing House, 1962.

Clarke, J., A. Cochrane, and C. Smat. *Ideologies of Welfare*. London: Routledge and Kegan Paul, 1987.

Crozier, M. *The Bureaucratic Phenomenon*. Chicago: University of Chicago Press, 1964.

Davies, B. P. *Universality, Selectivity, and Effectiveness in Social Policy*. London: Heinemann, 1978.

Davis, K. C. *Discretionary Justice*. Baton Rouge: Louisiana State University Press, 1969.

Donnison, D. V., and C. D. Donnison. *Social Policy and Administration*. London: Allen & Unwin, 1965.

Greve, Bent. *Advantages and Disadvantages by Local Provision of Social Policy*. Roskilde, Denmark: Roskilde University, Department of Social Sciences, 1994.

Johnson, Norman, ed. *Private Markets in Health and Welfare: An International Perspective*. Oxford, UK: Berg, 1995.

Lerman, Paul. *Deinstitutionalization and the Welfare State*. New Brunswick, N.J.: Rutgers University Press, 1982.

Lipsky, Martin. *Street-Level Bureaucracy: Dilemmas of the Individual in Public Services*. New York: Russell Sage, 1980.

Papadakis, Elim. *The Private Provision of Public Welfare: State, Market, and Community*. Brighton, England: Harvester Wheatsheaf, 1987.

Scott, D., and P. Wilding. *Beyond Welfare Pluralism*. Manchester, England: Manchester Council for Voluntary Service and Manchester Social Administration Department, 1984.

Smith, S. R., and M. Lipsky. *Nonprofits for Hire: The Welfare State in the Age of Contracting*. Cambridge, Mass.: Harvard University Press, 1993.

Taylor-Gooby, Peter. "Privatization, Power, and the Welfare State." *Sociology* 20, no. 2 (1986): 228–46.

Weber, Max. *The Theory of Social and Economic Organizations*. Edited by A. M. Henderson and T. Parsons. Glencoe, Ill.: Free Press, 1947.

Wilensky, Harold. *"The New Corporatism": Centralization and the Welfare State*. London: Sage, 1976.

XXV. CITIZENSHIP

Ackers, L., and P. Dwyer. *Senior Citizenship? Retirement, Migration, and Welfare in the European Union*. Bristol, UK: Policy Press, 2002.

Barnes, J., and D. Prior, eds. *Subversive Citizens: Power, Agency, and Resistance in Public Services*. Bristol, UK: Policy Press, 2009.

Barnes, M. "Caring Responsibilities: The Making of Citizen Careers." In J. Newman and E. Tonkens, eds, *Participation, Responsibility, and Choice: Summoning the Active Citizen in Western European Welfare States*. Amsterdam, Netherlands: University of Amsterdam Press, 2010.

Barnes, M., J. Newman, and H. Sullivan. *Power, Participation, and Political Renewal*. Bristol, UK: Policy Press, 2007.

Beckett, A. *Citizenship and Vulnerability: Disability and Issues of Social and Political Engagement*. Basingstoke, England: Palgrave, 2006.

Clarke, J., J. Newman, N. Smith, E. Vidler, and L. Westmarland. *Creating the Citizen Consumer*. London: Sage, 2007.

Coll, C. *Remaking Citizenship*. Redwood City, Calif.: Stanford University Press, 2010.

Coote, A., ed. *The Welfare of Citizens*. London: Rivers Oram Press, 1992.

Cornwall, A., and V. Coehlo, eds. *Spaces for Change: The Politics of Citizen Participation in New Democratic Arenas*. London: Zed Books, 2004.

Craig, G. "Citizenship, Exclusion, and Older People." *Journal of Social Policy* 33, no. 1 (2004): 95–114.

Friedman, K. V. *Legitimation of Social Rights and the Western Welfare State: A Weberian Perspective*. Chapel Hill: University of North Carolina Press, 1981.

Fung, A., and Wright, E. O. *Deepening Democracy: Institutional Innovations in Empowered Participatory Governance*. London: Verso, 2003.

Grimley M. *Citizenship, Community, and the Church of England: Liberal Anglican Theories of the State between the Wars*. Oxford, UK: Clarendon Press, 2004.

Huysmans, J. *The Politics of Insecurity: Fear, Migration, and Asylum in the EU.* London: Routledge, 2006.

Invernizzi, A., and J. Williams. *Children and Citizenship.* London: Sage, 2008.

Janoski, Thomas. *Citizenship and Civil Society: A Framework of Rights and Obligations in Liberal, Traditional, and Social Democratic Regimes.* Cambridge, UK: Cambridge University Press, 1998.

Johansson, H., and B. Hvinden. "What Do We Mean By Active Citizenship?" In B. Hvinden and H. Johansson, eds., *Citizenship in Nordic Welfare States: Dynamics of Choice, Duties, and Participation in Changing Europe,* 32–49. London: Routledge, 2008.

Lewis, G. *Race, Gender, and Social Welfare: Encounters in a Postcolonial Society.* Cambridge, UK: Polity, 2000.

Lister, R. *Citizenship: Feminist Perspectives,* 2nd ed. Basingstoke, England: Palgrave Macmillan, 2003.

Lister, R., et al. *Gendering Citizenship in Western Europe.* Bristol, UK: Policy Press, 2007.

Marshall, T. H. *Citizenship and Social Class.* Cambridge, UK: Cambridge University Press, 1950.

Meehan, E. *Citizenship and the European Community.* London: Sage, 1993.

Needham, C. *Citizen-Consumers: New Labour's Marketplace Democracy.* London: Catalyst, 2003.

Newman, J., and E. Tonkens, eds. *Participation, Responsibility, and Choice: Summoning the Active Citizen in Western European Welfare States.* Amsterdam, Netherlands: University of Amsterdam Press, 2007.

Newman, J., and J. Clarke. *Publics, Politics, and Power: Remaking the Public in Public Services.* London: Sage, 2009.

Siim, B. *Gender and Citizenship: Politics and Agency in France, Britain, and Denmark.* Cambridge, UK: Cambridge University Press, 2000.

Soysal, Y. *Limits of Citizenship: Migrants and Postnational Membership in Europe.* Chicago, University of Chicago Press, 1994.

Van Berkel, R., and B. Valkenberg. *Making It Personal: Individualising Activation Services in the EU.* Bristol, UK: Policy Press, 2007.

Willow, C., R. Marchant, P. Kirby, and B. Neale. *Young Children's Citizenship: Ideas into Practice.* York, England: Joseph Rowntree, 2004.

Young, I. M. *Justice and the Politics of Difference.* Princeton, N.J.: Princeton University Press, 1990.

XXVI. FAMILY AND GENDER

Abrahamsson, Peter, Thomas P. Boje, and Bent Greve. *Families and Family Policy in Europe.* Aldershot, England: Ashgate, 2005.

Bock, Gisela, and Pat Thane, eds. *Maternity and Gender Policies, Women, and the Rise of the European Welfare States, 1880s–1950s.* London: Routledge, 1991.

Connell, R. W. *Gender and Power.* Sydney, Australia: Allen & Unwin, 1987.

Dale, J., and P. Foster. *Feminists and State Welfare*. London: Routledge and Kegan Paul, 1986.

Daly, Mary. "What Adult Worker Model? A Critical Look at Recent Social Policy Reform in Europe from a Gender and Family Perspective." *Social Politics* 18, no 1 (2011): 1–23.

———, ed. *Care Work: The Quest for Security*. Geneva, Switzerland: International Labour Organization, 2001.

Daly, Mary, and Jane Lewis. "The Concept of Social Care and the Analysis of Contemporary Welfare States." *British Journal of Sociology* 51, no. 2 (2000): 281–98.

Dominelli, L. *Women across Continents: Feminist Comparative Social Policy*. Hemel Hempstead, England: Harvester Wheatsheaf, 1991.

Donzelot, Jaques. *The Policing of Families*. London: Hutchinson, 1980.

Drew, E., R. Emerek, and E. Mahon, eds. *Women, Work, and the Family in Europe*. London: Routledge, 1998.

Eisenstein, Hester. *Australian Femocrats and the State*. Sydney, Australia: Allen & Unwin 1996.

Fagan, C., and B. Burchell. *Gender, Jobs, and Working Conditions in the European Community*. Dublin: European Foundation of Living and Working Conditions, 2002.

Fraser, Nancy. "After the Family Wage: A Postindustrial Thought Experiment." In Nancy Fraser, ed., *Justus Interruptus: Critical Reflections on the 'Postsocialist' Condition*, 41–66. New York: Routledge, 1997.

———. "Women, Welfare, and the Politics of Need Interpretation." In P. Lassman, ed., *Politics and Social Theory*, 104–22. London: Routledge and Kegan Paul, 1989.

Glendinning, Carol, and Jane Millar. *Women and Poverty: Exploring the Research and Policy Agenda*. Brighton, England: Harvester Wheatsheaf, 1987.

Hantrais, Linda. *Gendered Policies in Europe: Reconciling Employment and Family Life*. London: Macmillan, 2000.

Hernes, Helga. *Welfare States and Woman Power*. Oslo, Norway: Norwegian University Press, 1987.

Hobson, Barbara. "No Exit, No Voice: Women's Economic Dependency and the Welfare State." *Acta Sociologica* 33, no. 3 (1990): 235–50.

Jenson, Jane. "Lost in Translation: The Social Investment Perspective and Gender Equality." *Social Politics* 16, no. 4 (2009): 446–83.

———. "Who Cares? Gender and Welfare Regimes." *Social Politics* 4, no. 2 (1997): 182–87.

Knijn, Trudie, and Arnoud Smit. "Investing, Facilitating, or Individualizing the Reconciliation of Work and Family Life: Three Paradigms and Ambivalent Policies." *Social Politics* 16, no. 4 (2009): 484–518.

Knijn, Trudie, Claude Martin, and Jane Millar. "Activation as a Common Framework for Social Policies toward Lone Parents." *Social Policy and Administration* 41, no. 6 (2007): 638–52.

Langan, M., and Ilona Ostner. *Gender and Welfare*. Bremen, Germany: University of Bremen, 1991.

Larsen, Trine P. "Work and Care Strategies of European Families." *Social Policy and Administration* 38, no. 6 (2004): 654–77.

Leira, Ann. *Working Parents and the Welfare State: Family Change and Policy Reform in Scandinavia.* Cambridge, UK: Cambridge University Press, 2002.

Lewis, Jane. "Gender and the Development of Welfare Regimes." *Journal of Social Policy* 2, no. 3 (1992): 333–66.

———. *Women's Welfare, Women's Rights.* London: Croom Helm, 1983.

———, ed. *Gender, Social Care, and Welfare Restructuring in Europe.* Aldershot, England: Ashgate, 1998.

Lister, Ruth. *Citizenship: Feminist Perspectives*, 2nd ed. New York: New York University Press, 2003.

McIntosh, Mary. "The State and the Oppression of Women." In A. Kuhn and A.-M. Wolpe, eds., *Feminism and Materialism*, 254–89. London: Routledge and Kegan Paul, 1978.

Millar, Jane. "Gender, Poverty, and Social Exclusion." *Social Policy and Society* 2, no. 3 (2003): 181–88.

O'Connor, Julia S., Ann Shola Orloff, and Sheila Shaver. *States, Markets, Families: Gender, Liberalism, and Social Policy in Australia, Canada, Great Britain, and the United States.* Cambridge, UK: Cambridge University Press, 1999.

OECD. *Babies and Bosses: Reconciling Work and Family Life—A Synthesis of Findings for OECD Countries.* Paris: OECD, 2007.

Orloff, Ann Shola. "From Maternalism to 'Employment for All': State Policies to Promote Women's Employment across the Affluent Democracies." In Jonah Levy, ed., *The State after Statism: New State Activities in the Era of Globalization and liberalization*, 230–68. Cambridge Mass.: Harvard University Press, 2006.

———. "Gender and the Social Rights of Citizenship: State Policies and Gender Relations in Comparative Perspective." *American Sociological Review* 58, no. 3 (1993): 303–28.

———. "Tendering the Comparative Analysis of Welfare States: An Unfinished Agenda." *Sociological Theory* 27, no. 3 (2009): 317–43.

Pascall, G. *Social Policy: A Feminist Analysis.* London: Tavistock, 1986.

Pateman, Carole. *The Disorder of Women.* Cambridge, UK: Polity, 1989.

Sainsbury, Diane. *Gender, Equality, and Welfare States.* Cambridg, UK: Cambridge University Press, 1996.

Sasson, A. S., ed. *Women and the State: The Shifting Boundaries of Public and Private.* London: Hutchinson, 1987.

Sipilä, Jorma, and Teppo Kröger. "European Families Stretched between the Demands of Work and Care (Editorial Introduction)." *Social Policy andAdministration* 38, no. 6 (2004): 557–64.

Skocpol, Theda. *Social Policy in the United States: Future Possibilities in Historical Perspective.* Princeton, N.J.: Princeton University Press, 1995.

Trattner, W. I. *From Poor Law to Welfare State: A History of Social Welfare in America.* London: Macmillan, 1974.

Ungerson, Clare. *Women and Social Policy: A Reader.* London: Macmillan, 1985.

Wilson, E. *Women and the Welfare State.* London: Tavistock, 1977.

Yerkes, Mara. *The Transformation of the Dutch Welfare State, Social Risks, and Corporatist Reform*. Bristol, UK: Policy Press, 2011.

XXVII. SOCIAL MOVEMENTS

Docherty, James C., and Sjoak van der Velden. *Historical Dictionary of Organized Labor*, 3rd ed. Lanham, Md.: Scarecrow Press, 2012.

Habermas, Jürgen. "New Social Movements." *Telos* 49 (1981): 33–37.

XXVIII. SOCIAL CAPITAL

Evers, Adalbert. "Social Capital and Civic Commitment: On Putnam's Way of Understanding." *Social Policy and Society* 2, no. 1 (2003): 13–21.

Franklin, Jane. "Social Capital: Policy and Politics." *Social Policy and Society* 4, no. 4 (2003): 349–52.

Hsung, Ray-May, Nan Lin, and Ronald L. Breiger. *Contexts of Social Capital: Social Networks in Markets, Communities, and Families*. New York: Routledge, 2009.

Putnam, R. D. *Bowling Alone: The Collapse and Revival of American Community*. New York: Oxford University Press, 1995.

Roberts, John Michael, and Fiona Devine. "The Hollowing Out of the Welfare State and Social Capital." *Social Policy and Society* 2, no. 4 (2003): 309–18.

XXIX. GLOBALIZATION, EUROPEANIZATION, AND WELFARE STATES

Alsasua, J., J. Bilbao-Ubillos, and J. Olaskoaga. "The EU Integration Process and the Convergence of Social Protection Benefits at the National Level." *International Journal of Social Welfare* 16, no. 4 (2007): 297–306.

Aurich, Patrizia. "Activating the Unemploymed: Directions and Divisions in Europe." *European Journal of Social Security* 13, no. 3 (2011): 294–316.

Börzel, T., and T. Risse. "Europeanization: The Domestic Impact of European Union Politics." In K. E. Jørgensen, M. Pollack, and B. Rosamond, eds., *Handbook of European Union Politics*, 483–504. London: Sage, 2007.

Caminada, K., K. Goudswaard, and O. Van Vliet. "Patterns of Welfare State Indicators in the EU: Is There Convergence?" *Journal of Common Market Studies* 48, no. 3 (2010): 529–56.

Citi, M., and M. Rhodes. "New Modes of Governance in the European Union: A Critical Survey and Analysis." In K. E. Jørgensen, M. Pollack, and B. Rosamond, eds., *Handbook of European Union Politics*, 463–83. London: Sage, 2007.

Crespy, Amandine. "When 'Bolkenstein' Is Trapped by the French Antiliberal Discourse: A Discursive-Institutionalist Account of Preference Formation in the

Realm of European Union Multilevel Politics." *Journal of European Public Policy* 17, no. 8 (2010): 1,253–70.

Crespy, Amandine, and Gajewska, Katarzyna. "New Parliament, New Cleavages after the Eastern Enlargement? The Conflict over the Service Directives as an Opposition between the Liberals and the Regulators?" *Journal of Common Market Studies* 48, no. 5 (2010): 1,185–1,208.

Esping-Andersen, Gøsta. *Welfare States in Transition: National Adaptations in Global Economies*. New York: Sage, 1996.

Falkner, Gerda. "European Union." In Francis G. Castles, Stephan Leibfried, Jane Lewis, Herbert Obinger, and Christopher Pierson, eds., *The Oxford Handbook of the Welfare State*, 279–90. Oxford, UK: Oxford University Press, 2010.

Greer, Scott. "The Weakness of Strong Policies and the Strength of Weak Policies: Law, Experimentalist Governance, and Supporting Coalitions in European Health Care Policy." *Regulation and Governance* 5, no. 2 (2011): 187–203.

Greve, Bent. "Indications of Social Policy Convergence in Europe." *Social Policy and Administration* 30, no. 4 (1996): 348–67.

Greve, Bent, and Jesper Jespersen, eds. *Globalization and Welfare*. Roskilde, Denmark: Roskilde University Press, 2003.

Grossman, E., and C. Woll. "The French Debate over the Bolkenstein Directive." *Comparative European Politics* 9, no. 3 (2011): 344–66.

Heichel, Stephen, Jessica Pape, and Thomas Sommerer. "Is There Convergence in Convergence Research? An Overview of Empirical Studies on Policy Convergence." *Journal of European Public Policy* 12, no. 5 (2005): 817–40.

Heise, A. "European Economic Governance: What Is It, Where Are We, and Where Do We Go?" *International Journal of Public Policy* 3, no. 1 (2008): 1–19.

Jacquot, S., C. Ledoux, and B. Palier. "A Means to a Changing End: European Resources—The EU and Reconciliation of Paid Work and Private Life." *European Journal of Social Security* 13, no. 1 (2011): 26–46.

Jessop, Bob. *The Future of the Capitalist State*. Cambridge, UK: Polity, 2002.

Jørgensen, K. E., M. Pollack, and B. Rosamond. *Handbook of European Union Politics*. London: Sage, 2007.

Korpi, Walter. "Welfare-State Regress in Western Europe: Politics, Institutions, Globalization, and Europeanization." *Annual Review of Sociology* 29 (2003): 589–609.

Kuhnle, Stein, ed. "Survival of the European Welfare State." Arena Working Paper No. 9. New York: Routledge, 1999.

Kumlin, Staffan. "Claiming Blame and Giving Credit: Unintended Effects of How Government and Opposition Frame the Europeanization of Welfare." QoG Working Papers Series, 2010, No. 26. Oslo, Norway, and Gothenburg, Sweden: Institute for Social Research and University of Gothenburg.

Kvist, J., and J. Saari, eds. *The Europeanisation of Social Protection*. Bristol, UK: Policy Press, 2007.

Leibfried, Stephan, and Elmar Rieger. *Limits to Globalization: Welfare States and the World Economy*. Cambridge, UK: Polity, 2003.

Martinsen, D. S. "The Europeanization of Welfare." *Journal of Common Market Studies* 43, no. 5 (2005): 1,027–54.

———. "Welfare States and Social Europe." In Ulla Neergaard, Erika Szyszczak, Johan W. van de Gronden, and Markus Krajewski, eds., *Social Services of General Interest in the EU*, 53–73. The Hauge, Netherlands: TMC Asser Press, 2012.

Martinsen, D. S., and K. Vrangbæk. "The Europeanization of Health Care Governance: Implementing the Market Imperatives of Europe." *Public Administration* 86, no. 1 (2008): 169–84.

Morgan, Hannah. "Disabled People and Employment: The Potential Impact of European Policy." In A. Roulstone and C. Barnes, eds., *Working Futures? Disabled People, Policy, and Social Inclusion*, 259–71. Bristol, UK: Policy Press, 2005.

Paetzold, Jörg. "The Convergence of Welfare State Indicators in Europe: Evidence from Panel Data." *European Journal of Social Security* 15, no. 1 (2013): 28–54.

Pennings, Frans. "The Cross-Border Health Care Directive." *European Journal of Social Security* 13, no. 4 (2011): 424–52.

———. "Introduction: Regulation 883/2004—The Third Coordination Regulation in a Row." *European Journal of Social Security* 11, no. 1/2 (2009): 3–7.

Radaelli, C. M. "Diffusion without Convergence: How Political Context Shapes the Adoption of Regulatory Impact Assessment." *Journal of European Public Policy* 12, no. 5 (2005): 924–43.

———. "Europeanization: Solution of Problem?" *European Integration Online Papers* 8, no. 16 (2004): 1–24.

———. "The Europeanization of Public Policy." In K. Featherstone and C. M. Radaelli, eds., *The Politics of Europeanization*, 27–56. Oxford, UK: Oxford University Press, 2003.

Sykes, Rob, Bruno Palier, and M. Prior, eds. *Globalization and European Welfare States: Challenges and Changes*. Houndmills, England: Palgrave, 2001.

Teague, Paul. "Deliberative Governance and EU Social Policy." *European Journal of Industrial Relations* 7, no. 1 (2001): 7–26.

Tsukada, Hiroto. *Economic Globalization and the Citizen's Welfare State: Sweden, the United Kingdom, Japan, and the United States*. Aldershot, England: Ashgate, 2003.

van Vliet, Olaf. "Divergences within Convergence: Europeanization of Social and Labour Market Policies." *Journal of European Integration* 32, no. 3 (2010): 269–90.

Verdier, D., and R. Breen. "Europeanization and Globalization: Politics against Markets in the European Union." *Comparative Political Studies* 34, no. 3 (2001): 227–62.

Verschraegen, Gert, Bart Vanhercke, and Rika Verpoorten. "The European Social Fund and Domestic Activation Policies: Europeanization Mechanisms." *Journal of European Social Policy* 21, no. 1 (2011): 55–72.

Wessels, Wolfgang, and Jørg Monar, eds. *The European Union after the Treaty of Amsterdam*. New York: Continuum, 2001.

XXX. JOURNALS

Administration and Society
Administration in Social Work

Adult Education Research in the Nordic Countries
Ageing and Society
American Historical Review
American Journal of Sociology
American Political Science Review
American Sociological Review
Analysis of Social Issues and Public Policy
Annual Review of Sociology
Asian Journal of Economics and Social Studies
Australian Journal of Social Issues
Benefits
Brookings Review
Comparative Journal of Social Issues
Comparative Political Studies
Contemporary Crises: Crime, Law, Social Policy
Critical Review
Critical Social Policy
Current Sociology
East-West Journal of Social Policy
European History Quarterly
Economic History Review
European Journal of Industrial Relations
European Journal of Political Economy
European Journal of Political Research
European Journal of Public Health
European Journal of Social Security
European Journal of Women's Studies
European Review of Economic History
History of European Ideas
International Journal of Health Services
International Journal of Sociology and Social Policy
International Labour Review
International Social Science Journal
Journal of Aging and Health
Journal of Common Market Studies
Journal of Economic History
Journal of Economic Literature
Journal of Economic Theory
Journal of European Social Policy
Journal of Family History
Journal of Income Distribution
Journal of Law and Social Policy
Journal of Medicine and Philosophy
Journal of Policy Modeling
Journal of Political Economy

Journal of Politics
Journal of Social Policy
Journal of Social Work Education
Journal of Sociology and Social Welfare
Labor History
Labour Market and Social Policy: Occasional Papers from the OECD
Philosophy of the Social Sciences
Policy and Politics
Policy Review
Politics and Society
Public Administration
Public Finance Quarterly
Quarterly Journal of Economics
Review of Economics and Statistics
Review of Income and Wealth
Scandinavian Journal of Economics
Scandinavian Journal of Social Welfare
Scandinavian Political Studies
Social Epistemology
Social Indicator Research
Social Philosophy and Policy
Social Policy
Social Policy and Administration
Social Policy Review
Social Policy Studies
Social Problems
Social Science Information
Social Work
Sociological Inquiry
Sociology
Work, Employment, and Society
World Politics

XXXI. WEBSITES

British Academy Portal   www.britac.ac.uk/links/res_petrw.cfm
   The British Academy's directory of online resources, which include several in the social sciences.

Centre for the Analysis of Social Policy   www.bath.ac.uk/sps/research/casp
   Part of the University of Bath. Aims to gather and develop the considerable range of research work that is underway in this field.

Centre for European Policy Studies   www.ceps.be

An independent policy research institute in Belgium that conducts policy research on European policy, which also includes aspects in relation to welfare-state analysis.

Council of Europe   http://hub.coe.int
Consists of representatives from all the European countries. The website includes useful information and viewpoints on social cohesion and social policy.

Economics Departments, Institutes, and Research Centres in the World
http://edirc.repec.org/
Gives information on more than 12,662 institutions in more than 231 countries doing research in economics. This includes several subjects of interest for welfare-state analysis, including financing, as well as social and labor market policy.

European Centre for Social Welfare Policy and Research   www.euro.centre.org
An international center for social research, policy, information, and training, and an intergovernmental organization focused on social welfare, affiliated with the United Nations. Various reports and books are available online in core areas of social policy.

European Foundation for the Improvement of Living and Working Conditions (EUROFOUND)   www.eurofound.europa.eu
A European agency set up in Ireland by the European Council, established to work in specialized areas of European Union policy. Its main area of research and analysis is in relation to living and working conditions in Europe.

European Social Welfare Information Network (ESWIN)   www.eswin.org
An European social welfare network with information on social policy and other related welfare-state issues, mainly on central European countries. Numerous links to international research in these areas can also be found.

European Union (EU)   europa.eu
The European Union has formulated various policies with an impact on welfare-state development in the member states. Their website contains information on these policies, along with data and analysis of the development in, for example, labor market policies and social inclusion. Description and comparison of countries is central in relation to the open method of coordination.

Eurostat   www.europa.eu.int/comm/eurostat
Eurostat's homepage gives up-to-date statistical information on social and labor market issues in the European Union member states.

International and Comparative Social Policy Group (ICSP)   www.globalwelfare.net
Contains information on comparative social policy issues and links to international organizations—governmental and nongovernmental—as well as activist groups in the fields.

International Council on Social Welfare (ICSW)   www.icsw.org
   Consists of a range of national and international member organizations interested in social welfare, social justice, and social development. Development aspects are central to this website.

International Labour Organization (ILO)   www.ilo.org
   Includes information on labor market issues, including safety at work, but also social protection and human rights.

Mannheim Centre for European Social Research   www.mzes.uni-mannheim.de
   Explores comparative tendencies and developments in social policy, mainly in European states, also looking at issues from the perspective of increasing European integration.

Max Planck Institute for the Study of Societies   www.mpi-fg-koeln.mpg.de
   The Max Planck Institutes in Germany are concerned with basis research in social sciences, which also have a relation to the development of welfare states. Links to other institutions in the field in Germany can also be found on the website.

MOST Clearing House
www.unesco.org/new/en/social-and-human-sciences/themes/most-programme
   MOST (Management of Social Transformations) is a research program designed by the United Nations Educational, Scientific, and Cultural Organization to promote international comparative social science research, with an emphasis on migration and international developments.

Observatory for the Development of Social Services in Europe
www.soziale-dienste-in-europa.de
   An observatory based in Germany established to follow the development of social services in Europe. It follows trends and perspectives in development processes in the area of social services in Europe.

Organization for Economic Cooperation and Development (OECD)   www.oecd.org
   The OECD mainly consists of the more affluent countries of the world. The organization's website lists detailed information about social and labor market policy. It is especially useful due to the fact that it features detailed analyses in a comparative perspective and provides access to data on such core issues as social and labor market expenditures, changes in demography, and other aspects of life. The OECD also publishes numerous reports, some of which can be ordered and downloaded online. Among these publications are those containing annually updated information on important labor market and educational issues.

Social Science Research Council (SSRC)   www.ssrc.org
   An international association devoted to the advancement of interdisciplinary research in the social sciences, especially in the following areas: HIV/AIDS as a

global challenge, children and armed conflict, economic growth, development and inequality, global security and cooperation, international migration, democracy, and the public sphere.

United Nations Research Institute for Social Development (UNRISD)
www.unrisd.org
An autonomous institution focusing on social aspects of development, as well as a variety of information and analysis in relation to social policy, migration, and other aspects related to societal development.

World Health Organization (WHO)   www.who.org
A UN organization that, as the name indicates, is mainly focused on health and health care throughout the world.

XXXII. RESEARCH ORGANIZATIONS

The following are some central research and other organizations from which information is available. In addition to specific information on the social security system in the United States, the U.S. Department of Health and Human Services circulates a publication containing an overview of social security programs throughout the world. This is a comprehensive book that deals with the institutional structure of programs and systems in different countries. It is made in collaboration with the International Social Security Association (ISSA), which consists of administrative representatives from most countries.

The ISSA and many other international organizations regularly publish information and research papers dealing with social security and its development. One important organization is the Organization for Economic Cooperation and Development (OECD). OECD studies focus on economic impact and consequences. They analyze member states of the OECD, which include European countries, as well as the United States, Canada, Japan, Australia, New Zealand, and Mexico. Furthermore, the OECD publishes regular studies that contain information on national development in individual countries. In addition, they publish an annual report entitled *Employment Outlook*, which provides information about developments in the labor markets, for example, social systems, which includes unemployment benefits and leave schemes.

Other important international bodies that concentrate on more specific issues are the World Health Organization (WHO) and the International Labour Organization (ILO). Both focus on health care and the labor market. The ILO, for example, publishes a yearbook of labor statistics. The World Bank and the International Monetary Fund (IMF) also analyze social problems, but their main interests are economic. Nevertheless, the World Bank has been interested in problems connected with poverty, changes in demography, and the impact on macroeconomic development. The IMF publishes information on public-sector expenditures, including expenditures on social security and welfare-state programs.

Such regional bodies as the Organization of American States (OAS) and the European Union (EU) also generate reports with references to the welfare state. The EU regularly publishes information on social security systems, for instance, its overview of community provisions on social security. Within the EU, the Mutual Information System on Social Security (MISSOC) recurrently provides information on the core elements in the social protection systems within the 28 European member states in a comparable manner. These reports, like those of the U.S. Department of Health and Human Services, are mainly institutional descriptions; however, this information can be supplemented with data from Eurostat. Eurostat is concerned with social security, migration, the labor market, and so forth, and can also provide statistics on development in European countries. Most data are based on macro-level statistics, but sometimes more micro-based data can be found.

The EU has several observatories as well. The subjects and focuses change from time to time. In recent years, there have been observatories on social exclusion, family, children, equal treatment, and employment. Reports from these observatories often provide good background material because they are based on national rapporteurs' information.

Finally, there is the Luxembourg Income Study (LIS), which consists of micro-data collected from household surveys in numerous different countries. Data may be requested directly from the LIS.

About the Author

Bent Greve received an M.A. in economics at Copenhagen University in 1977. He earned a Ph.D. in public administration in 1992, and a Dr. Scient. Adm. in public administration in 2002, both from Roskilde University. He is a professor of welfare state analysis in the Department of Society and Globalization at Roskilde University, Denmark.

Greve is an expert on the analysis of the welfare state and its development, mainly in a comparative European perspective. His research on the welfare state covers such areas as social security, the labor market, financing, and tax expenditures. He has been the Danish expert to several European Union Commission studies on financing and its implications, social and labor market policies, gender, teleworking, and free movement of workers. He has evaluated welfare state policies and initiatives in core areas of the welfare state, often in a comparative perspective. In recent years, Greve has also studied happiness and well-being in welfare states. In addition, he is regional and special issues editor of *Social Policy and Administration*. He has written several books and articles on welfare states, as well as the previous editions of *Historical Dictionary of the Welfare State*.

His publications include *Velfærdssamfundet: Myter og Facts* (*Welfare Society: Myth and Facts*), *Velfærdsstat and velfærdssamfund* (*Welfare State and Welfare Society*), *Vouchers—nye styrings—og leveringsmåder i velfærdsstaten* (*Vouchers: New Ways of Steering and Managing in the Welfare State*), *Fordelingsteori og fordelingsbeskrivelse*, *Væksten i de offentlige udgifter*, *Skatteudgifter i teoretisk og empirisk belystning*, *Social Policy in Europe: The Latest Evolution and Perspectives for the Future* (ed.), *Comparative Welfare Systems: The Scandinavian Model in a Period of Change* (ed.), *Choice: Challenges and Perspectives for the European Welfare States* (ed.), *Occupational Welfare, Happiness, Happiness and Social Policy in Europe* (ed.), and *The Routledge Handbook of the Welfare State* (ed.). Greve is also author of several articles in such Danish and international journals as *Social Policy and Administration*, *Journal of European Public Policy*, *Journal of European Social Security*, *Journal of Comparative Welfare*, *Central European Journal of Welfare*, and *Journal of Social Science and European Legacy*.